PIONEERS
IN THE
EAST AFRICAN REVIVAL

Pioneers
in the
East African Revival

H H Osborn

Apologia Publications
Winchester
UK

Copyright © 2000 H H Osborn

First published August 2000
All rights reserved.

Other books by the same author:

Fire in the Hills   Highland 1991
Revival - A precious heritage   Apologia   1995
Revival - God's Spotlight   Highland   1996
God and the antelope in the bush   Apologia   1996
Why search for God?   Apologia   1997
The greatest story ever told   Apologia   1998

ISBN   1 901566 07 2

Published in the UK by
Apologia Publications
5 St Matthew's Road
Winchester   SO22 6BX
UK

Printed by
Redwood Books
Trowbridge   Wiltshire   England

Contents

Preface

Some characteristics of the East African Revival were unique. Revivals, in the sense in which Evangelical Christians use that term, have occurred in Europe and North America since the 17th century. Here, Revival (with a capital 'R') is taken to mean an event or series of events in which a number of people, in the same geographical locality and at the same time, experience an extraordinarily powerful and unmistakable sense of the reality and presence of God, accompanied by an overwhelming conviction of biblical truth, especially as it relates to the relationship between them and God. This powerful working of God may or may not be evidenced by dramatic physical manifestations but is always characterised by very strong inner convictions and lasting evidence in changed lives—from immorality to purity and from dishonesty to uprightness of character— and a strong affirmation of biblical truth. Where these inner spiritual experiences occur without the extraordinary signs of Revival, the term 'revival' is used (with a small 'r').

A unique characteristic of the East African Revival was the merging of two streams of remarkable spiritual life. Revival did not begin in this part of Africa with the events generally understood as the East African Revival. Extraordinary signs associated with Revival can be traced to the late 19th Century in Uganda. In 1929, a seemingly insignificant meeting in Kampala of two men brought together the African and the European/North American streams of Revival.

However, a difference in the two cultures—Ugandan and English—has made the recording of the events of the East African Revival more difficult. Dr Joe Church kept a careful and detailed diary. He also wrote reports of his visits to countries beyond East Africa. Both he and Lawrence Barham wrote for 'Ruanda Notes', the magazine of the Ruanda Mission (CMS). In contrast, William Nagenda and Yosiya Kinuka were suspicious of putting things into writing. It was, so they felt, the sure way to make the Gospel and Revival an organised set of rules. Legalism of that kind could, so they argued, easily kill the living, spontaneous, freedom which was the true Christian life. It has, therefore, with a few significant exceptions, been much easier to obtain written records of the events of the lives of the English missionaries than of their African brothers and sisters.

It is customary, in English literature, to refer to a person by his or her first name. In African culture, it is usual to use the African name, even when that is preceded by a first or Christian name. The increasing use by Africans of the 'Christian name' to refer to each other has made it difficult to follow the two customs.

It would be impossible for me to list all those to whom I owe a deep debt of gratitude. Firstly, those, now mostly with their Master, who cared enough for me to help and encourage me while I was working as a missionary in Rwanda and Burundi. My many questions, and sometimes wrong reactions to what I was witnessing, were always met with a loving concern by the leaders of revival, about some of whom I now have the privilege of writing.

My particular thanks go to Joan Hall. Hers has been the driving inspiration for this book and it is largely due to her untiring efforts to interview people and encourage others to write down their experiences that such full accounts of the African pioneers have been possible. Of those who have contributed in different ways, I would acknowledge with especial thanks the collaboration of Zeb Kabaza. I am also grateful for the meticulous checking of the text by Mrs Judith Church.

Introduction

It is difficult to pinpoint a moment when it could be said that the East African Revival began. The first record of any events in East Africa which can be called 'Revival', in the sense in which that word is applied to the great Revivals of North America and Great Britain in the early 18th, and mid-19th centuries, occurred in the recently established church in Kampala, Uganda in 1893.

George Pilkington, a missionary of the Church Missionary Society, a gifted linguist engaged in translating the Bible into Luganda, the language of the area of Uganda around Kampala, and other members of the Church Missionary Society were very encouraged by the numbers who were being added to the Church of Uganda, and by the many who appeared to be eager to read God's word. They were, however, saddened by the very low level of spiritual life they observed in those who showed outwardly such eagerness to receive the Christian faith. The truths of the Gospel, which people appeared to accept with such enthusiasm, made very little impact on their moral lives. George Pilkington felt this dearth of spiritual life in the lives of those who professed to be Christians so keenly and was so discouraged that he spoke of giving up missionary work altogether.

Feeling very discouraged and depressed, George Pilkington "went alone for a visit to the island of Kome (one of the Sese Islands in Lake Victoria), and it was there that he learned the great secret of the indwelling power of the Holy Spirit, which transformed his whole life". [P225]

During that time at Kome, George shared a hut with a young African who was later ordained. The latter recounted how, one night, they both went to bed as usual, but, when George thought that his African companion was asleep, he got up and began to pray, sometimes aloud. The African fell asleep but George was still praying when he woke up in the morning. George was transformed with joy. He told his friend how he had experienced an overwhelming sense of the presence and power of God with him. He told the Christians around him in Kome what God had done for him. He returned to Kampala with a renewed vision and zeal for telling others of the Gospel he had known before, but which had become vibrantly alive for him.

In that year, 1893, the missionaries organised a mission in Kampala. They had hoped to invite speakers from the UK but that proved difficult because of communication problems. The first speaker was George Pilkington. On that first day and on subsequent days, there were remarkable scenes of 'great spiritual blessing' as men and women, some Christians of long standing, came under strong conviction of sin and found peace through the Cross of Christ.

During that mission, according to G K Baskerville, one of the missionaries who was present, "God showed us that we were the cause of the lack of zeal, of the low-level lives and of the absence of joy." Recognising that the obstacle to God working effectively was sin in their own lives, sometimes unrecognised as such, they sought cleansing through the Cross of Christ and asked for forgiveness of God and of each other. A surge of conviction of sin and then of joy and peace overwhelmed them,

The effects of the events of December 1893 do not appear to have lasted for long. A few missionaries, and some African leaders were transformed individually, but there does not appear to have been anything like a movement of Revival in Uganda. Nevertheless, from that time, the reviving power experienced in 1893, was kept alive in small groups of African Christians with no notable leaders.

It was from these relatively unknown products of Revival that, in 1929, one man emerged from obscurity to play a leading role in the Revival that was to begin in southwest Uganda and in Rwanda six years later.

Simeoni Nsibambi was born in 1897, of a high-ranking Buganda family. His education was interrupted by the First World War, 1914-1918, when he joined the African Native Medical Corps. He was converted in 1922. Later he underwent a transforming experience which he spoke of as the time when he was "spiritually overwhelmed" with the power of the Holy Spirit.

Meanwhile, in England, a young man, destined by his father to follow him as a clergyman, was leaving military service in the Tank Corps of the British Army, soon after the end of World War I. Joe Church was not a 'saved' Christian and did not look forward to becoming a clergyman as his father had hoped. A government grant to ex-servicemen allowed him to change the course of the life planned for him, and to become a medical student. While at medical school he was converted and met Decima Tracey, also a Christian medical student but at another hospital. They were married in 1930.

Joe offered for missionary service with the 'Ruanda General and Medical Mission', usually abbreviated to the 'Ruanda Mission (CMS)', was accepted and set sail for Uganda in 1927. He was located to Gahini, a new site in Rwanda, to build and equip a hospital. The work required all his energies, but he was able to visit Uganda from time to time. On one such visit, in 1929, in unremarkable circumstances, occurred the remarkable meeting between Simeoni Nsibambi and Joe Church which is often considered to mark the beginning of Revival in East Africa. It was, in fact, a merging of two streams - the Uganda stream with its links with the outburst of God's reviving power in 1893, and Great Britain, with its links with a number of powerful Revivals, the first associated with John Wesley and George Whitefield, in the 18th century, and others in the 19th and early 20th centuries.

Meanwhile another story was developing. A young English clergyman, ordained in 1925, was fulfilling his curacy at St James' Church, Hatcham, in South London, at the same time as a trainee teacher was attending the adjacent University of London Goldsmiths' College. Lawrence Barham was preparing to obey God's call to him to go as a missionary to China. Julia Leakey was expecting to return as a missionary to Kenya, where she had been brought up. In a series of events in which God's hand was clearly in control, China became closed to missionaries and Lawrence was guided to offer for service in Uganda. In 1928, Lawrence set sail for Africa and there he and Julia were married.

Lawrence was located to Kabale, the base centre of the Ruanda Mission (CMS) in Africa. It was natural that he would visit the sites in Rwanda where new centres were developing. So it was that Lawrence and Julia visited Joe at Gahini intending to spend a night there and see how things were progressing. Embarrassingly, Lawrence developed chicken pox in the home of his hosts. It was three weeks before he was fit enough to move on. During that time, Lawrence and Julia caught something of the fire that was burning in Joe. Both saw that God, working in power, as he had done in Revival in the past in other countries, in both missionaries and Africans, was their great need.

The pioneer work of establishing a church, medical and educational centre at Gahini called for more workers. Missionaries were needed, not, however, only from the UK but also from the adjoining country of Uganda. Ruanda-Urundi (as Rwanda and Burundi were known then), were not as advanced as Uganda in almost every sense - education, commerce and government.

Blasio Kigozi was the younger brother of Simeoni Nsibambi and it was largely through Simeoni's influence that Blasio became a Christian in 1925. Simeoni said of

him: "He was my firstfruit in Jesus." Blasio offered to the
Bishop of Uganda for service among the Pygmies of the
Congo forests. Immigration difficulties prevented this.

At just the right moment, Blasio met Dr Algie Stanley
Smith (one of the founders of the Ruanda Mission), who
explained the way God was opening up Rwanda to that
Mission. Kigozi's reaction was immediate. He recognised
that this was where God was calling him to work. In 1929
he arrived at Gahini to take over the leadership of the Evangelists' Training School. The driving force of his faith penetrated all sections of the work at Gahini. He was God's
man in the right place at the right time. In 1934, Blasio
Kigozi married Katharine, sister of Eva Nsibambi.

God works in mysterious ways! After a brief illness,
suffering from a virulent tropical disease, diagnosed, but
not confirmed, as tick or relapsing fever, Blasio died in
Mengo Hospital in January 1936. It seemed impossible
that the life of such a shining and promising light for the
Gospel should be cut short so abruptly. His going made a
profound impression on many people at Gahini, but none
more so than on his future brother-in-law, William Nagenda.

Nagenda was another of those who had been led to Christ
through Nsibambi. Like Blasio Kigozi, Nagenda heard the
call of God to serve Him anywhere, at any time. It was not
surprising that God should call him to follow in the footsteps of Blasio. He joined the team at Gahini. He later
married Sala, a younger sister of Katharine Kigozi.

Another strand in the tapestry of Revival was being wo-
ven in the district of Ankole, south-west Uganda. Yosiya
Kinuka was the son of a cattle-owning chief who died while
Yosiya was still young. He had no opportunity to learn to
read or write. As a young man he developed yaws - a disease marked by foul-smelling ulcers on the legs. In the
course of a medical safari, Dr Leonard Sharp, the co-founder
of the Ruanda Mission, visited the area where Yosiya lived
with his brother. The doctor could not treat him adequately
there and so invited him to go to Kabale Hospital for proper
treatment. There his remarkable qualities came to light.

He learned to read, write, dispense medicines to patients and to carry out other hospital duties. While there he met and married Dorokasi from the Bufumbira area of Uganda.

The great potential for Kinuka's abilities was noted by Dr Len Sharp and he was sent to Mengo Hospital to train as a Medical Orderly. In 1928, on his return to Kabale, he was invited by Dr Joe Church to join the staff of Gahini Hospital, still in process of construction.

Yosiya, although baptised, was only a Christian in name. He realised the emptiness of his life while he was working in the hospital at Gahini. In order to face the realities of his spiritual situation, he went to Kampala for a break from hospital duties. There he met Simeoni Nsibambi. Yosiya returned to Gahini a transformed person.

As God worked in reviving power in Uganda, almost every part of the church was affected in some way. Among those who saw what was happening but did not feel any need to go along with it, was a remarkably able and 'religious' pastor of an Anglican Church at Kinoni, not far from Mbarara, in Uganda. Erica Sabiti was a very dedicated, self-giving ordinand from Bishop Tucker Theological College, Mukono. He was ordained in 1933 and later married Geraldine. In 1939 he was asked to accompany the Bishop of Uganda on a visit to the churches of Rwanda and Burundi. There he came into contact with those whose lives radiated the living Christ and his life was transformed. He soon became one of the Uganda team of 'revived brethren'. Later, Sabiti's remarkable spiritual, intellectual and leadership qualities resulted in him becoming the first African Archbishop of the Anglican Province of Uganda.

The six couples of whom the following are brief biographies, were pioneers in the East African Revival, but they were not the only ones. Many were the men and women that God used in different ways in their own situations to testify to His reviving work in their lives. This is the story of the way God wove the lives of a few ordinary men and women into a powerful and effective witness to Him in the extraordinary circumstances of Revival.

Chapter 1

Simeoni and Eva Nsibambi

The early years

Simeoni Nsibambi was born in 1897 to Sezi Walusimbi Kimanje, (a Chief at Wakiso, Buloba, in the county of Kyaggwe, Uganda), and Tezira Wampanyo. He was baptised at Namirembe on February 14th 1902.

At an early age, Simeoni showed such exceptional qualities that, although not the eldest son, his father appointed him as his successor. As such, he inherited considerable property, some of which he later donated to needy causes.

Nsibambi attended Mengo High School but his further education was interrupted by World War I. Uganda, as a British Protectorate, became involved in providing support services for the war in Europe. Nsibambi joined the African Native Medical Corps which was engaged in nursing war casualties. He was promoted to Sergeant, a senior rank in the Colonial period, and was decorated for his services.

After his wartime service, Nsibambi returned to King's College, Budo. There he displayed such distinguished qualities of character and academic abilities that he was made the Head Prefect in his final year. He was recognised as "just, faithful, strict, highly disciplined and generous".

On completing his schooling in 1920, he joined the Kabaka's Government as a Chief Health Officer, a particularly suitable office as he was known to be meticulously clean. When the Kabaka (King) of Buganda offered him the post of Deputy County Chief at Wakiso, he declined because he considered himself too young for the post.

Nsibambi was a natural leader. Among his other accomplishments, he was a good singer, artist, footballer and wrestler. He won distinctions in both singing and football. He also enjoyed hunting for which he was granted a special licence to own a rifle and shot-guns.

The first indication of Nsibambi's spiritual search occurred while he was 16 years of age and still at school. In an act which typified his precision of mind and determination to follow what he believed to be right, on March 27, 1913, "he made a written pledge to God in which he resolved to stop taking alcoholic drink."

An experience while he was serving in the armed forces during the war years made a deep impression on him. He was on a ship sailing to Zanzibar. He had, so he told a friend, "a lot of worry in his heart." He saw that the ship was on a big ocean, but it had a captain who guided it. He saw that he needed a captain to guide him in his life and the captain he needed was Jesus.

He found that Guide in an event that changed his life. He wrote: "Our Lord saved me in 1922, and after, within a period of three years, He revealed to me many irregularities that existed in our Church here in Uganda. Whereas before my salvation I considered the clergy to be righteous people and envied them for their robes, wishing I were able to go to the Holy Table so that I could be as upright as they were, I found out later that this was not so. Some of these men were really defeated individuals." At that time, Nsibambi did not find a ready response to his challenges.

Nsibambi was greatly encouraged by a friend, Mulengera. On returning from a visit to Ethiopia, Mulengera shared with him "how he found the clergy there burdened to pray for their Government and its leader, the Emperor.

Simeoni and Eva Nsibambi

Joe and Decie Church

Kabale Convention

William and Sala Nagenda

September 1945

Lawrence and Julia Barham

Yosiya and Dorokasi Kinuka

Erica and Geraldine Sabiti

This challenged me to start praying for the leaders of our Church, that they may be endued with the same spirit of concern and responsibility towards our rulers."

As an avid reader, in English, as in Luganda, he read all available Christian literature. "There were a number of tracts, booklets and books from Britain and elsewhere which helped me to understand the ministry of the Holy Spirit," he wrote later. "For a whole year I gave myself to the study of the Scriptural materials with prayer. The reading of my Bible led me to complete commitment, and God filled me with the Holy Spirit. This is what I wrote in my Bible as a commitment, 'I have committed myself to God the Father. As from today I desire to be genuinely holy and never intentionally to do anything unguided by Jesus'."

"After that commitment," he wrote, "I was filled with power of the Holy Spirit of an unusual kind. I felt overwhelmed in my body and especially my head, and of course in the whole body."

On one occasion, when he had retired to the Rwenzori mountains for quiet and meditation, and while praying, he sensed clearly that God was telling him to take off his shoes for the place where he was standing was holy ground. From then onwards, he walked barefooted, even on official occasions.

He saw many things in the Church and government which appeared to him to be sin against God. He became unpopular as boldly he challenged drunkenness, hypocrisy, corruption, adultery and the seeking for prestige.

On August 25, 1925, he married Eva Bakaluba, the eldest daughter of Erasto Bakaluba, a Christian, who was one of the first African teachers at King's College, Budo.

The Bishop of Uganda, Bishop John Willis, recognised Nsibambi's special gifts and, in 1926, invited him to start a regular prayer meeting. These meetings were held every Tuesday, in the Hannington Chapel. Of these occasions, Nsibambi wrote later, "What gave me joy at the Hannington Chapel, with the prayer group, was that, even if I was there alone, I was able to have deep times of prayer."

Much of the Christian work in Kampala centred round Namirembe Cathedral and it was not surprising that Nsibambi found himself drawn there. He became a Warden of the Cathedral, sang in the Cathedral choir and took a very active part in many of its activities, including taking up the collection. He preached at some of the evening services—lay people were sometimes invited to do so while the leadership of the morning service was reserved for the clergy.

Nsibambi joined an organisation, named *Abasamaliya Abalungi* (the Good Samaritan Society), which had been formed in 1921, mainly by former students of Mengo High School, "to help the poor, the sick and the maimed". He was very generous with his own possessions. However, "Nsibambi became dissatisfied with the society because he felt that, although it practised high ideals and assisted the poor, it was not radical and vigorous enough to challenge people to renounce Satan and 'to receive salvation'"

Nsibambi contributed generously to the work of this society. He also realised that the greater need was for a change of heart which only Jesus Christ could bring about.

In 1927, the Church of Uganda celebrated its Jubilee. It was 50 years since the Gospel was first preached in Uganda. Despite the fact that he was relatively unknown, Nsibambi and two others, Kanyikire and Mayanja, were invited to speak of their Christian experiences at the Jubilee Celebrations. The contribution of Nsibambi made such an impression that he was thereafter frequently invited to speak at Christian meetings and to give 'Bible readings'.

Nsibambi became a well-known figure in Kampala where, in a quiet and unobtrusive way, he would challenge those whom he felt were not living lives according to God's standards, particularly church members. He was frequently seen in Mengo Hospital where he visited sick people with a message of encouragement, and also of challenge as he pointed them to his Saviour and warned them of an eternity apart from God if they did not repent of their sin and trust in Him. He also developed a special link with Dr Roy Billington, the missionary doctor in charge of the hospital.

Family life

Simeoni and Eva Nsibambi had twelve children of whom eight are still alive. The testimony of these children to life in their parents' home paints a remarkable picture of the integrity and consistency of their characters, individually and as a couple.

Dr John Nsibambi, Simeoni Nsibambi's heir, with his wife Salome, wrote: "Father will always be remembered by us as an exceptional person. He really loved his family and had a special place in his heart for all his children and grandchildren. He used to sit with us one by one when we came home from boarding school at the end of term, and he would go through our reports with us. He congratulated us on our achievements but did not spare us when our reports were bad. He put a lot of emphasis on good behaviour. He was particularly pleased when I (John) was made Prefect at Budo, as he had been the Head Prefect when he was there."

Janet Nsibambi, the eldest of the children, wrote of her parents: "My parents have influenced me to become the person I am today. While a child, my parents taught me the importance of being close to God. Their teaching helped me to grow knowing what is evil and what is good. Following in my parents' footsteps, I received Jesus Christ as my Saviour. My parents taught us how to pray every morning and evening and how to read the Bible every day. As we sang together with my father, we learned how to sing songs I still sing today."

The parents love for each other was very evident. In an unusual way, Simeoni entrusted Eva with the administration of their land and property and the overseeing of the education of their children, tasks which she performed with "rigour, foresight and imagination".

Professor Apolo Nsibambi, the Prime Minister of Uganda, who was also Head Prefect at King's College, Budo, and his wife Rhoda, wrote: "My father was extremely devoted to his family. He loved his wife very much and was absolutely loyal to her. She was also totally loyal to him.

He was a good administrator at home. Whenever there were disputes in the family, he used to listen carefully to both sides and invoke his highly developed sense of procedure and justice to resolve the problems. He would, of course, always urge us to refer all the problems to Jesus in the first instance.

"He was particular about discipline. Whenever we brought our reports from the school, he would first read the section dealing with character. ... One criticism must be made of my father. He tended to disregard the 'earthly world'. Since he used to allow us a lot of freedom of discussion, I once freely criticised him for having marginalised material things. His reply was: 'If one wishes to effect changes, especially in the spiritual sphere, one must marginalise certain things and concentrate absolutely on the desired ideals'."

Lucy, the fourth child, and her husband, Charles Mutawe, recall: "Our Mother was a hard-working housewife who loved her husband. She loved the children and looked after us in a special way. It was Mother who found the right schools for our education.

"One incident that particularly stands out in my mind was when an English Headmistress of Duhaga Secondary School near Kampala got to know my parents and offered them a scholarship for me to go and study at that school. So they took me there, but it was a completely different language they were using, and I did not understand it at all. I was so homesick and I cried and could not study at all. In fact, I was so homesick that they gave me someone to accompany me back home! My mother saw me at a distance and she called my father. She was an excitable lady, but my father was a very calm man, and he quietened her down! She called out 'Tata! (Father) Lucy is back! What shall we do?' But my father quietly said 'Mama, God has a reason'; and my mother was calm from there. Now these words have become our family motto: 'God has a reason'. When we face big problems in our family we remind ourselves of these words."

The experience which led Nsibambi to walk barefooted rather than wear shoes made its mark on his children. Lucy Mutawe commented: "Father was not shy and he always put into practice the things God was telling him to do. For example, he felt that the Lord did not want him to wear shoes and he felt he should walk barefooted. At that time my Father was a Health Inspector in the Government, but he felt he should listen to what God was saying and go barefooted despite his position in the Government. As children, we did not find this easy, and sometimes we felt ashamed at school to see him going about like this. Because we were confused, we used to ask him why he did not wear shoes, and he would tell us that he had his vision and that God had told him that he should not wear them and walk freely. He began to go barefooted in his early Christian life, and I never remember him wearing shoes."

Ezekiel Kimanje Nsibambi, another son of Simeoni and Eva Nsibambi, with his wife Victoria, wrote: "My father was very humble to everyone in the home, and he was very polite and he used to apologise as soon as he was aware that he had been wrong. If he knew he had hurt you, he apologised immediately to you and to God. He used to say, 'Forgive me, and God forgive me too.' He was very particular about our character. For example, if you brought a report which said that you had bad manners, he would cane us straight away."

Mrs Betty Ssekkadde, another daughter of Simeoni and Eva Nsibambi, underlined the example that her parents were to her: "Our parents loved each other so much that I learned that I should follow their example by loving my children, my brothers, sisters and other people. I learned from my father to repent and ask for forgiveness from the persons offended. I also learned that, through prayer, a person can achieve her cherished goals."

Mary Nsibambi, the youngest daughter of the Nsibambi family, added, "They sacrificed themselves to bring us up and to provide for our needs. Their great commitment to God was infectious to us."

Nsibambi's seventh child, Professor Sengendo Pilkington Nsibambi, wrote of life in his family: "What I remember most about our home was that our father was a very loving person who cared a lot about us, and was devoted to Mother. What I saw and I have never forgotten was that he was devoted to Mother, and after that he loved us, and I have sought to emulate that in my own marriage. That has become part of my understanding and of my life. My wife, Sarah, matters to me and is the most important person in my life and in my home. Although, as far as father was concerned, Mother was the most important person in his life and in the home, that did not mean that he never did anything in the home. When, for example, he ceased going out to preach because of his long illness, he was actually in the home more than my mother. If we were hungry or thirsty he would go and find something nice for us to eat or drink, and we would look to him to help us. We were often very demanding.

"My father was extremely artistic, and would frequently draw portraits of people who were in front of him. For example, he quickly sketched his grandchildren and would then give them the drawings which carried their likeness, even when crying! He had a natural talent for art. But if he felt it was taking over the place of Jesus he would give it up, and say that Jesus must come first.

"I sometimes felt a bit disappointed when I understood that our father could have been a very important person, maybe a Katikkiro (Prime Minister), because his life was being shaped for a senior post. He was a Head Prefect at King's College, Budo, a son of a great chief, and he could have gone far. But we used to discuss this with Father and he explained that we should really concentrate on life after death, and it made sense to me. Because he loved Jesus and was devoted to Him, he sacrificed much of his material possessions and positions, but he never forced you to do the same. He did not owe anything to anybody. He would go even to the Kabaka and challenge him about things he thought were not right."

"I was told that on many occasions he was sent presents of many kinds and he rejected them outright, commenting that if he accepted them, he would be compromised, He was very firm on this issue. He felt that if he accepted the gifts, he would not have been in a strong position to talk about the Lord and to challenge those donors.

"He was, in fact, very down to earth in the way he talked to us and discussed spiritual matters. He patiently tried to explain the costly way to the cross and salvation. He quoted the favourite verse: 'Seek first the Kingdom of God and His righteousness and the rest will be added unto you'.

"He listened to our youthful views and prayed for us. He would encourage us to make our decisions. He felt that I was very ambitious and proud, and he would do his best to try and get my focus correct! I was pleased that he recognised my early artistic inclinations and gave me the necessary support. When I was admitted to the University to pursue Art, he was very happy. Often during the holidays, he looked at my art works with much interest and we dialogued. However, he was not very comfortable with the human anatomy and nude life-drawings. As a compromise, I agreed to keep them away from him and my brothers and sisters. However, he realised that they were part of the core subjects of the discipline. Father believed in prayer which could change people and situations for the better. He encouraged us to pray for ourselves and for others."

Rhoda, the wife of Professor Apolo Nsibambi, Sarah, the wife of Professor Pilkington Nsibambi and Charles Mutawe, husband of Lucy, all recognised the humility and dedication to God of their parents-in-Law, and their full acceptance of them into the family.

Another great feature of their home was the large number of visitors who received a warm welcome no matter which part of East Africa they came from. He strongly discouraged anyone from thinking in terms of tribe or background, showing by his speech and action that Christ died for all the people and that no one should be despised. As with visitors, so with sons-in-law and daughters-in-law; they all knew that they were loved and accepted, and were made to feel very welcome in the family. When thanked for hospitality or a gift, he would say, "I am an unworthy servant"

"Father would never allow anyone to look down on anyone else," commented Lucy Mutawe, "and our home was always visited by a great number of people from any and every ethnic group, and all were made so welcome. Whether they came from Buganda or Kigezi, from Kenya or the U.K. no matter where they came from they all had the same welcome."

"We had so many guests in our home, and we had to entertain them and share whatever food we had with them." added Ezekiel Kimanje Nsibambi, another son of Simeoni and Eva, "All of us thought of him as a special or unique man. ... One thing we noted is that he never changed from his vision, and some of us, as we grew up, told him that he was awkward and embarrassing to us for not wearing shoes. It was difficult, especially at school, because children would laugh at us. But he would say, 'My children, I cannot change', and he did not change at all. The thing I found hardest about him was that sometimes I became fearful of doing wrong because I would fear that he could see through me, and this made me afraid of him sometimes."

A close friend of the family who was a frequent visitor to their home was Samwiri Bakiranze, a Nurse in training at Mengo Hospital. He was very impressed with "the way they brought up their children. How they worked together as wife and husband surprised me. If the children were stubborn, they would talk to them and help them. If they themselves had made a mistake in their dealings with the children, they would apologise to the children and so on. I felt that the way they dealt with the children was so humble and so loving. This was so different from the home that I came from where there was a lot of beating of children and no working together as a team between my Mother and Father. I had never seen a home like this before." The Nsibambi home was a testimony to the central place that Simeoni and Eva gave to God.

Ministry in Revival

In the late 1920's, a remarkable Irish Missionary Nurse, Mabel Ensor, worked in Mengo Hospital. In her zeal for the purity of the gospel, she felt that the Anglican Church of Uganda was dead because it did not preach and teach a true gospel. She was not alone in her concern. In her zeal, Mabel started a Bible class in Kampala for those who, with her, were prepared to look to the Bible alone for their source of truth of both doctrine and practice. She found a sympathetic cooperation in Simeoni Nsibambi. He was very aware of what he felt to be irregular and unbiblical activities in the national Church and he too, was concerned that the Church should proclaim a true and full Gospel.

It was to a meeting arranged by Mabel Ensor, in November 1927, that a recently arrived, young missionary, Dr Joe Church, was invited to speak. Among the listeners was Simeoni Nsibambi. He found within himself a sympathy for this new missionary.

Later, on Sunday 23rd September 1929, Simeoni had finished praying at Namirembe Cathedral and was walking in the grounds when he saw Joe Church. He approached him and reminded him of the meeting run by Mabel Ensor at which he had heard him speak. They arranged to meet on the verandah of the house which is now part of the Namirembe Guest House.

It was a meeting of two men who had had very real experiences of the saving power of Jesus Christ, and who were convinced that there was more for them if they but knew the way. On two consecutive days, Simeoni Nsibambi and Dr Joe Church studied the references in the Bible to the person and work of God the Holy Spirit. Both were searching for a new direction to their lives and they found it together as they prayed for God to make real in them all that they had been reading in His Word. Joe Church wrote, "I remember Nsibambi leaving his chair beside me and kneeling down as the Baganda do, and we took each other's hands and prayed for the fullness of His Spirit, and God answered that prayer."

Nsibambi had been zealous to win others for Christ before his meeting with Joe Church. After it, his zeal increased
greatly. On returning to Kampala, after that meeting in September 1929, Joe met a lay lady missionary who said to
him:

"What have you done to Nsibambi?"

"Why, what's the matter?" he asked.

"Oh, he's gone mad and is going round everywhere asking people if they are saved. He's just left my gardener," she
replied. She then advised Joe to go back to his work in
Rwanda as quickly as possible "because the Africans were
not ready for this teaching about sanctification and the Holy
Spirit." It was evident that Nsibambi knew more of God's
working in lives when given wholeheartedly to Him than
she did, and Africans were indeed ready for all God offered.

Nsibambi returned to his work in the Public Health De-
partment, but, on November 30, 1929, he resigned from
his post as Chief Health Officer. Thereafter, he gave himself
wholly to the task of sharing his faith with whomever he
could find who would listen. He gathered a small team
around him including Yusufu Mukasa, a senior hospital
worker, and Yusufu Byangwa, a gifted musician and singer.
This team soon became well-known in Kampala and in
Entebbe, the headquarters of the government.

For a time he continued to cooperate with the missionary, Mabel Ensor. She felt that liberal and 'high church'
practices had so permeated the Church of Uganda that she
had to separate from it. Nsibambi was not happy about
this. Despite the fact that he had been one of her strongest
supporters, he broke away from her Bible Class.

Writing of Mabel Ensor and her convictions, Shem
Ndimbirwe commented: "In the early days of God's Spirit
moving, there was a European lady who also lived in Kampala and worked at Mengo. She realised that the Church
was in many ways corrupt, and that people were persisting
in it, and so she talked to Nsibambi and said that she
thought it was right that she should leave the Anglican
Church and set up her own. As Nsibambi had the same

insights and concerns, she suggested to Nsibambi that he too should leave the Anglican Church of Uganda and that they should together start another Church in Kampala. His reply was that he too saw that people were corrupt, and many were perishing, but he said, 'Those who are corrupt in this church that I am in, are my brothers, and if I leave it, they will not hear, so I cannot leave them.' So Nsibambi stayed in the Church of Uganda. He continued to attend Namirembe Cathedral, but never lost an opportunity to talk to individuals about their need of coming to Jesus to be saved. Sometimes he would take people to his home and talk to them about Jesus. Although he was a Government servant his overriding passion was to tell people about his Saviour."

In the years that followed, Simeoni Nsibambi and Joe Church met whenever Joe visited Kampala, usually for medical supplies for Gahini Hospital. "He (Nsibambi) was often there to meet me just at the time I arrived at the end of my journey," wrote Joe Church, "He seemed to have a way of knowing the time even though I had not let him know." On one occasion, "We met in the small room at the back of the Synod Hall, and he brought some Baganda friends. We met in the late afternoon, and there were thirty-five in all. Nsibambi was gathering around him a little team of those whose hearts God had touched, who went out preaching and doing personal work with him." ᵠ74

Those meetings for fellowship and prayer were the beginning of a weekly event which continues in the same hall every Friday to this day.

During the years 1930 to 1935, Nsibambi was active around Kampala. He was concerned not only for the purity of the Church but also for Ugandan society in general. Ballroom dancing, common in Europe, had just been introduced to Uganda. This kind of dancing involved men and women holding each other and so coming into much closer contact with each other than was normal in Ugandan culture or in Ugandan dancing. "On May 25, 1935," recorded Joe Church, "I received a typical brief but appealing letter.

'The young people of Kampala have started dancing,'
Nsibambi wrote. 'When you ask them why, they reply that
the Europeans have taught them to do it. So when you
next come be prepared to let them know why it should not
be done. I hate it myself, because it will hinder them from
knowing their Master, the Saviour of the world.'" [Q114]

Yohana Bunyenyezi records how Nsibambi's love of clean-
liness affected his approach to people. "I remember
Nsibambi saying that after he came to the Lord he was busy
telling people how to keep their houses and compounds
clean and so on, but the Lord spoke to him about the more
important work of keeping their lives clean ... and that
prompting from the Lord was one of the major facts that
led to him giving up his government work. He would go
round to people's houses, sometimes going with Yusufu
Mukasa, and Yusufu Byangwa."

During this time, Nsibambi faced much opposition and
misunderstanding from within and from outside the church,
but, wrote Joe Church, "he never seemed to give way to
self-pity or self-vindication. He continued to go to the Archdeacon and to the Bishop at Namirembe to speak out when
he felt things were not right. Some said he was unbal-
anced, some said he was actually sinning. A senior missionary warned me that he had been seen after dark with a
woman on the back of his bicycle. I went down to his house
and asked him about it. He smiled and said, 'Oh that dear
missionary must be careful. It is true I did find an old lady
at Entebbe after a meeting who could not get back to Kampala, so I gave her a lift back on the carrier of my bike.'
There was even a rumour that he had made holes in the
knees of his trousers, and then sewn them up, so as to
show people what a man of prayer he was!

"These things happened long ago now and are all blotted out by the love of God," wrote Joe Church, " but it helps
us to realise the burden that Nsibambi had to bear and
carry to God in prayer, the load of misunderstanding. These
things made us warn people strongly in those days about
the subtle ways the Devil seeks to attack those who set out

for Revival, and those warnings may be timely for those who, we hope, as a result of Nsibambi's call, may set out to plead with people now in these days of even greater urgency."

When, in 1935, Lawrence Barham and Ezekieri Balaba, the leaders of the Church and of the Evangelists' Training School at Kabale, invited a team from Gahini to share in the ministry at a convention at Kabale, a number of Africans and missionaries were chosen from both centres to lead in the preparations and in the speaking of this team. Joe wrote: "The team looked to the three of us for leadership—Yosiya Kinuka, Blasio Kigozi and myself. We had become so used to working together in the daily teaching and weekend missions, but we knew that we must have Simeoni Nsibambi, so a letter was sent to Kampala. He knew at once that it was the call of God because, unknown even to his wife, he had had a dream in which he had been told to go to western Uganda, 300 miles away, to preach to the lepers; and the leper colony was near to Kabale. He had already begun saving money for the journey." Q116-117

That convention at Kabale, at the end of September 1935, was remarkable indeed. It was the first major public event at which God worked in unusual power. There was a great sense of His presence there. Many people were deeply convicted of their sin, and many of those found peace as their sins were blotted out by the 'blood of Jesus Christ', shed for them on the Cross at Calvary, and they began a new life with God living within them as a daily, continuing, reviving experience.

Similar manifestations of God's reviving power were seen in other parts of Uganda, Rwanda and Burundi. Many people, including missionaries, were perplexed by what they saw happening. There was an urgent need for guidance from those whom God was using in leadership. In Rwanda, these were Joe Church and Yosiya Kinuka—William Nagenda came later. In southwest Uganda, the leadership fell to Lawrence Barham and Ezekiel Balaba. In central Uganda, the leader was undoubtedly Simeoni Nsibambi.

During the years that followed, in evangelistic missions and conventions, in church services around Kampala to which he was often invited, and in his own home, Nsibambi's ministry was powerful indeed. He was not a great speaker, but his words were accompanied by great conviction on the part of the listeners. So clear was Nsibambi's testimony and so penetrating was his understanding of people's spiritual needs, that many would travel considerable distances to sit in "the chairs under the mango tree" of his home in Kampala, and share with him their problems and, often, their deep concern for their unconverted friends. Many Church leaders, missionaries and other visitors to Kampala would not leave without a visit to Nsibambi, and would often return home with a new challenge and blessing.

In February, 1938, a memorable mission was held at Kako, a centre of the Church of Uganda, about 80 miles from Kampala. "The Church was filled with silent, expectant, white-clad clergy, lay-readers and senior Christians of this CMS mission with its many years of history," wrote Joe Church. "There were now third and fourth generation nominal Christians, many sunk in worldliness and money making. ... We began, as at Kabale, with the subject of Sin. In the beginning God made man, but man sinned ... sins of act, such as stealing and cheating; sins of attitude, such as hatred and jealousy; sins of state, refusing God and being unsaved. So the Bible spoke, verse by verse being read and expounded and the Holy Spirit burning it into our hearts ... After a break, Nsibambi came in with his strong insistent voice and his long remembered and often repeated *Ekibi kibi nnyo*! - 'Sin is bad, very bad!'. Then came the mercy of God. That moving word *ekisa*—'grace' in Luganda—began to flow in and melt hearts as they heard Christ pleading, 'Come unto me'." Q139

Later that month, Simeoni Nsibambi, William Nagenda, Yosiya Kinuka and Joe Church spent a night at Bwerenyangi on their way for a mission in Hoima, Uganda. They were greeted there by a young Ankole clergyman, Erica Sabiti. He told them that "the number of 'saved ones' had grown from seven to seventy, with much dreaming of dreams and trembling." All—African and missionary—were given hospitality by the African Christians. ℚ140

At the Hoima mission, God seemed to put His finger on the sins of debts, dishonesty, immorality and, for the Africans, hatred of Europeans; and for the Europeans, despising black people. The team members testified to the 'light' God had brought into their lives. "So we went to the Cross as sinners together, the place where revival begins. Nsibambi's testimony of his life at Budo School went home to us all. We saw the danger, so common on the old mission stations of forty or fifty years' standing, of taking people for granted and of hiding sin." ℚ143

Simeoni Nsibambi, with the musician, Yusufu Byangwa, Paulo Gahunde from Shyira (Rwanda) and Francis Kaboyo and Erenesti Nyabugabo, from Tooro and Kabale, respectively, in Uganda, and Joe Church from Rwanda, formed the first team to visit Kenya and shared in the leadership of the Kabete Convention in April 1937.

Joe Church records an incident when a missionary, working at Maseno in Kenya, was asking for prayer to know "how to act in His plan for revival in Kavirondo." Nsibambi was in the car as the request was made. Nsibambi's contribution to the discussion is not known. That missionary wrote later, however, "That little sermon of Nsibambi's in the car just before you started was a blessing to me." ℚ146

The next year, in August 1938, another team visited Kenya. It included Simeoni Nsibambi, William Nagenda, Yosiya Kinuka, Erenesti Nyabugabo, Ezekieri Balaba, Ezra Kikonyogo and Yusufu Byangwa. At the 'African Keswick', held at the Alliance High School in Kikuyu, Kenya, September 1938, Simeoni Nsibambi, Ezekieri Balaba, and Erenesti Nyabugabo were taken to a meeting with elders of the Kabete mission. "They wanted to talk over some problems that had arisen since the convention in April last year ... The elders, some doubtful, some opposing, produced many of the old arguments—'these people think they are better than us; these people are really hypocrites'! How we

praised God as Nsibambi and Balaba dealt sympathetically
but firmly with these things, and then there seemed to be
joy and laughter again." 9157

"Nsibambi's army experience and knowledge of Kiswahili
was used of God to shake those hundreds of African Church
leaders sitting before him," Joe commented. "He also felt it
was right to speak to some of the older missionaries about
hidden sin in the Church, and the need of Revival. This led
to some criticism of us, but the love of God broke through
and something new began to happen in Kenya. Obadiah
Kariuki, a gifted school master and our interpreter was converted. He later became Kenya's first African Archbishop.
A movement of the Holy Spirit began that seemed raised up
of God to meet the challenge of Mau Mau in later years."

Joe Church recalls an incident in Nairobi. For relaxa-
tion between meetings, "A kind person took us all down to
the East Africa Railways engineering works where the
Garrett Anderson engines were maintained and repaired.
They demonstrated to us a huge hydraulic press that would
crush metal and bend railway lines. We went on to the next
demonstration, but Nsibambi stayed behind. We had to go
back to find him. We found him still watching the colossal
press working. We asked him why he had stayed on. "Oh!"
he said, "I just wanted to go on watching that press. So
many people's hearts are as hard as that metal. We need a
great hammer of God to bend us and break us."

Nsibambi was a member of the team which led a mission at Ngara and Katoke in Tanganyika, (later Tanzania).
This mission was notable for two things. It was, according
to Joe Church, one of the hardest places spiritually that
they had visited, and it was there that, a few weeks later,
"the most amazing transformation" took place. Mixed with
a very deep work of God in many lives, were scenes which
can only be described as 'excesses'—confusion and disorder in services with screaming and unintelligible noises. It
needed the wisdom and discernment of the team and others to distinguish between what was of God and what was
Satanic. K93

In August 1940 a notable convention was held at Namirembe, Kampala to which were invited "all these scattered *balokole* (saved ones), especially the leaders, for instruction, exhortation and Bible teaching. The team included Simeoni Nsibambi, William Nagenda, Erica Sabiti, Yosiya Kinuka, Godfrey Hindley, Lawrence Barham, Bill Butler and Joe Church. "This was a remarkable gathering," wrote Joe Church, "with a large team of Africans and white leaders working in absolute oneness and trust." 9180

At that convention in Kampala, the words of Simeoni's brother Blasio were quoted as a challenge: "Awake Uganda! Awake out of sleep!" The theme of the convention centred on 'entering the Victorious Life' that was in Jesus. Nsibambi's contribution was short but it was very effective.

The year following the Convention at Namirembe proved to be the last in which Nsibambi took an active part in missions and conventions. He played a leading role in the Convention in Tooro in May 1941. Then illness prevented any further public ministry. His influence did not cease, however. There followed many years of prayer and personal counselling of people who came to him in his home.

As others saw them

"Nsibambi was," quoting Peter Kigozi, "a man of true discernment, able to distinguish truth and error, not given to much talk, a man of prayer, generous, with a sense of humour; not so much a pulpit preacher as a personal evangelist; an artist and singer.

"Eva Nsibambi's mission in this life can certainly never be fully known, but it included a lifetime of selfless and loving care for the worldly affairs of a great man of God and the raising of a family of eleven."

Enoki Rugimbirwa noted how Nsibambi took every opportunity of speaking to people: "Because his home was near the road, people would suddenly run to his home for shelter from heavy rain and he never lost an opportunity to share the Gospel with these people. He would ask his friends to preach to those who were waiting for the rain to stop!"

Samwiri Bakiranze remembered: "Sometimes he would walk round Kampala just in order to talk to people about their spiritual lives, as he had such a burden for people to know Jesus Christ. He was a great personal evangelist, more than a great preacher. And he had tremendous insight into a person's spiritual life. Sometimes people would come to him and say that they were cold spiritually because they were the only ones in their family who were saved, so they were lonely. Or maybe they were the only ones in their Church who were saved. He would say, 'If you see Jesus, you will not see the lack of people. If you do not see Him, you will not see anything but your own position'".

"When I was convicted of my sins in 1939," wrote Ruth Badokwaya, "I did not know what to do. Then I heard some people say that they had seen Nsibambi walking near the hospital at Namirembe. At once I thought, 'That person, whom I hear is a thoroughly saved man, will not fail to tell what I should do.' So I decided to go and find him. Indeed, I met him at Mengo Hospital, fully determined to do whatever he would tell me. I asked him, 'Can Jesus forgive my sins?' 'That is what He came to do,' he answered. Whereupon I was very pleased and said, 'Good-bye,' to him. I did not say anything else to him, but I committed myself to the Lord and was saved at that time. I have been walking with Jesus since then till now, 1998, and I thank Jesus and rejoice in Him.

"From then on, Nsibambi was always a beloved brother. He was very straight with brethren and would tell them what he discerned about them. 'You are cold spiritually,' or 'You are striving," or 'You are legalistic,' or 'You are full of impurity.' Sometimes he would ask questions such as, 'Do you preach the Gospel? Are people saved when you preach?' 'Have you a burden for the perishing?' When he spoke to anyone very strongly, Nsibambi would repent of striving and ask for forgiveness. He also gave us advice, such as: 'Before you go to help anyone, first pray to God to show whether that person is hard or not, because people are not the same.' He was very humble."

James Katarikawe added his testimony: "Nsibambi never abated in his witness, in spite of ridicule that was poured on him from every side. Slowly he won some to Christ. Nsibambi was very much burdened by perishing souls. He realised very acutely the awfulness of sin and the judgment of God on unrepentant sinners. But on the other hand, he realised the power of the Blood of Jesus to cleanse away all sin, and he called all people to repentance. No one has ever met Nsibambi without experiencing his piercing, inquiring eyes. His time was mostly spent in prayer, Bible study and preaching."

Bishop Dick Lyth records an incident when he and his wife met Nsibambi. "In 1952, we were on leave from the Sudan and staying in Kampala. We were out for a walk on Namirembe one evening and met Nsibambi. We introduced our son Michael to him who was then seven years old. Nsibambi asked him: 'Are you a Christian, Michael?' And Michael said 'No.' We were out to supper that evening, but early next morning Michael came to our bedside and said, 'I tried to stay awake last night but I fell asleep. I wanted to tell you that I have asked Jesus into my heart. You know that yesterday that man asked me if I was a Christian and I said 'No!' Last night in bed I was thinking about that. And you know how you have always told me how Jesus wants to come into my heart, and I just have to ask Him in. So that is what I have done.' It was wonderful to see the change the Lord worked in Michael's life and how he straight away began to try to win his younger brother for the Lord. He is over 50 now and still in full-time Christian Service. And we still praise God for the simple question of a godly man and the love and caring that prompted it."

Doreen Peck was a missionary who passed through Kampala on her way to Rwanda. "In my first week in Uganda, January 1947," she wrote, "I was taken by Roy Billington to meet Simeoni Nsibambi at his home in Kampala. At this stage I knew very little about him, except that God had used him and Joe Church to open up the Anglican Church in Rwanda and Uganda to a reviving work of the Holy Spirit.

"I was a little overawed by this tall Ugandan as he looked at me, unsmilingly, in the eye, and said, with no other introduction, 'Are you saved?' 'Yes, praise the Lord, I am,' I managed to reply. 'Since when?' ... and the questions continued about my spiritual experience, and also about my family and their faith. When I said they were not really committed Christians, he said, 'I believe the Lord will use you to save those people.' Getting a little bolder, I asked him something of his own family, but he did not elaborate. Then taking up his Bible he read out to me, as a verse to take as a special 'word' from the Lord, Ephesians 3:16: 'That He would grant you, according to the riches of His glory, to be strengthened with might by His Spirit in the inner man; and that Christ may dwell in your hearts by faith ...' Although I knew this verse by heart, and was sure of being 'saved', it was some years before I began consciously to experience the reality spoken of in these verses."

Dr Harold Adeney, a missionary working in Burundi, remembers his first meeting with Nsibambi. "When I was a young missionary, Nsibambi was a greatly venerated leader, perhaps a prophet, of the Revival Movement. On a visit to Kampala, sensing my need of spiritual counsel and help, I decided to go to see him. I was warned what to expect. On entering his house you would be greeted. Then Nsibambi would say 'Excuse me' and he would disappear into another room to pray before coming to talk with you. So when I went, that was just what happened, and I sat in his front room with my own thoughts and prayers. Conscious of my many failures as a missionary, I wondered if he would bring a stern rebuke from the Lord to me. Or would there be some word of encouragement? It seemed a long time before the frail figure of the man of God appeared, and I waited expectantly for the word he would bring me. 'I have a problem, doctor,' he said, 'Could you help me? It is my constipation.' This was the last thing I had expected. I am sorry to say that I was not at all pleased. I think I gave him some simple advice, but I do not remember how the visit ended. I came out deflated and a little resentful.

"Reflecting afterwards, I saw that God was using Nsibambi to speak to me. I had gone to him full of self and my needs and problems. But God wanted to show me, through this humble servant of His, that I lacked love and real concern for others and their needs. In the centre of my thoughts was a big capital 'I' that needed to come to the Cross and pray: 'Lord, bend that proud and stiff-necked 'I'' ... I am still learning this lesson."

Meeting with Nsibambi for the first time left many people with impressions which stayed with them all their lives. Shem Ndimbirwe was one of these. "I first met Nsibambi in 1933. I went to Mukono to train, but was taken sick and so went to Mengo Hospital. While in the hospital I noticed a very smart man, dressed in a suit and tie, walking round the ward. He talked to people and I saw him weeping, and so thought they were his relatives and that he had had bad news. Before he left the bedside I saw him kneel down and pray, and so I thought that the person he was praying with must be very, very sick.

"Then he came to my bed, and looked at my chart where my name was written and said, 'Shem, are you at Mukono?' I replied that I was. He asked, 'Are you studying?' I told him that I was studying. He then asked me what my illness was and I told him about the pains I had. He then said that he knew that I was studying the Bible and learning at Mukono but was I saved? Did I have a personal relationship with Jesus? I had never really heard clearly about salvation. But also I took myself to be an upright person. I did not drink, or steal, and I did not sleep around with women, so that I was convinced that I was a good living Church person. I had never met up with people like this before, but in my mind I thought I had met a prophet. So he went, but before leaving my bedside he prayed, and then that night I had a dream.

"The next day I really wanted to see him again, and so I asked the hospital staff if the man who had visited yesterday would be coming back. They said they doubted if he would be back. On hearing this I was very disappointed, but to my great delight soon after midday I saw him coming back into the hospital ward. He came to my bedside and asked me how I was, and I told him about the dream I had had, expecting that he would help me to understand what the dream was about. But his reply was 'I understand, but you need to know that when a person is sick he or she often dreams'! Then he continued and said 'You are in a dangerous place, and God is calling you.'

"At the Kabale Convention in 1935, Simeoni Nsibambi was a member of the team of leaders. I listened to him and the others, but I did not consider that I had any great need, as I saw other people were overcome with sins which I did not openly commit. In the course of the week, Blasio called me and explained to me that I needed to repent, and he showed me that sin is a terrible thing and it must be judged, and that the grace of God is there for everyone who will come to Him in repentance. But I still could not understand what they were talking about.

"There was an argument in our family and I began to grumble at my wife for listening to things from my brother. At that time I was still studying at Mukono, and I was very angry with my wife. I decided I did not want to mistreat her physically, or argue with her, but I decided I would just keep quiet. This I did, and it really hurt my wife. I even wrote these things down in a book, listing all the things I had against her, so that if anyone asked me why I did not chat with my wife they could understand my reasoning. The Lord reminded me of the things I had thought and the things I had done and the things I had written and He asked me, 'Is that behaviour the behaviour of a man of God?' It was at that point that I began to repent of my sin. I went home and told my wife that I had been saved, and I got that terrible book and showed it to her, and apologised to her, and I burned the book. She could not believe that I had been saved. When I saw Nsibambi I told him what had happened and he was so pleased to know that I was saved, and he asked me with a twinkle in his eye 'Do you still trust your dreams?' I laughed, and thanked God for him."

Nsibambi's first remark to a visitor was often a disturbing challenge. This happened to Enoki Rugimbirwa. "I went to see Nsibambi as a young man, and he challenged me about the fact that I was not walking closely with the Lord, and I knew he was right. He especially talked to me about impure thoughts over a young lady with whom I had gone to see him. He said, 'It is not only you that is troubled by wrong thoughts, for I find I need to seek God's forgiveness too.' He was a man who knew how to come before the Lord in repentance. The other thing I remember about him was that he was a man who knew how to pray."

Zak Kalega was one of those who were, at first, afraid to meet the man about whom so many spoke. "When I was saved I was living at a village called Buloba, and there Nsibambi had a house, and I was living not far away. Other brethren told me that I should make time to go and meet him. But before I went I had heard so many stories about him and I got scared. They told me how straight he was, and how honest he was, and how he could just look at you and say what the Lord had shown him. I was told, before I met him, that he could say, 'Brother, I think that I am striving. I am not going to talk to you.' This sometimes dissuaded people from going to see him, and I personally made my excuses. But when I met him I understood that he had his own way. Often when he met people he would start by repenting himself of something he had been convicted of. For example, he would say: 'When you came I felt this or that, but may the Lord forgive me and will you forgive me too.' Then he would tell you what he thought you needed to repent of. He was a man of discernment and he was a good counsellor. If you talked to him about an issue, the Lord would give him something to say about it, and I never remember anyone telling me that they had been disappointed about the way he had talked with them ... it was always before people went that they had their fears and uncertainties as to what he was going to say. Afterwards, they would come away having been lifted up and encouraged. He was a man of vision.

"I subsequently met him on several occasions, but I never said much as I was always more interested in listening to him rather than talking myself. It was interesting that he never asked questions about your work, but he always asked about you spiritually. 'Are the people being blessed where you work?' he would say, or 'What about spiritual coldness?' He was always focusing on a person's spiritual walk. One of the things he said to me I shall never forget: 'We are in a world where people are spiritually starving, never go out of your house without food, people are hungry. You must have something to give them.' Those words were indelibly written on my mind, and I am so glad they were, for I want them always to remain with me."

While he was studying at Makerere in the early 1950's, Enoch Rukare visited Nsibambi. "I did not have much money in those days, and so I could not always afford to go home to Mbarara, but also I wanted to have fellowship with God's people. My father was not born again, and I was the only committed Christian in my family. During those days I heard about Nsibambi and sometimes I would feel God was telling me to go and see him, and so I went. To be truthful, he used to frighten me. His house was quiet and a bit lonely, it seemed to me. Sometimes I would wait in his sitting room, and he did not come out. My guess was that he was probably praying. Sometimes he came out sweating and would say, 'Hello Rukare, how are you?' I would say that I was all right but needed the Lord's grace, and he would tell me that he thought I was spiritually cold. He would bring me a cup of tea, and then the one thing that impressed me very much was that, after challenging me, he would tell me how *he* was spiritually, and sometimes he would say, 'I too am spiritually cold and I too need the Lord's grace.'

"To me, that was amazing. To come and see someone who was such a mature Christian, and he confesses to such a young person how he is spiritually, was very challenging and this encouraged me to return to see him from time to time. It also helped me to see that he was not condemning me but was being in the light about his own walk.

"He was a man who had no 'small talk'. He never asked
me how my studies were going, his main focus was spiritual. 'How are you?' 'Are you uplifting the Lord Jesus?'
'Are you preaching the Gospel?' 'Are you sharing your faith
with those people there?' I would never stay long with him
but he was always 'to the point'. His encouragement helped
me a great deal. Many people do not understand what we
mean by the word 'brokenness', but he was a 'broken' man.
We would always pray together before I left him, and I would
always return to Makerere feeling renewed and strengthened for the next few weeks. Although he was a sick man
he never said he was too busy to see me, and he never said
he was too sick to see me."

'Brokenness' to the revived Christians, meant a spiritual state of being 'broken' in the sense of having a humble
willingness to listen and accept the advice, challenges or
comments of others, particularly colleagues with whom one
worked closely. The 'stiff neck', representing 'unbrokenness',
is a picture of the person who says to God and to others, "I
am right. You are wrong!' So, the 'bent neck', representing
'brokenness', is a picture of the person who says to God
and to others: "You are right. I am wrong!" Even when the
person is not wrong, 'brokenness' is the willingness to listen and to be challenged.

"Nsibambi helped me in many ways," said Samwiri
Bakiranze. "One way in particular was over my attitude to
women. I found it so hard to come to accept that women or
girls could be saved! I thought that women were there for
men, and that was all! But God has a sense of humour,
and when I went into training in the hospital I found that
the majority of those learning were women, because they
were training as nurses. It was Nsibambi who helped me
to change my attitude to women. I was impressed because
I found young women who were really saved, and this
amazed me. He used to ask me if I was repenting of impure
thoughts towards them as I mixed with so many girls at
that time. I praise God so much because I found I had
such a lot to learn from them."

Malcolm Lea-Wilson was the owner of the tea plantation at Namutamba. "I first met Nsibambi in 1947, in his
home on the lower slopes of Namirembe hill," he wrote.
"He and my father, Leslie Lea-Wilson, were very close brothers in Christ and had a deep love for each other. In fact it
was through the testimony of Nsibambi and other saved
Africans that my father was challenged, and asked the Lord
to be Saviour and Master of every part of his life. At first I
found it difficult visiting Nsibambi. On arrival at his home
Eva, his wife, or one of the children would welcome me into
the sitting room, and there I would sit and wait, perhaps
even for as much as 15 minutes for Nsibambi to appear.
When he did, his smile and welcome would erase any impatience I might have had. His main concern was to know
how I was succeeding in walking closely with Jesus, and he
had spent those 15 minutes before seeing me asking God
to tell him what to say to his guest. He was a man of great
discernment, very open and honest about his own shortcomings, but also of the Lord's saving Grace.

"Even when he could no longer move far from his room,
he kept very up to date with all that was going on in politics, in the Church and in the country as a whole, as well
as overseas, and he spent many hours praying for all these
things as well as the spiritual well-being of many individuals of any nationality.

"When Nsibambi visited us at Namutamba, I got to know
him well, and no longer feared his loving challenges. After
all, he never spoke out of criticism or jealousy, or hurt pride
etc., but always out of love for His Lord and a longing for
me to experience fully the Spirit-filled life—the joy of walking with the Lord Jesus with nothing between— and that
this could be something very real and practical for me, a
young Britisher working on our family tea estate and dairy
farm, with a labour force of over 400.

"When my father died in 1953, the whole farm was left
to me, even though, like Nsibambi, I was not the oldest
child. The English accountant we employed to audit our
accounts urged us to turn the whole concern into a Private

Company, so that we would not lose vast sums to Inland Revenue in super tax. It seemed such a sensible idea. We discussed the whole matter over a period of two years, with relatives and close friends, both black and white. We also talked and prayed about it with our senior supervisors on the farm. The whole matter was gone into in detail, and yet no 'green light' lit up with regard to any of the possibilities.

"I happened to visit Nsibambi one day in Kampala, and whilst talking about various other matters, he suddenly asked a question. 'Malcolm, if Namutamba becomes a Company, will you have complete freedom to follow the Lord's leading in the future?' And then he added, 'Don't worry about the tax side of things; the Lord can so easily look after that.' It was such a simple question, but it cut right across my thinking and planning. I went home and we prayed about the company question once more. Very clearly the green light shone on the decision to forge ahead uncluttered by any company, and there was agreement from the family too. Interestingly enough, for the next 20 years, until we had to leave Uganda, we never ran into Supertax! But we did run into all the difficulties of the Amin years, and had Namutamba been a Company at that time, I think Amin would have confiscated it and given it to one of his friends, as happened to many other estates.

"So I go back to that simple question that my dear brother Nsibambi asked me and which brought us to make what I'm quite sure was the right decision. His one main concern for all who came to visit him was the closeness of their walk with Jesus. 'How are you?' he would ask, and then with a smile he would add: 'spiritually'. There was never any condemnation in his voice or what he said, just a pointing back to Jesus."

His son, Dr John Nsibambi, noted a characteristic of Nsibambi which distinguished him from many of his time. "He was not tribe conscious. People of all tribes used to visit our home, no matter what their tribe or nationality. He loved the Lord's people very much, irrespective of their background."

"Another thing I noticed," said Samwiri Bakiranze, "was the fellowship between these people. The embracing fellowship of the saved people is very touching and impressive. It embraces people of all backgrounds and conditions. Folk from all over the world would meet to share the Good News together, and to listen to what God was doing in other parts of the world. The Namirembe Friday meeting was very special to so many people. People come to the meeting once a week, but all of them attend their own church on Sundays."

"Even the inter-tribal relationships came as a matter of course," said Zeb Kabaza and Revd. Peter Kigozi. "If you were a Munyankole, the Muganda is your brother, the Mutoro, is your brother, the expatriate is your brother. That helped even the missionaries with their aloofness. In the past, when you visited missionaries, they would come and greet you on the verandah but you never knew them. But when the Holy Spirit worked, and we began walking in the light and confessing our sins, we found that we needed the same Saviour. The spontaneous love of God moved us."

Sam Bakiranze was not alone in noting that "Nsibambi was not a great pulpit preacher. He could go into the pulpit and just give you one or two words or sentences, and people could be touched or brought to Christ by these few words. Then other people would continue with other messages. His voice was so interesting."

Enoki Rugimbirwa remembered that "one of his favourite passages was 'Whoever wants to come and drink of the water of life should come.' He stood up at a Convention and everyone thought he was going to preach on this passage, but he read the passage, and to everyone's surprise he sat down. During those days when people visited him in his home this was the passage of the Bible he would frequently use. Even when he was ill he was very frank, and told you what God had put on his heart to say."

It is a surprise to some people to learn that Nsibambi was a great reader. Most of this reading was in English as the only two books in Luganda at that time were the Bible and Pilgrim's Progress. Nsibambi read a great deal about

the Revivals in Europe and North America and would refer
to the works of Charles Finney which he knew well. "But he
held to books quite lightly," remembered Malcom Lea-
Wilson, "and with a chuckle used to say 'Yes! In England
you have many books, many good Christian books, but do
you have Revival?' He had seen many well-taught and well-
read Europeans in Uganda, but so few who had been able
to pass on the simplicity of the way of walking with Jesus
and being filled with the Holy Spirit. The Bible was his text
book and constant friend and often he would ask a guest to
read out a verse of particular relevance."

Even Joe Church found it difficult to describe "this lov-
able, magnetic, yet strange person. He had a quiet dignity
that was built into his character. He would take quite a
time to answer a question, and more often than not he would
answer, in African style, by asking you one back, with a
chuckle. He would keep you waiting, quite a time sometimes before emerging from his inner room. It must be said
that for the last ten or even twenty years he remained a
great deal with his family and grandchildren around him
in his nice little modern Buganda home. He suffered for
many years from poor health which was a trial to him, but
which God used, by people coming to visit and consult him
at his home.

"He had a remarkable gift of discernment. He would
speak gently, but sometimes, when he felt it was necessary, with embarrassing directness, he would touch the really sore spot that you did not know that he knew about.
He was quite fearless, yet remarkably tender when he felt
he had been too hard. He would break off the conversation
and say, 'I'm sorry. Perhaps I've been striving—*okufuba*—
in Luganda. Sometimes he would stop in the middle of a
sentence and say 'I'm sorry. I have something I must put
right, something that I must repent of ...' Then he would go
on again. But occasionally, with a very difficult person, he
would go quite silent rather embarrassingly and just say,
'I'm sorry. I feel tired, I must stop. Let us pray.' And then
the Good-bye would come, rather disconcertingly.

"His English was never perfect and he could sometimes be rather blunt unwittingly. In this way there grew up around him a tremendous sense of respect and love and gratitude, but also with some people a fear of him, and others were annoyed.

"Nsibambi had a great ministry among people who came day by day to bring news of what was happening elsewhere and to share their testimonies. He was quick to spot anything that seemed to be taking the place of Christ, or anything that was added to people being saved by grace only. Some converts who longed to 'go all out' for God and to keep nothing back from Him, can easily fall into 'works'—shouting in prayer, all night singing of hymns with much repetition. We all loved times when the Spirit of God was clearly moving us, but when sacred things become mechanical and dry the Holy Spirit is grieved away.

"Nsibambi loved these times of the moving of the Spirit and would join in with abandon. His hearty laugh and joyful singing could be clearly heard. In all this, Nsibambi was one of the first to come in fearlessly with a challenge when, what came to be called *gufuba* (striving) got in. In looking back over the years, these times are remembered as the most moving and heart-warming. We learned something of the true 'fear of God', which is really a true reverence and awe of the Holy Spirit. If Nsibambi saw some one or a small group of enthusiasts beginning to 'strive', he would walk up to them firmly with a smile and say, 'Brother or sister, you are striving'. Then there would be repentance and the peace of God would come back."

Simeoni's leadership in spiritual matters, firm yet always with great humility and grace, was accepted by all the revived brethren. Criticism there was from onlookers, but within the fellowship there was something very powerful in the way the brethren would submit to each other without anyone feeling cowed or rejected. Simeoni and Eva Nsibambi were living testimonies and examples of the Gospel they proclaimed. From near and far, people came to their home knowing that they would meet with Jesus.

Later years

Nsibambi was 44 years of age when he played a leading role in a Convention at Kabarole, in Tooro, in Uganda, in May 1941. After this he was taken ill and he was thereafter almost entirely confined to his house. His ministry was not, however, at an end. Although unable to take an active part in missions and conventions, Nsibambi was a source of inspiration as, in his home, he received people, and from his home he kept in touch with all those whom God was using in the Revival.

Despite his physical limitations, "Simeoni had a vital role in Revival, with his finger on the pulse of things," wrote Joe Church, "He followed every movement and expected reports to be brought to him. I once said to him, 'How do you keep up so well with all that is going on?' 'Oh,' he replied, 'My Eva brings me all the news!' There were many, like Eva, who brought him news of what was happening and everything was taken to God in prayer. But the greatest of these sources for prayer was, I believe, the prompting of the Holy Spirit Himself."

The serious rift which Revival appeared to bring in the Church of Uganda in 1943, was blamed by some church leaders on the Ruanda Mission, of which Joe Church was a missionary. The Executive Committee of the Ruanda Mission drew up a reply to the accusations made, but before submitting it to the Bishop, three of the members, including Joe Church, "went to Nsibambi armed with our Minute and the account of our efforts at reconciliation. He listened patiently to the story of the meetings at Buye, then he walked over to his bookshelf and pulled out a well worn copy of Finney's 'Revivals of Religion'. He pointed to a passage and asked me to read it ... 'if those who are labouring to promote them (Revivals) allow themselves to get impatient and get into a bad spirit, the Revival will cease.' He pointed to the words 'bad spirit' and asked me to read them twice. Then he said, 'Isn't there another word in English ... 'sweetness'? Be careful not to lose sweetness'." [203] It was advice which he himself followed.

In 1945, William Nagenda and Yosiya Kinuka became
involved in what came to be known as the 'Crucifying-the-
old-man' controversy of which more details are given elsewhere. Nagenda brought the matter to Nsibambi who resolved the issue with the words: "Don't you know, William,
that your old man was crucified for you, long ago, at Calvary!
... Go home and rest, brother, rest in the finished work of
Calvary." Such was the authority of Nsibambi that both
Nagenda and Kinuka accepted this as from God. The testimony of the truth which emerged from that experience was
taken by Nagenda and Kinuka, and quoted by others, to
many in East Africa and further afield who were seeking a
'second blessing' through 'striving' for it.

During the years of the active, public ministry of
Nsibambi, there was a less publicised feature. Groups of
Christians would meet regularly for prayer, with no fears,
no sense of inferiority or superiority by members of different racial, ethnic or language groups, all 'one' as they prayed
in the one name which bound them together, that of Jesus. One small group was known as 'the three ladies'—
three women whose hearts were 'knit together' in prayer—
Eva Nsibambi, Keziya Matovu and Marjorie Kireremerwa.
The leaders of Revival, and Nsibambi foremost among them,
recognised the fundamental importance of the prayer of
revived Christians as the Gospel was preached to sometimes ignorant listeners but also to antagonistic ones from
whom there was often severe opposition.

A serious threat to the unity of the revived 'brethren'
occurred when a separatist movement emerged. A number
of 'revived brethren', including Yona Mondo, a very close
friend of Nsibambi until this time, felt that their purity and
holiness were being weakened by the ways of the world.
They called themselves the *Abazukufu* (awakened ones) or
the *okuzukuka* (awakening). The group, led by Mondo, laid
down rules for 'holiness'. It was, for them, sinful to borrow
money, to arrange their hair in an unnatural way, to sweep
their houses, wash their clothes or bury the dead on a Sunday. Many other such restrictions were imposed on their

members. There were also clashes of personalities, notably between some of the less educated and those who had had a better education.

Of these two errors Shem Ndimbirwe wrote: "By the 1940s, there were many saved people, and many who loved to 'walk in the light', and this time the enemy came in to make people strive. They found themselves striving to be holy, and to put on the 'new man'. If the 'old man' had died, it meant that no one could sin any more. There would be no more being annoyed, no more sin. People followed this teaching, but Nsibambi saw through this, and warned them of the dangers that Satan was bringing.

"Then Satan brought another trap, and this time it was that of fleeing from the world (*okuzukuka*). Some people went to Entebbe (although Nsibambi did not go himself) to try and sort things out. This problem was very subtle, as indeed all the devil's works are, as they seem to be so near to the truth. On their return from Entebbe some said they had found a new way, but others felt that the enemy was coming in so as to get in between His people.

"For Nsibambi, it was a puzzle at first, and he did not find it easy to see what the Lord was saying. But after a while he understood that this was another trap brought by the enemy in order to get God's people to strive. Part of the reason that made him hesitate was because he was a man who did not make quick decisions, but carefully considered them first. When he saw through the issue he wrote to the leading people in *okuzukuka* disassociating himself from them and telling them that it was not the right way to go. He then went on to pray for them."

An article written by Nsibambi to make clear the errors of the *okuzukuka* was entitled: *The nature of Revival and how the grace of our Lord helped us to receive it here in Uganda and East Africa and the danger that can destroy it if it is not safeguarded.*

"To serve God in a Revival," he wrote, "demands from the person that God uses, a humble reverence, free from pride, as the example of Moses. He was frightened at first.

And Jeremiah was afraid, despising himself saying, 'I am
only a youth.' There were many ways through which the
Lord was guided, through brokenness and obedience, which
were out of the ordinary. 'Although he was a Son, he learned
obedience.' (Hebrews 5:8) When a person is called to participate in the work of Revival, God gives him the Holy Spirit,
to enable him to be strong and courageous and not to fear
the people among whom he is sent to work ..."

Nsibambi then described how God led him into a complete commitment to Jesus Christ and into God's working
in revival. Extracts from this are quoted elsewhere. "After
that commitment, I was filled with the power of the Holy
Spirit of an unusual kind. ... It was due to this personal
experience and encounter with the working of the Holy Spirit
and many other reasons that I became sensitive to any heretical tendencies developing in Revival—here in Uganda
or elsewhere."

Nsibambi saw that in time to come there would be those
who would look for other phenomena instead of looking at
Jesus. He saw the *okuzukuka* as a heretical movement
which brought Christians into legalism and spiritual bondage. "The Holy Bible refers to groups of people who became
heretical in these terms," he wrote and quoted: "'And from
among your own selves will arise men speaking perverse
things, to draw away the disciples after them.' (Acts 20:30)
This concerns all Christians, the body of Christ. 'You are
severed from Christ, you would be justified by the law, you
have fallen away from grace.' (Gal 5:4)   And 'They make
much of you. They want to shut you out, that you may
make much of them.' (Gal. 4:17) But if you read Col.2:20-
23, 'If you died to the elemental spirits of the universe, why
do you live as if you still belong to the world? Why do you
submit to regulations: do not handle; do not taste; do not
touch; referring to things which all perish as they are used,
according to human precepts and doctrines? These have
indeed an appearance of wisdom and promoting vigour of
devotion and self-abasement and severity to the body, but
they are of no value in checking the indulgence of the flesh.'"

"Coming under a heresy of any form is a very dangerous thing in the Church and kills the hearts of Christians and destroys the Revival. The only remedy for a plague and to stop it spreading quickly, is to put into quarantine and segregate the 'sick' from those who are not. Those who read Church History will know the truth of what I am saying. This is what led St Paul to challenge St Peter when he saw him putting emphasis on teaching Jewish traditions in hypocrisy which was leading many astray. Paul stopped him until Peter repented. (Gal 2:14-21)

"The greatest sources of heresy are: 1. The love of money and wealth. 2. Jealousy, envy and the lust for power and self-aggrandisement. 3. Impurity leads many astray by blindly quoting the Bible. 4. Lack of teaching of Scripture and thus following other teaching, either of their denomination or heretic doctrines extracted out of the Scriptures.

"It is also taught that if a person accepts the Lord Jesus as his Saviour and is saved, he must immediately become 'awakened'. This awakening has been exalted, taking away the pre-eminence of our Lord Jesus and the Salvation through him is no longer important without 'awakening'."

Nsibambi had indeed perceived the error in the ways of the *okuzukuka*, that of striving to gain righteousness and holiness by the laying down of rules and regulations of conduct and raising any Christian experience above that of walking with Jesus. "To have a Revival in a nation is a matter of great blessedness and to allow it to deteriorate would be a matter of great sadness which should not be handled with complacency."

It is typical of Nsibambi that when William Nagenda was about to leave for the UK, in 1947, he said to him, "You may think the Lord is taking you to England to do great things, and that through you many Europeans will be saved. But remember, if you return to Uganda and it turns out that *one* person of the Lord's choosing has been blessed, then your visit to the UK will have been 100% successful."

The reality of Jesus Christ and the 'world of the Spirit' filled Nsibambi's horizon. Everything else was secondary.

He was also driven by a passion to pass the Good News on to others and to challenge them as to where they stood in relation to God and their eternal destiny. This did not diminish a very real understanding of human life and the importance of events and suffering in this world, but these were seen from the point of view of the eternal, spiritual world which was even more real to him.

Dr Joe Church wrote, "One of those questions which only God can answer is why such a gifted man had to suffer so much from sickness in the later years of his life. Only eternity will reveal how many men and women will be in heaven because of the faithful ministry of this great and humble man."

"In later life Nsibambi did not leave his home very much but spent much time in prayer," added Shem Ndimbirwe. "He had a deep burden for Revival, praying constantly that God would revive His people. The Lord used him greatly."

Of the last years of Nsibambi's life, Dr Manual Muranga wrote: "A life of extensive journeys to spread the Gospel, often under harsh conditions, had resulted in a weakening of his physical body. Debilitated by *diabetes mellitus,* Simeoni was forced to stay at home during the last years of his life."

Simeoni Nsibambi died on February 14th 1978 at the age of 81. A thanksgiving and memorial service was held for him on June 16th 1978, at which the retired Archbishop Erica Sabiti described him as 'Our father in Christ'. Nsibambi was, the Archbishop observed, "a man who could have been the 'katikkiro' (the leading government official) of Buganda, but who instead, devoted his life to bringing people closer to God."

Eva Nsibambi died on October 14th 1990 at the age of 84. She was buried beside her husband in the grounds of the church at Buloba.

The number is uncountable of those who were influenced by the lives of Simeoni and Eva Nsibambi. There were, and there are still today, many who praise God for every memory of them.

Chapter 2

Joe and Decie Church

The early years

John Edward Church was born on 10 August 1899, the eldest surviving son of ten children, five boys and five girls, born to the Revd Edward and Florence Church. John later came to be known as Joe. Edward Church was the Rector of the parish of Burrough Green, Cambridgeshire. The Rectory of that parish was the centre of life for John in his early years. It was into the study of that Rectory, normally 'out of bounds' to the children, that Joe's father called him one day to show him a leather-bound, handwritten diary with entries dating back to 1660. Among other fascinating entries was the story of Mary Church, who "listened to the preaching of Whitefield and Wesley after they had been greatly blessed through meeting the Moravians".

The diary went on to record that Mary "entered into the joy of the Lord and she ceased to worry and found rest in the power of the blood of Jesus". For Joe, the memory of this incident gave him great joy in later years. It was also significant to him in the light of what was to follow subsequently in his own life.

Joe attended the local village primary school, which he did not enjoy. At about this time, he acquired a pronounced stutter and also a very dry skin condition from which he was never free. For his secondary education, he attended St Lawrence College, Ramsgate. He revelled in the school games and made many friends but he carefully avoided the Christian Union. He became a prefect, sang in the school choir and gained his hockey colours, a much envied distinction in that school.

In January 1918, the last year of World War I, at the age of eighteen, Joe was selected from among the senior boys of St Lawrence College, to train as an officer in the Tank Corps of the army. As in school, so in the army, Joe pursued what he described as a 'merry-go-round' existence in a ceaseless round of activities.

He was stationed for a time near Poole, Dorset, and there he became an ardent sailing enthusiast, an interest he carried into later life. He founded the famous Walrus Cruises on the Norfolk Broads in 1924, and they still continue.

At the end of the war, he elected to remain in the Tank Corps for two years in order, so he claimed, to put off the day when he would have to decide whether or not to read classics and train for ordination in the Church of England and so fulfil his father's hopes.

Although outwardly gregarious, Joe was essentially a lonely, sensitive person with deep concern to find an answer to the question which occupied much of his thinking—what was to be the direction of his life. Despite his Christian upbringing and the future proposed for him as a clergyman, not once during his army career did he seek advice or help from the army chaplains. Although unwilling to make any sort of Christian commitment, he would, from time to time, slip into a church or chapel seeking something, he hardly knew what.

Early in 1919, he learned that the government was making grants to ex-service men to enable them to complete studies interrupted by the war. He knew that his father could not support him financially at a university and he would have to be largely responsible for his own further education, if any, and so he filled in the necessary application forms for a government grant.

In a series of events which he later attributed to God's gracious intervention, he gained early demobilisation and the promise of grants to cover university tuition for five years. He was now independent of his father's aims for him and, as he had become increasingly attracted to medicine, he applied for and gained a place at Emmanuel College, Cambridge, as a medical student in October 1919.

His parents had moved to the vicarage of St. Andrew the Less, Cambridge, and Joe was able to lodge with them, but he was careful to take no part in parish activities. He avoided the Christians who met in the CICCU (the Cambridge Inter-Collegiate Christian Union), even though this meant also avoiding some of his friends from St Lawrence College. Apart from academic studies, Joe divided his attention between hockey and a second-hand Triumph single cylinder motorbike!

Some of his old school friends who, unknown to him, had been praying earnestly for him, invited him to join them in a seaside 'CSSM house-party' at Whitby, Yorkshire. This was a Christian evangelistic outreach to children in a seaside town. To his own astonishment, he agreed to go. He loved being with children, so it was not difficult for him to enter into their games, give them rides on his motorcycle and organise treasure hunts. As he listened to the simple talks given to the children, he became aware that God was there and was speaking to him. On the 29th August, 1920, he found himself praying the words of a chorus they had been teaching the children:

> Cleanse me from my sin, Lord,
> Put Thy power within, Lord,
> Take me as I am, Lord, And make me all Thine own.
> Keep me day by day, Lord,
> Underneath Thy sway, Lord;
> Make my heart Thy palace And Thy royal throne.

That same evening, Joe gave his testimony to what God had just done for him—He had made him, Joe, His own. Following his conversion, Joe was warmly welcomed into the Christian Union and he joined eagerly in its activities. He worked even harder at his medical studies.

In the Autumn Term, 1920, Joe suffered a severe shock when he twice coughed up blood! He had been conscious of a persistent cough and a painful chest which affected his hockey. With a deadening horror, he realised that he might be suffering from the then dread disease: tuberculosis. In those days it could spell the end of a medical career. He prayed desperately that God would not let that disease prevent him living his life for Him. He wrote later: "I prayed and made a solemn vow that I would surrender every bit of my life, and quit absolutely all known sin, and would claim, in faith, the victorious life and revival and would give my life to be a missionary anywhere in the world if He, for His part, would cure me. Yes, cure me, then and there. I had had these chest pains for weeks and I bowed to His will, but asked for healing."

 In what cannot be described as anything less than miraculous, Joe's health began to mend and, by the end of the term, he appeared cured. Years later, a routine radiogram scan revealed some old scar tissue on his lungs.

In June 1922 Joe learned that he had successfully passed all his preliminary examinations for his medical degrees. He left Cambridge and continued his medical studies at St Bartholomew's Hospital—usually abbreviated to Bart's Hospital—in London. There, while working hard, Joe also found time for sport. He played hockey strenuously and won a much coveted cup for rifle shooting.

In the same family home where Joe lodged, there was also a young medical student from the Royal Free Hospital named Decima Tracey. Decima was the tenth child of a family doctor, a keen Christian, with a medical practice in Devon. A friendship between them grew rapidly.

After qualifying as a doctor, in 1926, Joe completed six months as casualty officer and Resident Anaethetist at

Addenbrooke's Hospital, Cambridge. While there, he attended a missionary breakfast at which the speaker was
Dr Algie Stanley Smith, one of the founders of the Ruanda
Mission (CMS). As he spoke of a remarkable opening in
that part of Africa for Christian medical work, Joe recognised God calling Him to that work. He offered himself for
service with that Mission. He was accepted and very soon
travelled to Brussels, in Belgium, to practise French and
study for the Diploma in Tropical Medicine and Hygiene.
He returned to England the following February. In June,
the CICCU invited Joe to a farewell tea in Cambridge and
there he announced his engagement to Decie.

In October 1927, Joe set sail for Africa.

The first mission centre in Rwanda, then part of a single
territory, Ruanda-Urundi, administered by the Belgian government, had recently been started at Gahini by Geoffrey
Holmes. He was joined by Revd Bert Jackson and Kosiya
Shalita, a young Rwandan whose parents had fled from
Rwanda some years previously and who had received a good
education in Uganda. He spoke English very well in addition to his native language. It was there that Joe was located with the aim of developing a medical work—building
and staffing a hospital as well as going on medical safaris.
With him went Yosiya Kinuka, a young man from neighbouring Ankole, who had volunteered to be a member of
the pioneer medical team at Gahini.

Life was very full for Bert, Joe and Kosiya at Gahini. It
was made even more difficult by a severe famine in north
Rwanda. In 1929, this reached such proportions that local
aid became totally inadequate and help was requested from
beyond Rwanda. Without any direct action from Joe, his
plea for assistance in Uganda was published in England,
in 'The Times' of 16 April 1929, and then in the international press. The plight of the famine sufferers appeared to
be a criticism of the Belgian government to which Ruanda-
Urundi was 'mandated territory', under similar conditions
to those under which Great Britain governed Uganda as a
'protectorate'.

The matter was discussed in the Belgian Parliament and considerable assistance was granted. The CMS Ruanda Mission, and, in particular, Dr J Church, were officially thanked for their cooperation.

In 1929, the team of Joe Church, Bert Jackson, Yosiya Kinuka, and Kosiya Shalita was increased by the arrival of Blasio Kigozi, a brother of Simeoni Nsibambi. Blasio, who had been converted through his brother, came to Rwanda in 1929 with a strong sense of a call to reach the 'unsaved'. He met a kindred spirit in Joe Church. The influence of Blasio was far greater than might be indicated by the shortness of his life. After his death, Joe wrote a brief biography of him entitled: 'Awake! An African calling.'

That year, Joe felt that he needed some rest and time to think and pray over the hectic life he, with other members of the Gahini team, had been leading in the development of the work—evangelistic, educational and medical—at Gahini. In a borrowed car he drove to Kampala and it was there, in September 1929, that he and Simeoni Nsibambi met.

"I had been praying for a long time," wrote Joe in his diary, "that God would lead me to one saved African with whom I could have deep fellowship." God answered that prayer in Simeoni Nsibambi. "Yesterday a rich Muganda, (in contrast to the poverty in Rwanda), in government service, rushed up to me at Namirembe and said he had heard me speaking at a small meeting run by Miss Ensor. I had spoken about surrendering all and coming out for Jesus. He said he had done so, and had great joy in the Lord, and had wanted to see me ever since. And then he said in his own words that he knew something was missing in the Uganda church and in himself: what was it? Then I had the great joy of telling him about the filling of the Spirit and the Victorious Life ..." [66]

They met on two consecutive days and together followed through the references to the Holy Spirit in the Scofield Bible. Together they decided to "quit all sin in faith, and have claimed the Victorious Life and the filling of the Spirit ... Our hearts truly did 'burn within us' those days, as with the two going to Emmaus when Christ himself in his risen glory 'expounded unto them in all the Scriptures the things concerning himself.' I have often referred to this time in my preaching in later years as the time that God in his sovereign grace met with me and brought me to the end of myself and thought fit to give me a share of the power of Pentecost. There was nothing very spectacular, nothing ecstatic; it is easy to become proud if one has received a special gift. The only special gift is the experience of the transforming vision of the risen Jesus himself." [968]

The two men separated to go their different ways. For Joe it was to go on to Nairobi to take delivery of a new car for the work at Gahini. On returning to Kampala, he heard a critical account of the change in Nsibambi as expressed in his renewed and revitalised evangelistic zeal.

Joe realised that "the devil was fighting and I wanted someone to pray with, so I ran out to the home of Dr Cook (the missionary Doctor in charge of Mengo Hospital) at Makindye, where Dr Algie Stanley Smith was staying, and together we asked God to guide and protect His own work. Algie said, 'If this happens when you have asked for a new filling of His Spirit, then we must trust that what follows must be His will'." [970]

The New Year, 1930, opened at Gahini with encouraging signs of rehabilitation after the terrible effects of the famine. Joe wrote: "Gahini has come through the ordeal and has reached the stage when real advance can be made." [971]

Further encouragement came from several conversions which showed deep spiritual changes. One, in particular, impressed Joe. He was walking near the football field with an 'intelligent junior chief', from whose hand he had removed a small tumour and for whom the hospital staff had prayed that 'God would heal him and save him.' Joe reminded him that he could be saved there and then. They knelt together on the grass. The man prayed, "Lord Jesus, I have heard your words. I believe in you. I am like a blind man, open my eyes that I may see." [971] The next day he began to tell his family of his new-found Saviour.

Family life

Two and a half years after their engagement, Decie arrived from England at Nairobi railway station, in the company of Dr and Mrs Len Sharp. It was there that she was
met by Joe. They were married in Namirembe Cathedral,
Kampala, on Monday, 19th May, 1930. Three weeks later
they arrived at Gahini, which was to be their home and
that of their five children for many years.

Joe and Decie found, as do all missionary parents, that
there is a strong tension between the demands of missionary activity to which they were committed and to which
they had been called by God, and the demands of the family, equally the gift of God.

"It was at six years old," wrote David Church, the second son, "when our family moved home from Gahini in
Rwanda to Kabale in Uganda in 1938, that I first became
fully aware of my father's missionary calling, and of my
mother's quiet dedication in supporting him.

"My father was usually up first in the morning, and I
can remember him coughing as he stepped out into the
thick Kigezi mist. My mother would have early morning tea,
and we would love to creep into her room and slip into the
warm double-bed while she read Daily Light. We were all
expected to follow Dad into the cold bath and to do ten
'push-ups' to keep ourselves fit. After breakfast our family
routine would be to gather in our father's study for short
family prayers. We were encouraged to participate by praying out loud, but I recall the anxiety when it came to my
turn to think of something original to say, and inevitably
the prayers became stereotyped. My mind would drift to
the huge fir trees outside the window and the happy antici-
pation of climbing and building tree houses with our friend
Ngunzu, younger brother of our cook Filipo. I was also
aware of the piles of letters on father's desk and the row of
specimen bottles on the shelf above my head. These con-
tained foetuses at different stages of development, so my
education on the facts of life started from as early as I can
remember.

"In the evening, after supper, we would often gather around the fire in the living room for Bible study and fellowship with our house staff, and with any visitors. Exhausted after an active day out of doors, we children would often slip off to bed, leaving the older folks to sing and chat into the night. Mother would always tuck us in and pray with us in the darkened bedroom. She knew how much I enjoyed the physical loving contact of having my back rubbed. I remember her caring for the many flowers in the garden at Gahini. She played the harmonium in church and loved to play the piano when possible. My earliest recollections of my father were of the things he made for us to play with, the scooter and the soapbox car.

"Mother did not enjoy cooking. She grew up as a child in her large family home in Devon with cooks and housemaids. In Africa she rarely ventured out to the smoky kitchen across the yard where Filipo or Isaaka would create memorable meals on primitive wood-fired stoves. One exception was at Christmas time when she would set up a small paraffin cooker on the back verandah and prepare delicious fudge as Christmas presents, always keeping back enough for us to sample. On returning to England in 1946, it was Dad who impressed on us that, for Mother's sake, we would have to get used to life without servants. He drew up the rota on the kitchen door and we each had to take our turn at stoking and cleaning the solid-fuel cooker, and washing up the dishes. However, the novelty of competing for who could make the neatest bed soon wore off!

"Close family life effectively ceased for us when we were sent off to boarding school, firstly in Kenya and then in England. It was Mother who kept in touch with us with regular letters, giving all the latest news. Father would write occasionally in a more light-hearted style, sometimes assuming the character of one of our pets. It was in these times of separation that I realised the strength of my parents' teaching and example at times when I had to face the many temptations that arise from trying to keep in with one's new school friends.

"Overhearing discussions in the home, as a child I was aware that Father felt inhibited by the restrictions imposed on him by senior missionaries and by the bishop, and also I was aware of his criticisms, and sense of competition against the Roman Catholics. It was years later, when I became an architect in Uganda in the 1960s, that I found myself working closely with many Catholic clients on schools, hospitals, churches and cathedrals, and came to appreciate how much they had in common with my father's enthusiasms and beliefs. At first I felt that I was letting him down by accepting these commissions, but later realised how much he had always supported me in my developing career.

"Being the son of my father, I know how difficult it can sometimes be to accept the authority of one's superiors, particularly when convinced that they are misguided. Every new generation inherits its own seeds of rebellion. It can often be harder, therefore, for children brought up in an atmosphere of Revival to rediscover reality for themselves. For me, as a student in the 1950s, after two years of relative spiritual claustrophobia in Rwanda, a whole new world opened up; and yet the things I found most exciting, sport, sailing, flying, old motor cars, music and parties were the very things that had inspired my father a generation earlier. Looking back I am deeply grateful for the example he set when I think of the times when I could have been tempted away from my fundamental Christian beliefs by the first waves of liberal morality which were to sweep the world in the 1960s.

"By today's standards my parents were old fashioned. They did not drink alcohol, they did not smoke or swear, they considered dancing and cinemas as morally unhelpful and therefore best avoided. I would have been disgusted if I had ever seen my mother wearing earrings or make-up. And yet they lived full, exciting and creative lives together. They were faithful to the end, not only to each other, but also, through good times and times of danger and anxiety, to their own Creator in whom they both deeply trusted."

Ministry in Revival

Missionary activity was sometimes described as being like a three-legged stool. The primary aim was the establishment of a church. This required the combined elements of evangelism and Bible teaching, medical outreach and educational development, at first the teaching of reading and writing. The three legs—evangelism, medical care and education—required that all those engaged in the three areas work together harmoniously, otherwise there would be a lack of balance and also there would not be that witness to unity which was so essential. Although the importance of each of the 'three legs' working together was recognised, it was not easy to achieve a 'oneness' between those engaged in the different sectors.

At Gahini, Joe realised that it was not only important for all the medical staff to be united in their work, but that oneness should be seen between all the sectors of the work. This unity had to begin 'at home', so to speak, and Joe was very conscious that relationships between the members of the hospital staff were not in a happy state at that time. The problem lay in the fact that some of the staff were only nominally Christian. The dramatic conversions of two of them—Yosiya Kinuka and Paulo Gahunde—in 1931 changed the spiritual atmosphere not only in the hospital, but in the other sections of the work at Gahini.

In addition to the problems of working together in the different sectors of missionary activity, two other factors contributed to making evangelism difficult. The first was the strong pressure to conform to the Anglican system of church government. After all, the Ruanda Mission of the CMS was an Anglican mission. The second was the very hostile attitude of the Roman Catholic Church in Ruanda-Urundi. This was Belgian administered territory and Belgium was a predominantly Roman Catholic country.

Joe found it difficult to conform to structures when they appeared to him to obstruct rather than help in the evangelism and church establishment which was their God-given task as missionaries.

Joe was not a rebel, however, as his diary record of an event in 1930 demonstrated: "One Sunday morning, before Bert (Jackson) went on leave we were walking up the station for the morning service. We were following the pattern of our older stations, Namirembe and Kabale, of having two morning services running simultaneously. So I left Bert to take his service in the school, and I walked on up to the hospital. I noticed that there were only two or three rows of students at Blasio's school, and after that only a handful of people in the school-room. I could just begin to see the hundreds packed at the hospital. A thought came that changed the pattern of our morning worship. I asked myself: 'Why not have one Sunday morning service at which all on the station can take part—doctors, parsons, hospital staff and Bible School, all together—and have another simple Gospel service in the evening in one of the wards for the patients and their friends? Why haven't we done this before?' Then I seemed to hear a voice saying, 'Weren't you a little proud that you had such a crowd to preach to at the hospital, and your brother missionary only had a handful?' I said, 'Yes Lord, I did feel proud.' I shared this with Bert and asked him to forgive me, and at once we set to work to plan a joint morning worship.

"We opened the Book of Common Prayer and began thinking about a shortened form of service. We soon came to the Absolution. Surely it is vital, we thought, in an African territory that is being administered by a country of strong Roman Catholic tradition, to try to avoid giving the impression of a 'priestly' order in our church as long as possible? Bert tried to remember what he had learned at Ridley Hall, and we both felt certain that it was right in the circumstances that a layman or lay reader, authorised to conduct the service, should be able to pronounce that sins were forgiven to all those 'that truly repent and unfeignedly believe His Holy Gospel'. So when it came to my turn in the newly-arranged joint Sunday morning worship I read the Absolution." [972] Although it was unusual for Joe not to 'keep to the rules', his action was reported to the Bishop.

Joe and Decie returned to the UK on leave in April 1932. They returned to Gahini in 1933 and it was in August of that year that Lawrence and Julia Barham visited them on a tour of Rwanda before returning to the UK on leave. They were delayed due to Lawrence suffering from chickenpox. What happened on that occasion is part of the Lawrence and Julia Barham story.

The following month, September, the first Ruanda Mission missionaries' conference in Africa was held on the small picturesque Sharp's Island, near to Bwama, the leprosy hospital and settlement. At the conference, serious conflicts, internal to the Mission, were exposed. These centred on the fact that the Ruanda Mission (CMS) was an Anglican mission and it was expected, therefore, that an Anglican form of church structure would be imposed, with all its regulations, rites and ceremonies. The Mission was predominantly lay in its leadership, and there was strong opposition to introducing forms of service and structures which appeared to conflict with their evangelical interpretation of the Christian faith. To follow the English parish system was seen by Joe and others to place too much authority in one person—the vicar, and so ignore what Dr Algie Stanley Smith referred to as "the immense reserves of spiritual power in the laity".

"Most of us were in agreement about the dangers of thrusting upon the African the complete Church of England Anglican liturgy and set-up," wrote Joe Church in his diary, "and we were also agreed that mere change in itself was of little value. We knew that real genuine revival of the whole church was the vital and only thing that mattered and we were beginning to praise God for the moving of the Spirit." 996

The danger of 'high church' or 'sacerdotal' forms of worship and especially their interpretation of the service of Holy Communion was recognised. "Our efforts at Gahini", wrote Joe, "to help the emerging church to see the dangers of encouraging the routine baptism of infants, and the reading of the Absolution by laymen to make people realise what it means (backed by intensive Bible teaching) had met with strong opposition from a few and I had been reported to the Bishop." [996] The issues were clear, so it seemed to Joe, but putting them into practice in the fellowship of all the missionaries appeared to be a very difficult task.

A 'small Keswick convention' was arranged in 1933 with the Revd St John Thorpe, Chairman of the Council of the Ruanda Mission, as the visiting speaker. "It was hard for our Chairman," wrote Joe, "straight out from parochial England to grasp what we were feeling after, and he felt that it was his duty to curb us and to encourage the rapid diocesanisation of the Church that was growing so quickly. He pressed for the speeding up of ordinations of African clergy—the very thing we feared." [997]

It was difficult for clergy from England who were used to the Anglican parochial system there, in which the vicar was always the highest ecclesiastical authority on the spot, to understand the apprehensions of a predominantly lay leadership in a church-building situation.

At Christmas of that year, Joe was encouraged by an unexpected response to a request by him to the hospital staff to meet at 5 am for a prayer meeting. They smiled. They were, so they said, already rising for prayer before that hour in any case. The following morning the staff appeared on the verandah of Joe and Decie's house and they prayed together for two hours, until daylight.

A convention for local churchgoers was arranged over Christmas. Missionary, Geoffrey Holmes, some of the hospital staff, and Joe and Decie had been praying for God to work in a clear and life-changing way at these meetings. They felt disappointed and somewhat depressed when things did not go as they had hoped. They decided to continue the meetings for another day. An extra prayer meeting was arranged for that afternoon, the last day of that year. There was half an hour of fairly formal prayers. "While everyone was bowed in prayer, one of the African Christians stood up and began confessing some sin he had committed. Then all sat up. It seemed as though a barrier of reserve had been rolled away. A wave of conviction swept through them all and for two and a half hours it continued, sometimes as many as three on their feet at once trying to speak." [99]

Some appeared to see visions and there were several very real conversions. That last night of the old year, 1933, was one to remember and there was much praise as the new year was drummed in.

This was no passing emotional event. The days which followed saw many more than usual offering to serve as church teachers in the outlying districts, and a deep fellowship began to develop between the leaders at Gahini—black and white—and also between the leaders and the other, less educated and often illiterate, people around. There also appeared to be a greater zeal among the Christians to witness to their Saviour.

For Joe personally, there was an unexpected sequel. He felt convicted that he had not really shared with his vicar-father what was happening to him and Decie. He knew of his father's suspicion of 'over-emotionalism' and his dislike of hymns about the 'Blood of Jesus', and he did not want to alienate him and had kept silent about the nature of some of the things that had been happening. Now he wrote more openly of what was really happening—the problems, the disappointments as well as the joys. It is probably because of this new openness between Joe and his father that, a few years later, when Joe's father died, there was found beside his bed, written in his own hand, the words of William Cowper's hymn:

There is a fountain filled with blood,
Drawn from Immanuel's veins ...   [100]

The years 1934 and early 1935 saw an encouraging number of signs that God was working at Gahini. A number of men and women were converted. Some older Christians began to pray more freely and fervently and with increasing expectancy that God was going to answer their prayers. At Kabale, 90 miles over the border in Uganda, there was a similar encouragement to prayer that God would act in confirmation of His word that was being faithfully taught.

In September 1935, Joe received a letter from Lawrence Barham inviting him to take a team to join him at Kabale for a convention of local Christians and church-attenders.

The 1935 Kabale Convention proved to be the moment when God began to work in reviving power on a much bigger scale than in the isolated moments of encouragement in the previous two years. The leaders were drawn from Uganda and Rwanda. The themes for the meetings followed the customary pattern: *Sin* on the first day, then *Repentance*, the *New Birth*, 'Coming out of Egypt'—*Separation*, the *Holy Spirit* and, on the last day, the *Victorious Life*.

There were remarkable scenes of confession of sins that had previously been glossed over or not considered as serious enough to require repentance. There was restitution as stolen goods were returned, and forgiveness was asked of those who had been wronged. Many had dreams which convinced them that God was speaking to them personally about some course of action they should take. For some, verses from the Bible were taken as commands from God directing them to put away heathen practices, drinking the locally brewed powerful alcoholic drinks and other practices not, until then, considered wrong. Some formed teams to go out to those in the district around to tell them of their new-found faith, the reality of the living Jesus and the power of God to overcome sin and Satan.

After the Kabale Convention, Simeoni Nsibambi went to Gahini for two weeks. It was during that time that Nsibambi brought to Joe a challenge which was to influence his thinking about the future. "At the end of one of our times of prayer one afternoon in his house, Nsibambi called me aside and said, 'I have a very important question to put to you, Joe, one that may affect all the rest of your life. But I will not do it now, I will come up to your house tomorrow morning to see you when you have finished the morning ward round.'" [9][119] Nsibambi's challenge was that Joe should leave his medical work to become a full-time evangelist.

This challenge was confirmed when Archdeacon Arthur Pitt-Pitts also asked Joe to consider giving up medical work

to devote his time to 'whole-time missions and evangelistic
work'. "My call to evangelism was so strong", wrote Joe in
his diary, "that I knew it would entail my not being able to
keep up my medicine. God had overruled this. He had given
me a wife better qualified than I. ... So, after much prayer
and heart-searching, I asked that I might continue with
part-time medical work." [Q119]

In December 1935, both Decie and their eldest son, John,
suffered severe attacks of malaria, and it was with reluc-
tance that Joe left them for Uganda to obtain essential
stores. While passing through Mbarara, and despite his
desire to return to Gahini to his ill wife and son, he accepted a request for a team from Gahini to visit the church
there in ten days' time. Hospital duties prevented him from
attending that convention in January 1936, but a team went
which included Yosiya Kinuka and Blasio Kigozi. For several reasons, that convention was a memorable one. It was
the last attended by Blasio Kigozi. He died within a month
from what was probably relapsing fever. It was also memorable because Blasio, probably sensing that he had not long
to live, added a new theme to the scheme Joe had introduced: To "*Sin* ...through to ... the *Victorious Life*" was added
kurimbuka: "to perish, to be doomed, to be lost". [Q121]

That addition, underlined by the sudden and unexpected
death of Blasio Kigozi, never left Joe. It added an urgency
to his preaching. It was reinforced by the occasions when
people, listening to the preaching of the Gospel, would experience a desperate fear of an eternity in Hell—apart from
the Holy God they were, at that moment, unfit to meet.
Where there was repentance of sin and faith in Jesus Christ,
this 'fear of Hell' was replaced by the overwhelming joy of
sins forgiven and unobstructed fellowship with God.

The year 1936 saw extraordinary happenings in south-
west Uganda and in Ruanda-Urundi, as it was called then.
At Gahini, there were dramatic incidents in the Girls' School
which are recorded elsewhere, [F15ff] and in the local churches.
God was doing something far greater and wider in its implications than was happening through Joe's own ministry.

Nevertheless, God had given him a role in proclaiming the truths which God so powerfully highlighted in Revival. Joe also saw the danger of preaching an experience, a system of teaching, or a particular way of doing things. He had a mission to preach Jesus, Him crucified and Him only. In later years he would refer to the scene in the Upper Room, when the disciples were praying and the Holy Spirit came upon them like tongues of fire. "Those disciples", so Joe would say, "could have gone out and proclaimed 'the Upper Room experience', the 'tongues of fire experience', or the 'speaking in other tongues experience', but they didn't. They went everywhere preaching 'Jesus'."

It was at this time that a dual truth became very real for Joe: *In Revival, God leads people to pray; and, when people pray God brings Revival.* The two go together and it is impossible to say which comes first. This conviction led Joe to seek to extend the circle of those who prayed for the work of God in the area in which he was working.

In April 1936, a pamphlet written by Joe, and entitled: *A Call to Prayer,* was published by the Ruanda Mission (CMS) in London. "There is only one thing that matters," Joe concluded, "that is, to be linked up to the Source of all Power. Do pray that we may be unhindered channels for His Power to flow through till it becomes a mighty flood-tide."

At the invitation of Bishop Cyril Stuart, Bishop of Uganda, a team led by Joe Church was invited to lead a mission at the Bishop Tucker Memorial College, Mukono, Uganda. It was a difficult time in many ways. There was opposition to the message, and to the messengers, from the staff, but there were also many who came into a joyful experience of salvation in Jesus Christ. Joe wrote to praying friends in the UK: "We could feel the barrage of prayer you were putting up for us in England. A crowd of thirty students ran down the main road singing the mission hymns and choruses as we drove off in our cars." There was a reminder too of the past as they sang: "What can wash away my sin, nothing but the blood of Jesus." "It was one of Pilkington's hymns," an old Muganda woman reminded them.

The year 1936 proved to be a very formative one in the thinking of Joe—really of Joe and Decie—as they thought and prayed over what was happening. The single-minded aim of proclaiming Jesus and the Cross as the key to everything that the Gospel meant had already been seen very clearly. Increasingly, Joe saw the amazing ways in which God answered prayer, the prayer of individuals, yes, but ever more so, the prayer of teams and groups of people who not only met for prayer, but lived and worked in fellowship with each other. Wherever God worked in power, there could be found groups of people who prayed together in fellowship.

The *Call to Prayer* of April 1936 was followed by *Victorious Praying* in September of that year. In it Joe wrote, "Here, then, in simple obedience to Him lies the secret of blessing, and here only can real Revival Prayer be prayed and mountains be moved. That is why we stress it now. ... How miraculous is the result of this praying!

"Revival is like an African bush-fire. As it burns and spreads over the mountainside, all that lurk in the long grass, the snakes and the rats, have to flee for their lives.

"Revival is like the storm of long-expected rain which comes at the end of the dry season and brings life again from the dusty veldt. But before the reviving rain falls, black clouds will appear and trees will bow and fall before the wind.

"Revival is like a delicate and beautiful flower that can only thrive and bloom in prepared soil. The soil is the surrendered heart, and the flower looks upward to the sun. All 'roots of bitterness' must be daily weeded out.

"Revival is the fruit of the Spirit, and is, therefore, normal spiritual life. God's command is : 'Be filled with the Spirit' ...

"And so we ask you in Jesus' name to take up the burden of prayer for Revival, and to enter into this invisible bond of fellowship with the bands of men and women who, fired with a new life, are carrying the flame of Revival into these Central African kingdoms. Effectual praying might bring about a mighty movement of God's Spirit from Congo to Kenya and throughout the whole world. ... Let this prayer, well known, but so searching, be ours daily:

'Lord, bring Revival, and begin it in ME.

For Jesus Christ's sake. Amen'."

Even wider than this vision for that part of Africa was that for evangelistic teams worldwide. "We began to feel the invincible power of a consecrated team who were absolutely one, who could give themselves to care enough for another until that one came into the place of victory. It was not uncommon to find two brothers with tears in their eyes praying and pleading with another who was still resisting."

God was doing something new at that time, at least new to that area. God was giving teams of people—husbands and wives, hospital workers, school teachers, pastors and church workers—a great concern for the spiritual and physical welfare of each other. They would weep when they sensed resistance to the pleadings of God in their lives. They would challenge what they felt was blindness to sin in their colleagues. Where this loving concern and challenge was received, there developed a great depth of fellowship. Where it was resisted, or where it was exercised unwisely or harshly, there was often strong reaction, not only against the persons concerned, but also against the truths they sought to live out.

In 1936, the team at Gahini, decreased by the death of Blasio Kigozi, was increased by the arrival of William Nagenda. Soon he, Joe and Yosiya Kinuka formed the leadership of the outreach work on that church centre.

Joe's brother, Howard, was a CMS clergyman at Kabete, in Kenya. He invited Joe to lead a team on a nine-day mission there in March-April 1937—it was the first team to visit Kenya since the beginning of Revival. "The church was packed every evening," wrote Joe. "We insisted on African and European leaders sitting with us and joining in the planning. ... I stress this because I believe here lies the secret of blessing and revival in Kenya; mistrust between European and African must be broken down." [9][145]

Joe and Decie returned to the UK on leave in May 1937. In March 1938, Joe returned to Africa while Decie and their three boys stayed on in England till September of that year. Joe moved to Kabale where he shared a 'bachelor's' house with Archdeacon Arthur Pitt-Pitts until Decie's arrival.

In June, Joe attended the first Ruanda-Urundi Church Council held at Buye. (This was then known as Ibuye, until it was pointed out that this was the mistake of someone who did not know the language well. 'Ibuye' was really 'i Buye', that is, 'at Buye'). The theme set for consideration by the Council was 'Hindrances to revival'.

It is typical of Joe's pictorial thinking that, at evening prayers, he should choose the picture of the *agatimba*, the mosquito net, to illustrate these hindrances. "In the evening we took the subject of barriers, and the 'mosquito net' picture for the first time. ... I talked on the *agatimba* or barrier that comes down around one and forms the barrier on both sides, between yourself and Christ, and between yourself and your neighbour at the same time. If there is no repentance, the barrier gets thicker and the darkness deeper till it becomes a little prison, and many stay in that prison of jealousy or unforgiveness for a long time, even years. But Christ is there nearby, knocking to come in. In a moment, as 1 John 1:7 says, we can call to Him and repent, and the darkness is dispelled; the barriers come down and we 'walk in the light' again with our brother or sister, feeling safe— cleansed by the blood of Jesus." [9]153-4

In the months that followed, this 'oneness in Christ and in the light" did not go unchallenged. In Rwanda, in particular, some of the Christians became so eager and zealous that they became known as the *Abaka*—'those on fire'. In their enthusiasm they would challenge older Christians as to the reality of their faith and particularly about sins which they appeared to cover up and not recognise as such. This was frequently resented. The deep fellowship between some Christians, particularly Christian leaders, was, at the same time, accompanied by dissension and division among others. It was a time of great testing for Joe.

The Ruanda Mission Missionaries' Conference in July, 1938, was a memorable one as the missionaries faced the 'hindrances to revival' in their own lives. Joe felt keenly the fact that not all missionaries were, outwardly at least, as strongly in favour of pursuing what was happening in Revival as he was. Although not all the differences were removed, there was such a movement of God's Spirit at that conference that one senior member of the Mission, Dr. Norman James, wrote of it that it was "the most remarkable time the Mission has ever known."

Away from the hospital at Gahini, Joe was able to focus on a new role of concentrating on taking the message of Revival, preferably as part of a team, wherever there was an invitation.

In August 1938, Joe led a team of the 'Keswick' Convention in Kenya. With him were Simeoni Nsibambi, William Nagenda, Yosiya Kinuka, Ezekieri Balaba, Erenesti Nyabugabo, Ezra Kikonyogo and Yusufu Byangwa. "It was a humbling time," wrote Joe, "God convicted me of 'bossing' my African brothers, so the five weeks together were spent in absolute oneness in Christ, with Him as our leader as never before."

The 'Keswick' Convention was attended largely by European missionaries who regarded it as a kind of retreat where they were away from their normal activities and could listen to speakers in English. It was followed by the 'African' 'Keswick' Convention at the Alliance High School, Kikuyu, where the speaking was by translation into two or three of the African languages.

As happened frequently, when some action or way of doing things was proposed, theological issues arose. Where the one missionary leader was in charge, his or her word was often accepted without challenge. It was different when the leadership was a team. A simple suggestion as to some way of doing things threatened to bring disunity. Such a situation arose at this convention. "There were some differences between us over the timing of the teaching," wrote Joe. "Canon Butcher and Rowland Pittway felt strongly that conviction would come if we moved on quickly to the teaching of the Holy Spirit, but we (the team) felt from experience that we must, if necessary, preach more about the Cross till conviction came."

William Nagenda and Yosiya Kinuka continued to plead with people to repent of their sin, trust in Jesus Christ, and so be right with God. The testimonies of those who responded confirmed the rightness of this course of teaching. "God seemed to tell us clearly to stress sin and repentance, centring it all around the Blood of Jesus," commented Joe. When and where the Blood of Jesus cleanses, the Holy Spirit fills, became strongly attested truth.

Later, in September 1938, Joe with Ezra Kikonyogo, led a mission at the Kaloleni Church centre in Mombasa. It was again among the leaders of the church work that God worked in convicting power. It was becoming very clear that, not only among missionaries but in the African church, Revival began with the leaders. Where there was resistance to the message of sin, repentance and forgiveness by the 'blood of Christ', there appeared to be less response from the ordinary listeners.

In Europe, there was the threat of war. Decie Church with their three boys was returning to Africa on a German boat. There was a fear of possible internment. Due to the action of Decie's elder brother, who was Acting Governor of the Sudan, the family was taken from that boat and put on a Nile steamer travelling south to Juba, in the Sudan. Joe was able to conclude the Mission at Kaloleni, Kenya, go on to be reunited with his family at Juba, and then on together to Kabale. Travelling with the family was Eileen Faber who was to teach the three Church boys. The conversion of an old garage into a classroom and the addition of the son of the District Commissioner, marked the beginning of the Kabale Preparatory School. The School still bears the marks of Joe's artistic abilities.

At this time, Anglican churches were in the majority of Protestant churches in Uganda, Rwanda, and Burundi, so it was natural that most of the invitations to the 'Revival teams' should be from among these churches. Denominational differences, which are powerful in Europe, had not yet developed so strongly in East Africa. It was, therefore, especially significant that, in January 1939, a team from Uganda, Rwanda and Burundi met at the Danish Baptist Mission centre, Musema, in Burundi. Those who gathered included missionaries and Africans from the Friends' Mission and the Methodists' Mission.

Hans Jensen, the leader of the Danish Baptist Mission, wrote later: "The Revival here is going deeper and stronger all the time. There have been scores of heart-breaking confessions since the convention and people have got victory. They are really walking in the light, there is no doubt about that. To us personally this experience has made all the difference. It is another life. The Revival is spreading further out to the villages and to the outstations. What a joy to visit them now! Indeed the Lord has been good to us." [9164]

For Joe and the team, this was a confirmation that Revival knows no denominational, racial or geographical boundaries. In Revival, where these barriers exist, sometimes almost unrealised, they are broken down and there emerges a deep fellowship which is a foretaste of heaven.

In early March, 1939, Joe faced a disturbing situation at Gahini. "For several weeks reports have come from surrounding district churches that services have been held up on Sundays by much weeping and confession," wrote Joe. He took Jack Symonds and four others to investigate.

"When we were four miles from one place we saw crowds of people streaming up the hillsides and through the fields going to a church. ... We began the service at 10 am with the hymn, 'What can wash away my sin, nothing but the Blood of Jesus'. During the first verse people began to weep and cry out. I stopped the hymn and told them all to sit down." At another church "people were prostrate, weeping and crying, while others sat quietly waiting. There was so much noise that it was impossible to hold the service. ...

"Fortunately I had prepared a list of texts on assurance We read these slowly together in Lukiga. The result was wonderful to see. It was a new experience for me of the power of the Word to comfort as well to convict. Joy began to be manifest on all their faces. We left about 4 pm and all along the roads and paths were lines of people returning to their homes singing hymns." Q164-5

Later that month, Joe, Decie and William Nagenda travelled north to visit some of the leaders in the Sudan, whom they had contacted when Joe went to Juba to link up with his wife and three sons the previous year.

The significance of this visit was not lost on Joe. Revival had started at Lui, in the Sudan, in a dramatic way. "A senior schoolboy, who had been convicted of sin and challenged by the Gospel ... was filled with an unquenchable passion to leave school and return to his home to preach. He ran away and arrived at Lui cut and bleeding, having fallen off his bicycle. He ran around the station almost beside himself, calling all to repent and naming the sins of many people openly." Q165

There followed many who were strikingly convicted of their sin and were immediately converted. Some had particularly vivid dreams, saw strange lights and some appeared to preach in very wild ways. This had been attributed by some missionaries to hysteria or to Satanic powers.

Joe's questioning soon showed that the preaching of the missionaries and the senior African clergy had been exactly the same as that of the leaders in Revival in Uganda, Rwanda and Burundi. God was working in reviving power in the Sudan, apparently independently from anything that was happening further south. This was, indeed, a further indication that God was working throughout that part of Africa, using different people in His purposes. The common factor was the same message of the Gospel of Jesus, the sinfulness of sin, the need for repentance, the cleansing power of the Cross and the indwelling of the Holy Spirit.

On their return to Kabale, Joe was invited urgently to go to Buye to face the problem which had arisen at Gahini, that between the *abaka* (those on fire) and those who, although Christians, did not associate with them.

The important question faced was: If *Revival*, which claimed to lead to unity in Christ, was expressed in events which caused divisions, was it really *Revival*? The nature of these seemingly divisive events was discussed at length— the emphasis on personal repentance in relation to God's saving grace, the confession of 'unseemly' sins in public, bold challenging of people to be 'in the light', the meaning of being 'saved' in view of the extraordinary experiences of those believed to be already 'saved' ... Missionaries were obviously divided in the way they interpreted what was happening. It was inevitable that these divisions in inter- pretation should threaten the spiritual unity of the mis- sionaries themselves.

It was agreed that the Revival being experienced was undoubtedly a work of God. However, the interpretation of what was happening varied from person to person. The discussion turned into prayer that God would forgive a spirit of wrong destructive criticism which had harmed fellow- ship, and a lack of love and grace in pursuing openness and 'light' in others. The group affirmed their oneness in Christ across any of the divisions which had occurred, and a determination not to fall into complacency when error crept in. 'Oneness in Christ' was accepted as a priority when seeking to interpret what God was doing. The refusal to accept division as the answer to differing views lead to a strengthening of the fellowship. As time went on, the term *Abaka* was replaced by the more inclusive Uganda term: *abalokole*—'the saved ones'.

In April 1939, at the invitation of Bishop Chambers, Joe Church, Simeoni Nsibambi, Lawrence Barham, Ezekieri Balaba, Tito Masozera and Erisifati Matovu formed a team to visit Tanzania. They were received by Lionel Bakewell, an Australian missionary who was the Principal of the Teacher Training College at Katoke, as Bishop Chambers was on leave in England. The team divided into two and meetings were held at Katoke and Ngara. There were few signs of a spiritual impact although the response at Ngara was greater than at Katoke.

It was some five weeks later when remarkable things began to happen. A number of well-known Christians of repute came under sudden powerful conviction of sin in their lives. Bishop Chambers, now returned from England, wrote to Joe, "It has been to us a terrible revelation of the inner lives of those whom we had looked on as good Christians. Many of these are communicants. They have all got it perfectly clear that confession does not save, but that they must confess and make restitution if necessary—and are longing to get out and especially to get home, to tell of their experience to others." [Q170]

Commenting on this situation, James Katarikawe wrote, "In this new excitement of great salvation to many, the leaders forgot that discipline was very important. In the school, where evening prayers usually lasted twenty minutes, they now went on for two hours. This created problems."

In the weeks that followed the error crept in of going beyond recognising unusual happenings as manifestations of inner spiritual working, to looking for the unusual happenings themselves. The leaders of the churches at Katoke and Ngara were inexperienced and they allowed meetings—especially testimony meetings—to get out of control. Bishop Chambers was so perturbed by what he saw happening that he wrote to Joe: "I am greatly disturbed over the confusion, disorder and unseemly conduct of meetings conducted by the Africans which Mr. Bakewell regards as the work of the Holy Spirit, and which he connects with your visit to Katoke." [Q171]

He described a meeting: "As darkness drew on, hands and arms waved to the rhythm of popular hymn tunes and choruses ... some finished their hymns with a hollow, mocking laugh, then followed cryings, screamings, shoutings, noises like those of animals such as cat calls, the yelping of dogs, snorting of wild beasts—most of the congregation were in a kneeling posture. There were loud utterances, unintelligible to others, mutterings and murmurings ... Bakewell was kneeling in the midst of the assembly. There were about seventy in the congregation." [K95]

Bishop Chambers added, "I have instructed Bakewell to cease such forms of devotions ... anywhere in connection with our Church or in this Diocese." [9171]

As soon as he had heard of these excesses, Joe had dissociated himself from them but this did not prevent some church leaders in Tanzania blaming them on him and his team. James Katarikawe has made some pertinent comments on these happenings: "When people pray for Revival they do not always understand what is involved. When Revival comes, it produces shocks and many things are turned upside down, the long held norms are shaken to the foundation. So one has to pray that in it he may keep looking at the One who is the giver of all life. This does not at all mean that Revival brings chaos, far from it. But what we need to be clear about is that Revival shakes the powers of Satan to release the long held captives, therefore Satan in his rage cannot fail to do anything to discredit the power that is ousting him. If we can look at it in this way then we shall be able to be less critical, and we will in fact be sent on our knees to ask for more blessing from the Saviour to meet the challenge.

"All the problems which tormented the Church in East Africa at this time originated from the fact that many missionaries and nationals alike failed to see this subtle attack of the Devil. Instead of discovering the enemy who was bringing all these excesses and misunderstandings, they looked at the people and their mistakes and then failed to see the power of the Holy Spirit who was at work reviving His dead Church, driving out the powers of evil from His people which had held them for generations. Yes, when Revival comes, lives have to change in order to give glory to God. While cryings and screamings were common signs wherever Revival came into the Church, the making of animal noises, yelping as dogs or snorting as wild beasts which Bishop Chambers observed at Katoke, to the writer's knowledge, had never happened before anywhere else either in Rwanda or Uganda where the power of the Spirit had been at work for some time, neither has it happened elsewhere in East Africa ever since. The only conclusion we can make about it is that human enthusiasm plus the cunning ways of the Devil brought all this about. Bishop Stuart got the point when he wrote to Bishop Chambers and said. 'Can you have Revival in Africa without excesses? I doubt it, and certainly in Rwanda, and Uganda we have found that they do get through these outward signs and go on to real deep faith and changed lives." [K96]

During the years of World War II, travelling world-wide was restricted and Joe's ministry was confined to East Africa. The 'Mukono Crisis', part of the William Nagenda story, occupied Joe's attention during much of 1940.

From a tour of centres of the Ruanda Mission in Rwanda and Burundi in 1942, there emerged what Joe referred to as a "visual aid in our quest for holiness". It was a small flag inscribed with the single word: HIGHEST? That word followed Joe to the end of his days. The author remembers when, almost unable to speak, Joe could whisper that word that symbolised his life's ambition and which put a question mark to his every activity—was it *the highest*?

Joe, with Lawrence Barham and Godfrey Hindley, responded to an invitation to visit South Africa in 1944. Despite urgent pleas, permits were refused for William Nagenda and Yosiya Kinuka to join the team. *Apartheid* was strong in those days.

At an official welcome in Cape Town, attended by about eighty pastors and evangelical leaders, Joe spoke on "where two or three are gathered together in my name, there am I in the midst". He wrote: "We said how God had been meeting with the three of us on this incredible long journey and how Jesus had been very near to us. We had come to talk about Him—that is Revival—when two meet with bowed heads at the foot of the Cross and shake hands again. There is the V for Victory. That is where Revival begins. That is what the world is seeking. ... Lawrence and Godfrey followed on and were very good—a wonderful time, ... There were some tears and re-consecrations then and there. ... We said plainly that Revival could not come if they had no (apparent) intention of getting down to colour-bar. ... There was warmth, personal talks, decisions, but we felt a deep undercurrent of resistance against the insuperable barriers of colour-bar and sectarian exclusiveness. ... We couldn't help thinking, what would have happened if William and Yosiya *had* come!" [9212]

The Protestant Alliance of the Missions of Ruanda-Urundi united several missions of different denominations in those countries—Methodist, Baptist, Nazarenes and Anglicans. In June 1945, representatives of these missions met at Mutaho, in Burundi, to "seek a deeper unity before God". Some of the American missionaries felt that 'English reserve' was a barrier. "So we decided to have a time of prayer about this," wrote Joe. "We were thirty-three CMS missionaries. Some of us felt that our natural reserve made us reticent about giving our testimonies to having been filled with the Holy Spirit, and so we were missing God's blessing. One by one we came forward, and kneeling, repented of this reserve and claimed new filling. One or two of us asked for special friends to come and lay their hands on us at the same time if they so wished. Leonard Sharp, a naturally silent person, said, 'Let me be the first!' It was a very personal and very intimate spontaneous time which we will never forget." This experience proved to be a turning-point in the spiritual lives of some of the missionaries but it also raised strong questioning on the part of others.

A few weeks later, just before the 1945 Convention at Kabale, a Quiet Day was arranged for the team of convention leaders. News was exchanged of God's working in the various areas from which the members of the team came. This included a report of the 'laying-on-of-hands' from those who had been at Mutaho'. "It nearly ruined the Kabale Convention of 1945," wrote James Katarikawe. "Some of the leading African brethren challenged it as it could turn into 'striving' and would easily provide another divisive element in the Revival and stop people from seeing the Grace of God. The memories of the 'crucifying the old man' were still too fresh to entertain anything of this nature. The brethren from Rwanda and Burundi quickly saw the danger and were willing to drop that which had been a blessing to them. Then God worked in a marvellous way to shower blessing at the Kabale Convention. Again God had averted another danger which could easily have led to a split." [K137] Here was a noteworthy example of 'submitting to each other in love'.

The practice of 'laying-on-of-hands' could, so wrote Joe Church, "lead to works and waiting for an experience instead of grace and humbling at the Cross. We went on till dark laying this and other things before the Lord, some bowing and admitting that this good thing nevertheless could become a 'plus' and so easily could be copied." [Q220]

From then onwards, Joe and other leaders in Revival avoided any act, such as the laying-on-of-hands, which could detract from seeing God's activity as 'all of grace'. If God was going to confirm the preaching of His word by deep conviction of sin, of the Cross and of the indwelling of the Holy Spirit, then it was important not to distract from that being seen as 'all of God's grace' by implying that some other activity, however good it might seem, was necessary.

Between the Protestant Alliance meetings at Mutaho, Burundi, Joe attended a weekend of meetings at Byumba, Rwanda in July 1945. The testimony of a Rwandan chief, Kilimenti Semugabo, at the end of one of the meetings was to lead to the 'bowed neck' picture which Joe used to illustrate his talks. Joe never forgot the dream which that chief recounted. It formed part of his testimony, as recorded later in this chapter. From it grew the 'bowed neck' motto cards which became, for Joe, "basic doctrinal visual aids." [Q219]

The end of World War II opened the way for travel worldwide. In June 1946, Joe and Decie, with their family, sailed from Mombasa to England by troop ship. In 1947, after their leave in England, Joe and Decie returned to Gahini where Joe worked part-time in the hospital. Their sons, John and David, were left at St Lawrence's College, in Ramsgate, England.

In the following years, Joe, usually with William Nagenda, Yosiya Kinuka, or others, responded to invitations to visit

and hold conferences or missions, in England and Switzerland in 1947; Switzerland, France and Germany in 1949;
Nyasaland, now Malawi, in November 1951; Angola in
March 1952, India in May 1952; the USA in May to August
1953; Israel in September 1953; India and Pakistan from
January to April 1954; Ethiopia November to December
1954; Angola 1956; South America January 1959. Joe write
reports of all these tours to circulate among praying friends.
Glimpses of events in these tours give an indication of the
ministry of Joe and his teams.

The visit to Switzerland in 1947 was at the invitation of
a group of people influenced by an ex-Rwanda missionary,
Berthe Ryf. To a meeting of the Cathedral Parish Council
in Geneva, held in the 'staid precincts of the State Church',
the team gave their testimony. "The three of us," recorded
Joe Church, "from the equally reserved Church of England,
told of how the Holy Spirit had come down on us away in
Africa and had released us and brought new life into our
departments of hospitals and schools. ... Then, in reply to
further serious questions we likened our visit to a doctor's
consultation; you can do nothing if the doctors do not tell
you frankly the condition of the patient. Whereupon the
Moderator, a great man, said, 'I am not going to tell you the
need of the patient only, I am going to start with my own
need. ... The cold walls of the 'Salle de Paroisse' in the an-
cient precincts of Calvin are beginning to warm."

William Nagenda and Yosiya Kinuka joined Joe Church
and Lawrence Barham in England in 1947. A notable consequence of that year's ministry was the formation of a
'Revival team' in the UK. Of this team, the two most well-
known leaders were Roy Hession and Stanley Voke. A series of annual Christian Holiday Conferences was started
which continued for many years and, although under different leadership, are still held.

Of the French border city of Strasbourg, during the visit
of October 1949, Joe wrote: "This city of many wars ... has
known hate. William and I have done what we do in each
big town. We have bought a map of the streets, had a coffee

in the 'grande place', and looked at people's faces. We began our meetings in one of the central churches and they
were continued every evening until Sunday night. We sensed
a feeling of apathy at the beginning. We wondered if things
had been as well arranged as elsewhere. But I believe we
were meant to see the true state of this town. The people
are listless and apathetic. But the church filled right up,
including the galleries, on the last night. We knew that the
only hope for that great town and for Europe was that they
should come, each man, again to Calvary to be forgiven
and then go on to forgive one another. ... So we arranged a
special meeting each afternoon in the parish hall where we
all sat round in a circle, about eighty people, and got down
to the question of relationships. ... There were reconcilia-
tions in that room. Germans and French forgiving one another, and we praised God that there in that humble parish
hall was growing up a true united nations council, and the
answer to Europe's need."

Across the frontier into Germany, to the amazement of
the team, the church at Ottweiller was packed. "Such is
the hunger in Germany," wrote Joe. "William and I mounted
the high pulpit as we talked on Nicodemus and John 3:16.
People would not leave the church, so we went on till about
10 pm, telling them of Jesus and how He is healing race
and tribal hatreds in Africa. What a strange thing—an Eng-
lishman and an African speaking to these Germans in the
Saar, but we had all forgotten our nationalities as we went
back to Calvary."

During the visit of a team of three—Joe Church, William
Nagenda and Dora Skipper—in November 1951, to
Nyasaland, now Malawi, a severe ulcerated mouth prevented
Joe from taking part in the first meetings at Blantyre. This
provided William and Dora with an opportunity to recognise and repent of a subtle sin which had, till then, been
kept in the background. It was the sin of the 'fear of not
doing what Joe wants'. "That is rather a long title for it,"
wrote Joe, "but it came as a real revelation from God and,
once repented of and cleansed, we were free and rejoicing

again. O the joyous liberty of the children of God, when we
are simple as little children with Him over sin. That sin
could have cramped this tour. It is easy in teams to be held
up by each other."

Meetings followed in missionary church centres. At
Chiole, the team used a new picture—that of two kingdoms:
the Kingdom of Light and the Kingdom of Darkness and
their kings. "It's been a good day," wrote Joe, "but we felt
there was opposition. Here is an old-established Evangelical Church, with hundreds of grey-haired Christians, yet
one wondered where they stood. Their faces were lined and
wistful and they seem to have not grown spiritually." The
lack of any evident testimony to a saving experience of Jesus Christ among those they considered their leaders saddened the team. William, in particular, felt deeply that the
Africans seemed "stunted spiritually and completely lacking in joy and freedom. They were so 'hat-in-hand' to the
Europeans."

On the Sunday morning, the team decided to give a clear
presentation of the Cross and spoke, "verse by verse,
through the story of Nicodemus. ... It was one of those times
when one felt that hush and softening of the Spirit. We
wondered how any heart could be so hard as not to break
before the pleading of the Spirit."

At the end of this tour, Joe wrote, "Never before, I think,
on these tours, have we been led to stress so emphatically
the absolute necessity of being born again. 'Go and wash!'
came as an insistent command from God. ... At several
stations people told us they were wondering when we were
coming to the point! They had had many missioners in the
past, they said, with some special message to stress—the
'second blessing', 'healing', 'fasting', 'praying for Revival' and
so on. How we praised as we saw what God was doing
through preaching only Christ and Him crucified. Everywhere, we hear, men are repenting and getting right with
God and finding peace, simply as a result of the plain
preaching of the Cross. 'I, if I be lifted up, will draw all men
unto me. ... God has been showing us our pride in trying to

add anything else, as if God was pleased with our self-dedi-
cations, our long prayers, special methods, or agonisings.
All *we* do, all our righteousness, are as filthy rags. God
only sees His righteousness in us, not our own. ... we found
much 'striving' amongst the devoted and hard-working missionaries, and much nominal Christianity in the Africans.
Some were trying fasting, so we felt we ought to advise
against the reading of certain of the keen evangelical
papers that stress this terrible error of fasting for Revival,
and so obtain blessing. If the Lord is our Shepherd, that is
all we want. He promised us that He must needs go, so that
the comforter could come and abide with us for ever. The
Holy Spirit glorifies Jesus and points us to the Blood of
Jesus for cleansing when we may have grieved Him on the
way. That is all we need." [N10]

While in Uganda, Rwanda and Burundi, Revival occurred
mainly in the Anglican churches, in Tanganyika there was
a considerable work of Revival among the Mennonite Baptists. It was as a result of the testimony of Mennonite missionaries in the USA that a team was invited to America in
1953. The team—Joe Church, William Nagenda, Roy and
Revel Hession—"sped down the great motorways with light
hearts, asking God to teach us more about what it meant
to preach 'Christ and Him crucified' only." [9245] "This, and
only this, is our theme as we seek Revival in America. The
simple name, JESUS has been printed and pinned up on
the oak panelling above the platform. May God make this
truth more than ever clear here where everything, including evangelism, is so mechanised and mass-produced—
where some 'new thing' can so easily creep into one's Gospel message and be copied." [A9]

On the last day of their first residential conference which
was attended by about 350 people, the theme of 'Jesus only'
was continued with readings from Revelation "where we
see Jesus crowned, but before that, we see Him crowned
with thorns and climbing up Calvary's hill wearing my sin-
stained garments in place of His royal robes. For an hour,
testimonies have gone forth. ... Many have testified that

they have found the solution to their struggles and the end of their striving for Revival and holiness, they have seen Jesus as their sanctification, their power, peace, Calvary love, fullness, healing and second blessing." [A9]

At their next venue, the team faced many people who questioned what they were saying and the teaching of the well-known *Calvary Road* by Roy Hession. "We are cutting away props," wrote Joe, "even the 'Ruanda', WEC and *Calvary Road* props, as we are being driven out by the Spirit of God."

In 1953, an invitation was received from the Revd Ronald Adeney, a missionary in Jerusalem of the Church Mission to Jews, brother of Dr Harold Adeney, a missionary of the Ruanda Mission, to visit Israel. The outstanding thing about this tour," wrote Joe, "was the blessing that it was to the missioners themselves." [Q246]

At a meeting for some fifteen people, mainly missionar-ies, Joe and William spoke of the land God had promised Israel, "a land flowing with milk and honey, plenty and sweetness, satisfaction and fullness. ... We met with many more in Nazareth in the Hospital in the cool of the evening, and took much the same line. Several talked till late, deeply concerned about their lives. We saw that revival is only being *satisfied* with Jesus. The Christian's Promised Land still flows with milk and honey if we are obedient, but like the Jews, we are always going off after other gods." [PL6]

"We all met in the hospital prayer room in the evening, and God led us to base our talks on Isaiah, chapter 6. We asked God to cleanse us from prejudice, and other subtle sins that close our lips, and take away our testimony. We saw how there are some hidden sins of Christians that make us 'Go quiet,' and 'hide' from one another. We saw how unbelief in this very town had closed their eyes, and blinded them to the Son of God. Then we saw the Lord, high and lifted up again, and some in the room bowed, and were revived. The Lord really met us in that room in a new way. One, even though she was a missionary, testified the next day that she had been truly born again." [PL7]

William and Joe were asked to speak at a united prayer meeting in Jerusalem for workers in all the Christian missions there. "We were told that people were wanting to hear news of the Revival in East Africa," recorded Joe, "but we have to tell them, as we often do, that we cannot talk about 'the Revival', because, if we do, there is such a danger of people trying to copy it, instead of going back to Jesus. ...

"We felt we must stress the need for deeper oneness between mission and mission, between the missionaries and the Jews and, as we know in East Africa, in the home between husband and wife. And to bring our testimony up-to-date we felt we should tell them that the Devil, the arch divider of souls, had found his way in a little between William and me when we separated and took our meetings separately in Nazareth and Tiberias, and there seemed to be more blessing in one place than the other. But the Holy Spirit had already pointed this out to us, and we had brought it to the Lord for cleansing. The Devil can so easily say that it is such a little thing, or that two brothers working for the Lord shouldn't really have to talk about things like that, but this demonstrated what we mean by going deep with Jesus, and going deep with each other. No sin must be glossed over and left unrepented of. I believe that is why so many Christians are so poverty-stricken and poor today, because they don't repent." [PL12]

Joe and William were able to fulfil a desire that they had shared before embarking on this tour of Israel—"to do the walk to Emmaus". They were not, in fact, able to complete that walk as it became dark early and a meeting was scheduled for that evening. "Before turning back," wrote Joe, "we spent a time in prayer in the darkness, in the shadow of the hills, and we praised that the Lord was no historical figure. He was still with us and He still gives the burning heart as we talk about Him and talk with Him.

"After supper, the large room in the Dawsons' house filled up with friends, and we based our talk on Luke 24, so fresh in our minds, and trying to find the secret of walking continually with Jesus; in fact, revival is having our hearts continually burning within us. It is not a thing that should come and go, Christ does not come and go. People often ask us how it is that the Revival in East Africa keeps on, and hasn't died out, people seem surprised to think that revival is a thing that lasts. Revival is only walking with Jesus day by day, until we die." PL17

The following year, 1954, Joe Church and William Nagenda visited India and Pakistan. They took as their theme for the tour, "As ye have therefore received Christ Jesus the Lord, so walk ye in Him." (Col 2:6) The need for a simple message soon became apparent as Joe and William found that "the evangelical denominations, that are doctrinally one, are being grievously divided by 'special emphases' and 'non-essentials', here, a special emphasis on Believer's Baptism, i.e. that it is necessary for a Christian to be re-baptised by immersion. Several leading Europeans and Indians have done so." PL16

Of the first morning meeting at Madras, Joe wrote: "We turned to our Bibles and prayed that God would show us the simplicity of the walk with Jesus, and the 'oneness' there is in Him—letting the Word melt and speak to us by His Spirit, but we were led to see those things that hinder and which can so easily 'beguile us' as Paul says. Many leaders of Christian work were there, and we felt we must not be afraid of going into the re-baptism controversy. It was a deep time and people were moved, but we are not all one on this subject. After lunch, two of the leaders of a certain group have come round in their cars to say they must publicly disassociate themselves with our statement. It was good of them to come and to be in the light with us.

"We had a packed church tonight. We spoke on 'Come and see my zeal. (1 Kings 10:16) As we saw, it was Jehu's unguided zeal—so we, in pride, want to show off our 'works,' or our 'keenness', or our 'Revival', etc. We coupled it with our testimonies of Africa, and the word of the woman at the well, 'Come, see a Man, that told me all.'" 16

At the Dohnavur Fellowship, Tirunelvelli, the 'House of Prayer', "We turned to the story of Nicodemus," Joe recorded,

"He was told to 'receive Jesus' to be born again and enter the Kingdom, and then we looked at the daily application of cleansing, the need to keep on being saved, every day, and to have our sins washed away. They are experiencing in India the world-wide problem of children being brought up in Christian homes, and becoming nominal Christians, just as we are beginning to find in Africa. William has a convincing testimony to being saved from nominal Christianity in Uganda. ... William spent some time ... giving our testimony of East Africa, of how at times we had found ourselves looking away from Jesus, and looking at 'Revival', as a 'thing' that could save us.

"We found people in different parts of the world falling into this trap, looking to 'people' to bring Revival, or to a formula, or to a name, like Ruanda. Even a good book, like 'Calvary Road', we found could be read and marked with great care, yet people missed the things that it is trying to portray—what revival means in the heart, which is walking with Jesus. God helped us, it was a deep time."

At 3 o'clock and at 7 pm, during long sessions, God blessed us and gave us freedom, all our speaking being in English. ... Pastors have been coming for talks with us all the time, a few have repented deeply. These repentances are very costly. We all, as brothers together, have gone back to the Cross for cleansing. At midday we felt we should close the meetings in order to have more time for private talks, so we went back and told them. This led to some consternation, but eight or so came up for individual talks. We feel this is a crisis time, an hour of decision in the Church of South India. There is a danger of Christianity just becoming one of the many religions of India, into which you enter by the fact that your parents were Christians.

"We feel this is the centre of the attack of the Devil, as he knows this is the key to Revival in South India. ... We have tried faithfully to challenge several things, such as the long prayers, intoning and dramaticism in prayer, long repetition of hymns with drum, cymbals and bells, the working up of excitement. We came to the end of ourselves this

morning and asked God to vindicate His power, as we felt
our weakness so much. He has answered. ... A change is
coming over the place, the singing is less wild, and the
prayers and testimonies are given in real simplicity."

William Nagenda returned to Africa after the tour in India leaving Joe to go on to Pakistan. This he was reluctant
to do, preferring to work in a team. The first event of this
part of the tour was a convention at Ludhiana. "Again, as
in South India," wrote Joe, "I made the 'V' Picture the theme.
Each Bible study and address seemed to go back to, and fit
in with this. The two stiffnecked I's, bowing and saying,
'Yes, Lord,' thus forming the 'V'.

"We very soon saw as the light of the Spirit shone, that
here, as everywhere in the Christian world, the great need
is for daily victorious living amongst us leaders. I believe
more and more, the whole world is waiting for one thing,
not to see a great mission, or a great missionary, or a great
organisation, or to hear wonderful words, but to see Jesus
in us. Barriers were broken down, and hearts began to melt,
but there were some battles."

At Lahore, Joe was feeling the strain of continual ministry when God gave him a gracious reassurance. He wrote:
"I felt tired, as this was coming at the end of about two and
a half months of continual conventions and meetings. I
asked for two or three others to join with me as a sort of
team to help with the speaking; but this plan did not seem
to have God's seal on it, so we left it.

"I returned to my room to lie on my bed and get some
rest. Before I slept I said to God, 'I cannot go through with
another convention alone, I am empty.' Then I prayed, 'Lord,
do a miracle as You did at Salem, because I can't do it
myself, fill me with Your Spirit for Jesus' sake.' Then His
voice clearly seemed to say, 'Repent! Repent of doubting
Me, and of trying to get those extra speakers when you
could see they had not come prepared. Have I ever let you
down before?'

"It was a very clear experience to me, and I knew I had to
bow and just repeat to myself those two words that I knew

had got to be my text, 'Yes, Lord.' At once a flood of light came and every address from beginning to end seemed to be flung as though on a screen, before me. 'Take the theme you took at Elfinsward,' the Voice said, 'the theme of the Promised Land - How to enter - How to live there - How to rest there - from Joshua, Deuteronomy, Hebrews, Acts.

"I felt His infilling of power and a sense of assurance and urgency. 'Time will be all too short,' He clearly said. I turned over in my bed and said, 'Thank You, Lord,' and slept. It was one of those spiritual experiences I shall always remember. I knew William would be praising with me too, if he were here. ... So I left India, learning only very slowly how costly it is to obey those words—'Yes, Lord.'"

At a missionaries' conference in the tour of Ethiopia, November to December, 1954, Joe and William based their thoughts on the appearance of Jesus to His disciples in the Upper Room and His words to them: 'Peace be unto you.' In the following three days, the themes centred on *Our Commission* - 'As my Father has sent me, even so send I you'; *Our Comforter* - "He breathed on them, and said unto them, 'Receive ye the Holy Ghost"; *Our Calvary* - 'He showed unto them His hands'.

"William and I have felt so unworthy of being called to speak to a crowd of missionaries like this, but God has answered our prayers, especially today. Jesus has truly appeared among us, asking us if we have His Peace. There have been many heartbroken repentances and testimonies; it has been holy ground."

At Soddu, a crowd of about 4,000 people met in a specially arranged arena with seating facing a kind of platform called a 'banda' in East Africa. The speaking was handed over entirely to William and Joe. They took as their theme "the prison picture that we had taken years ago at Kako," wrote Joe, "starting with Colossians 2:13-14, 'Blotting out the handwriting of ordinances that was against us ... nailing it to His Cross.'

"We drew on the blackboard the picture of the prison cell, with the prisoner sitting rebellious on his stool and

looking at his charge-sheet and shaking his fist—the door
tightly closed. Then there comes the knock at the door and
the call to leave, and as the prisoner steps out in faith and
repents he sees the Cross in the second picture, and his
charge-sheet nailed to it as he passes by, free. ...

"A moving picture came from 2 Samuel 14:14, 'For we
must needs die, and are as water spilt on the ground, which
cannot be gathered up again; ... yet does He devise means,
that His banished be not expelled from Him.'

"Many bowed and yielded up their hearts to the Lord as
they saw how He had devised means to bring them freedom
after they were as water spilt on the ground—never to be
retrieved. Many of the Ethiopian leaders of this movement
are here with us, but we have found that there are many
problems which we have talked and prayed over. ... We have
seen faces relaxing, and eyes filling with tears as the Holy
Spirit has pointed to the love of God." [E5-6]

Two days later, Joe and William were in Hosanna. "This
convention is much the same as Soddu," wrote Joe. "Today, William and I have both spoken twice, and the burden
of the message that God has given us, using the blackboard again, is the picture of the pit from Psalm 40, verse
14: 'He brought me up out of an horrible pit ...', especially
stressing sin. God has made the picture of the pit live to us,
I think almost more deeply than ever in the past. In a way
there is doctrine in a nutshell in a living parable like this.
We saw the man in the pit as he is in the state of sin. It is
not so much the sins that matter, but his state of sin—
being cut off from God. Then we saw repentance as an attitude and not only an act: the man must leave the pit to
repent truly. We saw the whole story of the love of God, how
that, seeing the plight of man, He sent His only Son right
down into the pit, to be sealed by the stone, but yet to rise
again, opening the way for all mankind to follow. We saw
the scarlet rope that must be held and trusted in by faith;
we saw the man being born again, coming out of the top by
grace, singing a new song and then walking with Jesus
along the Highway.

"We have felt great freedom in preaching, and we were not tired, even though there were three long meetings each day, sometimes with two interpreters (the Government ordered that Amharic and the local tribal language be used). There has been no special break spiritually. But it has been one of those conventions when people go away quietly facing a new and deep challenge as to their whole standing before God. Many are praising, including the sixteen missionaries who have just sung the Doxology a few minutes ago at our last hymn-singing and fellowship meeting. We are praising for an unmistakable sense of victory through the preaching of the Blood of Jesus. After all, the very name of this place is *Hosanna*. Praise has been the keynote!" [E6-7]

While in Addis Ababa, William and Joe were called to the Royal Palace to meet the Crown Prince of Ethiopia—the Emperor was away. Once the introducing formalities were over, "we talked freely about the Lord," wrote Joe, "and our call to Ethiopia, and answered many questions His Highness put to us. He speaks perfect English. He knows the Kabaka of Uganda and talked to William about him. ... So we praised very much for the opportunity of seeing the dignity and grace of this God-fearing royal house of Ethiopia. ... Tonight the Evangelical Church was full, including the gallery, and God has spoken clearly on the line of decision, 'Choose you this day'. Many are testifying to blessing."

Of the last two meetings of the Ethiopia tour Joe wrote: "We have just finished this evening one of the most wonderful times William and I have ever had. At the meeting we felt compelled to invite those who had decided for Christ to stay behind. They were not very many, but about thirty-five remained. We have instructed them and linked them up with the activities of this church. God has been very much with us at the two morning services. William, at the Ethiopian service, preached on Noah's Ark, and how people stood mocking, even as the rain began and the doors of the Ark were closed. 'Enter into the Ark before it is too late'— that was the call. He felt compelled again to make an appeal, and about three hundred remained behind. There was a time of open prayer, many praying together at the same time. ... We have just finished the final meeting in the Ethiopian Evangelical Church. It has been packed, many having to sit outside in their cars and listen to the service relayed through loud speakers. ... My heart looks back with gratitude and praise for all that the Lord has done in Ethiopia during these three and a half weeks." [E13-14]

For a full tour, the medical responsibility of Gahini Hospital had been undertaken by Dr Bill Church, Joe's brother. When Bill and Janet returned to England on leave in 1957, Joe, backed up by Decie, resumed the responsibility for the hospital work there. During that time Joe accepted no invitations to lead teams elsewhere.

In January 1959, Joe Church and Roy Hession travelled via Jamaica to Brazil, South America. To the many meetings and conferences for leaders which they addressed, they usually began with their testimonies. For Joe, "mine was that of a missionary belonging to a keen evangelical Mission, going out to Africa to teach the Africans about the love of Jesus, and how He died for them, and about the victorious life; but very soon, under the testings that God allowed to come upon us in those early days at Gahini, it was not more about Jesus, but less and less about Jesus, that the Africans began to see: and then God, in His goodness, led me to a saved African, away in Kampala, in Uganda, and there He gave a new vision of Revival. I began to see slowly that much more of me had to die, first I think it was my anger, that I called 'righteous anger'. Secondly was the sin of departmentalism: independence in running *my* hospital and not wanting others, especially my fellow-missionary, a clergyman, to 'interfere' in it. Thirdly, there was a deep-seated, but subtle, despising of the Africans as being somehow inferior to me, who was the superior paternal missionary. These things and others had to die." [B12]

In Jamaica, Joe and Roy were driven to St George's Church, "crowded to the doors, with a full robed choir, the Bishop, the Assistant Bishop and the Archdeacon, all waiting to process in with us ... We both preached on the text,

'If the Son shall make you free, you shall be *free indeed*.'
We felt we should tell them the story of the revival in East
Africa, especially of how God raised up a witness during
the terrible Mau Mau times, when many of the 'saved ones'
were willing to face martyrdom rather than give up their
testimony to the Lord Jesus. Christ has made them free—
'free indeed'—from fear, from unforgiveness, from hatred of
the white man and of their own fellow men who were seeking to kill them."

In Sao Paulo, Brazil, Joe and Roy addressed a Pastors'
Conference. On the second day, Joe wrote: "Yesterday was
one of those rather hard days of studying the Word and of
going back to the Lord for help in one's weakness. This
drove us back more to prayer, and God gave more of a hunger for holiness. We definitely asked God to vindicate Himself as we tried to go back in brokenness to Calvary. Today,
as we have seen many times before, He has answered our
prayers, there has been a break-through with repentances
and a consciousness that God was melting hearts.

"We have had an outstanding time around the Word of
God—Luke 23:39. Two thieves were crucified with Christ,
one on the right hand and one on the left, both on their
crosses, both equally bad. Their condemnation the same,
but their destination vastly different. They differed in their
attitude to Jesus, one had a stiff neck the other bowed.
One protested his innocence, the other cried for mercy. One
said, 'I'm all right', the other said, 'I'm all wrong'. One died
resenting, the other died repenting.

"What are the crosses that we are on? A cross is anything that crosses our wills: a hard word from another,
uncongenial circumstances which we would not choose for
ourselves, even a tiresome little child may be the nails of
our cross. The determining factor is our attitude to the Lord
Jesus. That word from my wife this morning! Is it, 'I'm
right, and she is wrong'? Is it self-vindication or forgiveness? Is it revival or dryness? We cry out for our rights,
when, if we got our 'rights' we should have to go to hell! Is
it peace, or is it bitterness? If it is the latter, we see no

significance in Jesus hanging on the Cross next door to us; we don't see any meaning in the power of the Blood, because it was for sinners and not for us. If we are not wrong we don't need it, the other person does!

"We are then, in effect, railing on Him. We join those on their way to hell, protesting our rights to the end. How different was the story of the thief, who, after first resisting, bowed to Jesus. He said, 'Thou art in the same condemnation, and we indeed justly, but this Man has done nothing amiss.' He asked not for justice, but mercy. Confessing his cross as his due reward, he becomes a fit object for the grace of God. What broke him? It was the sight of the suffering Son of God. He didn't bother to defend Himself. There was a meekness the world had never seen before. Look at Him lying on the ground to be nailed, holding out His hand and saying to the soldier, 'Yes, that's the place to put the nail.' How can any man remain unmoved? But we do, we lie awake half the night arguing to ourselves with the man who has wronged us, and winning every argument! Wiping the floor with the other man! If you are like that, you will never see Jesus, the Cross will be just foolishness.

"Our prayer of the early morning that the Holy Spirit would come to help us was answered. A spontaneous sense of melting and joy began to come down upon us."

At Bello Horizonte, near Rio de Janeiro, Joe wrote, "There is still much misunderstanding about the Fullness of the Spirit, so at the afternoon and evening meetings we spoke about the Holy Spirit. It has been a memorable day, as if the Holy Spirit Himself came and put His seal on our Bible studies. The big church in the main square was packed, and there was such conviction of sin that to give an invitation seemed easy. When we did ask them, they came up from all over the church, until there were about fifty kneeling at the communion rail—a few were weeping aloud. We gave them an opportunity altogether to pray aloud, and openly to ask God's forgiveness and the filling of His Holy Spirit. We had given the East African illustration of Christ going round, Himself, to each one, one by one, to fill their cups with the Water of Life. After the congregation was dismissed we stayed on to talk for some time with those who needed help. To many it was the entry into life and to the fullness of the Holy Spirit."

At Jacotinda, near the end of their visit to Brazil, Joe wrote, "God led us to that amazing conversation of Christ with Peter, (John 21:15-17) when He said three times: 'Lovest thou Me?' using twice the deepest word in the Greek language for love. It came to us that He was saying, 'Have you got Calvary Love for the world?' Have you got that quality of love that drives you out to 'feed My sheep'? Have you real 'caring', when all around you are those who 'couldn't care less'? Have you heard the cries of a perishing world? It seemed to us that Jesus implied that at Pentecost this love for the lost, this gift of divine love, would be given by the Holy Spirit.

"There was one thing that we felt we lacked on the team," added Joe in his report on this visit to Jamaica and Brazil, "that was one of the Africans from East Africa. Perhaps William will come one day, or one of the others."

Joe never found preaching easy, in English or Kinyarwanda (the language of Rwanda) but he had a forceful way of communicating what he wanted to say. An example of this is a talk he gave at the Grace Abounding Convention held in London in 1963: "I wonder how many of you have brought Bibles! Shall we hold them up for a minute. Yes! nearly everybody. Please turn to Isaiah 6. There are several of us who are going to speak this afternoon—it is a sort of testimony meeting. We have been meeting here together as a band of brothers, and God has been meeting with us.

"'In the year that king Uzziah died I saw the Lord sitting upon a throne, high and lifted up and his train filled the temple.' Isaiah saw—he had a vision. On the day of Pentecost the disciples had a vision. They had seen it first on that mount of transfiguration, but Christ said to them, 'You must not talk about it yet, not until you have seen my Blood shed for you.'

"We have been talking about Revival. We want to be revived, but you cannot see Revival until you have seen again the Blood of Jesus, flowing from those hands to you and then covering that sin.

"What was the vision Isaiah saw? I believe that in the Bible it is always the same vision where people have seen visions - the same vision Jacob had as he saw that ladder going up to heaven - the same vision that Moses had of the burning bush and then of the glory of God come down on the Tabernacle. In the Old Testament and the New, the glory is the glory of the Lord Jesus. I believe that, on the day of Pentecost, that is what the disciples saw. Those two on the way to Emmaus, tired and grumbling and full of complaints - they said: 'We have seen Him!' 'Old men will dream dreams, young men will see visions.' So the vision we will see won't be something like the roof coming off, but it will be another vision of Jesus.

"Here Isaiah had a terrible testing. He felt that the whole bottom had fallen out of life. The one he really loved and respected and rather worshipped, and perhaps he copied the way he did things, the King *died*! And everything seemed to have come to an end. My testimony is a little bit like that.

"I was saved at Cambridge. I thought I knew a good deal and I thought I knew a lot about the Bible and I even talked about Revival. In those days of 1928,1929—I was tested in all sorts of ways. Here it was like that with Isaiah. He was chastened by death. With me, I don't know how many things went wrong—we had a famine, my hospital was turned over to dying people. I had to go round with my African assistants, Africans who had come to help me but they weren't saved, and they certainly did not see Jesus in me! We just went round the hospital to take the bodies and throw them down in the valley for the animals to eat. We hadn't time even to dig graves. Everything seemed to go wrong. I wasn't married in those days. I was just engaged. My fiancée, away in London, began to go down with what looked like rheumatic fever. Everything seemed to come to an end.

Then the time came to be married and I did not know what
to do. I really felt that she wasn't well and I'd better call my
engagement off. Then I remember going back to Kampala
on my motorcycle. It was 333 miles and I took a couple of
days to get there. On the way I was stranded and I lodged
in a little rest camp. I remember that night. Before God
blesses, He often brings you to a very dark place, and I
remember almost giving up all the mission field, as a failure. I remember lying in my bed and I could not go to sleep
but somehow the Lord would not let me go, and I had to lay
hold in faith in Him, the One who saved me, and He said,
'Hang on to me though you pass through the valley of the
shadow of death. Hold on to me.' And then I had to cry, as
I so often have done, even here, to the Holy Spirit. Are you
praying to the Holy Spirit? We have been praying to the
Holy Spirit here. And what does He do? He leads us to
Jesus.

"I arrived in Kampala on a Saturday. I had to have a
good wash after all that long way in the dust. Sunday morning came and I walked up to the cathedral in Kampala, the
capital of Uganda. I was walking up there in my hunger—I
had determined even in the dark to hold on to Jesus, but I
was cold and there was no Revival in me. I remember walking up to the Cathedral and there was an African there.
His name is Simeoni. He is still in Kampala now—that was
in 1929. I was at the very end of myself and there he was,
standing by the Cathedral. He had heard me speak and he
called and said, 'Hullo! Dr Church. Haven't you got any
more to give us?' I suppose that my face easily showed that
I hadn't got anything. I think that he was feeling hungry
too. Praise the Lord that there were two of us; two feeling
hungry and we were going to be made \ and / — V for
victory. As we were both hungry, we both had time for two
afternoons to read through the Bible—this Bible—we went
through Scofield's references to the Holy Spirit.

"We went right through the Old Testament and back to
the New and our hearts began to warm. I remember coming to this very text which I have chosen for this meeting.

I do not know quite what happened, but I know that God began to show me the finger that had been pointing at my Africans—'You, you poor Africans. You can't do your hospital work. You are lazy! But I was like Isaiah, that dear prophet of God. He was a most wonderful prophet, and evangelical prophet, just as I was in a way, only I was a feeble one. 'Woe unto them that join house to house and lay field to field.' All these things he was saying, ' Woe unto you, woe unto you.'

"I was just like that as a paternal missionary right up there and the poor Africans right down there. That is the way I saw them. But now, praise God, He has brought me down, I don't know whether I am brought down low enough, but I love travelling with brother William here. And we forget colour together.

Somehow the Lord seemed to say, 'Can't you see it? Look, one finger pointing *that* way, and there are three pointing *this* way. Well, I don't know if that has ever come to you, but God seemed to ask me, 'Can they see Jesus in you?' and I knew that they couldn't. 'Was I revived?' Sometimes I talked about it but could they see 'revival' in me? It was when I got to those words, 'Then said I, "Woe is me for I am undone, for I am a man of unclean lips",' that the light began to shine. The trouble with my lips was that I was always getting angry. I called it 'righteous anger' and argued from the Bible that it must be righteous anger. Then I seemed to hear the Lord say, 'I must touch your lips, there must be sweetness on your lips, you must not hide sin when you see it, but you must learn to have grace.'

"Well, I can tell you that I went back to my station from those wonderful days, and, one by one, people began to be saved. Only then can I say that God began in His mercy to give us Revival. God gave us a vision of teams. We heard the voice that Isaiah heard. We heard the voice of the Lord saying, 'Whom shall I send? Who will go for us?' And we said, 'Here am I, send me. We began to go out in teams. ... The teams that are here today are something to do with then, and there are other teams going all over the world.

"And so, in those days, God began to light us up. God showed us the true meaning of repentance. God showed us fellowship. God showed us what it is to walk in the light. I found that I was hiding all sorts of things from my African friends. Then we began to be brothers, we began to travel together. A new openness came to us as we walked the highway together. People began to dream dreams. They began to see visions. Strange things happened. People began to cry out in meetings.

"I remember going one Sunday to a meeting in a little place called Byumba, in the north of Rwanda. When we had finished preaching, a man stood up and said, 'Please may I tell you my dream?' It was the most extraordinary dream I think that I had ever heard and could only have come from the Spirit of God. He saw God in heaven, he said, and the Lord Jesus sitting beside Him. Then he saw God call the Lord Jesus and Jesus stood in front of Him in heaven. God asked him three questions: 'My son, are you willing to go down to that earth down there, that Satan has spoilt, and live in a poor life and be despised - You, my Son!' In the dream Jesus was dressed in all His splendour. He bowed to His Father.

"The second question was this, 'Are you willing to suffer a terrible death on the Cross, a very painful death, My son— to have nails put in your hands and your feet and to die?' Again Christ in His splendour bowed to His Father and said, 'Yes! My Father.'

"And then, in that dream, one more question. God said to Jesus, 'Are you willing for Satan to think that he has won the day, for Satan to think that he has conquered You, My Son. And are you willing My Son, for Me, your Father, to turn away My face and not be able to look on as You suffer for the sin of the world?' 'I saw Jesus standing quite still, just for a moment,' the man went on, 'then He bowed His head and said, "Not my will but Thine be done."' As he looked on, this man remembered the words, 'they delivered Him to be crucified, and when He had received the vinegar He said, "It is finished", and He bowed His head.'

"The man, who was a chief, went on, 'As I was watching I seemed to hear a voice which said to me, "You are a thief!" I said, "I am not a thief. What have I stolen?" I felt my neck getting stiff. I said, "I am not a thief." Then I seemed to see the Lord Jesus bowing His head for me. Then God helped me to say, "Yes Lord, I am a thief. I have been stealing poll tax money, and I will have to pay it back." Then He went on, "You have been despising the Bahutu, your slaves." Again, God helped me and I bowed my head again.' It was true.'

"Did not that dream come from the Holy Spirit. I pass it on to you. I don't think that you will forget it. I have never forgotten it. ...

"I was in Kampala with a fellow missionary, Bill Butler, and we were reading Galations 2:20 where Paul writes, 'I have been crucified with Christ. It is no longer I who live, but Christ who lives in me.' It is: 'Not I, but Christ.' I like doodling on paper with a pencil and suddenly I saw a little pin-man standing up with his neck very stiff saying, 'Not I!' - the 'I' that says 'No!' when the Holy Spirit speaks to us. Then we hear the Holy Spirit say, 'It is you. Jesus died for that sin—that unforgiveness, that impurity, that deceit, that dishonesty, those hard words, that grumbling, that anger, that bluffing, that wasting time—and we bow our neck and die. It is: 'Not I, but Christ.'

"I remember asking Bill Butler to write me a chorus and I will close by reading the words:

> Lord bend that proud and stiff-necked I,
> Help me to bow the neck and die,
> Beholding Him on Calvary,
> Who bowed His head for me."

Two cards illustrating these truths were widely used by Joe. The card entitled, 'NOT *I*, BUT CHRIST, depicted the stiff-necked, rebellious man standing rigidly upright as *I*, and the 'bent-neck', humble man on his knees as C. The card entitled: 'YES, LORD", depicted the source of Victory by two kneeling figures with right hands clasped, \ and / , to form the V.

As others saw them

Bill Butler first met Joe Church as a visiting speaker while he was in training in London for missionary work. "Joe certainly didn't strike us as anyone very special," wrote Bill, "A slight unassuming figure with a small moustache and a rather diffident manner, and yet he'd been given such a build-up. How was it Godfrey Buxton had described him? A man filled with the Holy Spirit? We fancied ourselves at the Missionary Training Colony, a unique establishment where 'men were men and women were only in the way', and we regarded ourselves, in all humility of course, as a sort of élite corps of hand-picked pioneers to be.

"It was to this unusual set-up that our speaker, Dr Joe Church of the Ruanda Mission, had been invited for a few days and we wondered what sort of powerful, dynamic figure he would prove to be, this man filled with the Holy Spirit. True, we had been warned that he was no speaker, a fact that soon became apparent. And yet we quickly became disarmed by his evident sincerity and transparency. He was so real, so honest in all that he shared with us, that even the most critical or suspicious among us was captivated and challenged. He spoke humbly and frankly, in a way we had never heard before, of the spiritual battles encountered on the mission field, the strains and tensions not only between black and white but often between missionary and missionary.

"We loved the Colony and were very happy and proud, perhaps too proud, to be there and of our reputation as Colony men... And yet, as Joe Church spoke we could not help but recognise situations amongst us which needed to be dealt with. Uneasy relationships and hard, unloving, critical attitudes which were far from Christ-like. Then, very simply, he went on to tell of the way God had broken through in Revival on his station, Gahini, in Rwanda; of the overwhelming conviction of sin they had experienced followed by deep and costly repentance, sometimes with tears, and of the restitution which often followed. When he spoke of the power of the precious Blood of Jesus to cleanse from all sin, and of the subsequent melting, breaking and uniting of Christians, one with another, we felt as that were indeed standing on holy ground. Friends said to me later, 'I could have listened to that man all night.' It was all so different from what we had expected, no powerful preaching, no tricks of eloquence, just a humble, unselfconscious, Christ-centred man pointing to Calvary and the shed Blood. Was this what Revival was all about? It certainly seemed so to us that evening as we sang the familiar chorus which we had sung so often in the past, but which now seemed to take on fresh meaning: 'Spirit of the living God, fall afresh on me...'"

David Church added to the testimony he gave about life in the Church family with this comment about his father in a wider context: "Father grew up as the eldest son in a strong supportive Christian family, his father being a Church of England parson. He needed, and enjoyed, this support, but was by nature a free-thinker, always seeking reality within the situations in which he found himself.

"This was to become the essential strength of his convictions in the early years of Revival in East Africa, when in spite of urgings from other Christians to break away from the established Church, he remained convinced that revival should be in finding new life in the old body, following the example of Jesus Himself who taught and prayed in the synagogues while at the same time not being afraid to speak out against hypocrisy and spiritual death within the establishment. Father, however, was not a great preacher as many of his friends and colleagues were, but when he spoke he would often start by opening his well-worn leather-bound Bible, covered with his own margin notes, and listeners would feel that they were being invited to share his latest exciting discovery.

"Christians are often urged to be more Christ-like. For Father, one sensed that he developed a deep empathy with Christ as a direct outcome of his daily study of the Gospels. His message may have lacked eloquence but it did seem to have authority. He often referred to Lake Muhazi as Ruanda's Sea of Galilee, and he certainly found spiritual relief away from the noise and crowds at the hospital, by retreating to the lakeside and taking to the water in one of his boats. Similarly he tried to avoid being drawn into political disputes, concentrating on the Gospel teaching of the need for personal repentance, regardless of one's status in the political system.

"His single-mindedness, particularly in his younger years, was seen by some as lacking a broader perspective, but almost until his death at ninety he was fascinated by new ideas, and would fill scrapbooks with cuttings from newspapers on the latest developments in science, technology and Christian thinking."

Later years

In July 1959, the Mwami (King) of Rwanda died in circumstances which raised many political questions. Although succeeded by his son Kigeri, the latter was never established as king, and the country began a long period of internal conflict. It was inevitable that, while not engaging in political alignment with either of the two opposing sides, *Hutu* or *Tutsi*, missionaries became involved because of their close relationships with many of the African Christians of both ethnic groups. Joe and Decie had been able, in the past, to be of medical help to the royal family. It was, therefore, inevitable that they would be considered to be on the side of the *Tutsi* people among whom figured the royal family and all the chiefs of the country.

From the end of 1959, onwards, violence flared up all over Rwanda and many *Tutsi* families were killed or forced to leave their homes to become refugees on the borders of the country or in neighbouring countries.

The situation deteriorated even further in 1961, and, on returning from the Butere Convention, Joe and Decie found an urgent letter awaiting them from Dr Godfrey Hindley, the field secretary of the Ruanda Mission, informing them that the British Consul-General had advised the Mission that it would be wise for Joe and Decie to leave the country. The Consul gave as his reasons that Joe had become a

centre of political controversy in the Gahini area, and he
feared for his safety. It is not difficult to understand his
reasoning. "All our missions have been involved in looking
after refugees, including the Roman Catholic stations," wrote
Joe soon after the event, "Sometimes one has to act quickly
without much thought of consequences. For example, a
year ago the 'Mugabikazi' (Queen Mother of the King
(Mwami)) arrived for treatment at Gahini. While with us
her official home and property were destroyed and her cattle stolen or killed, so she turned to us for protection. One
of our senior staff offered her his home, and for nine months
this brave and dignified lady was our guest. But this, and a
number of other instances have drawn the fire on Gahini
and on me personally. I have protested my neutrality as a
doctor and a preacher of the Gospel, and of our non-par-
ticipation in politics; and so, later, with the permission of
the Belgian government, I took the Mugabikazi into Uganda
for refuge. As Gahini has continued to seek reconciliation
and peace, we have been accused of holding up the trend of
the country."

    "I hasten to add", wrote Joe when writing to the UK
about the situation, "that I would never have left Gahini at
this time of worse testing and threatened attack unless I
had been ordered to go. But somehow I have a feeling that
God is behind this move, and we are resting in Him and
going on a step at a time."

    It was a sad day for Joe when, on 15 October 1961, he
crossed the border from Rwanda to Uganda "using my pink
resident's pass but feeling that I no longer belonged to
Rwanda, even after 33 years, and having been one of the
oldest European residents". [RN156.21]

    In the August prior to leaving Rwanda in 1961, Joe had
visited Fort Portal, Toro, in Uganda for the laying of the
foundation stone of the new Kabarole Hospital. It was to
there that they moved from Gahini. In the next three years,
in collaboration with their son Dr Robin Church and his
wife, Joan, Joe set about the reconstruction and development of that hospital.

In August 1964, Joe reached his 65th birthday and he and Decie officially retired. After a brief visit to England, they returned to Uganda, to Lweza, a site on Lake Victoria, with the intention of building it as a centre for those concerned with Revival. For a time Lweza became a retreat to which people came from other parts of Uganda and beyond. "One of our visions for 'Lweza'", he wrote in a circular letter, "was that friends on world travel could drop down out of the skies and visit us, as we are only thirteen miles from the international airport at Entebbe on Lake Victoria."

For a time Lweza proved to be a fruitful centre of fellowship for many who visited there, from Uganda, and further afield. Joe's vision for Revival was undimmed but there were difficulties to be faced on all sides, even from within the circle of those who had once been fellow-workers in his ministry. Misunderstandings among some of these led to the situation at Lweza being untenable, and Joe and Decie moved to a house in Kampala. They hoped that they would be able to live out the rest of their lives among the people who had meant so much to them, and among many of whom they were indeed 'brethren' in Christ.

During this time, Uganda passed through the turmoil of the Obote regime and this was succeeded by that of Idi Amin. Erica Sabiti, who was made Archbishop of the Church of Uganda in 1966, encouraged Joe and Decie to stay in the country, despite the breakdown of law and order that was destroying the peace it had enjoyed for so long.

As security became more difficult, not only for foreigners but also for Ugandan Christians, the limitations on visitors as, well as threats to their own safety, led to Joe and Decie being persuaded to leave Uganda and settle in England. It was during this time in Kampala that Joe began to prepare the material which would eventually appear as his biography, *Quest for the Highest.*

In June 1972,Joe and Decie flew out of Uganda for England as Idi Amin was ordering the explusions of the Asians from that country. As from Rwanda, so from Uganda, it was 'just in time'!

Joe and Decie settled in Little Shelford, near Cambridge, in a bungalow, 18 Church Street. "Number 18," Joe would point out "in CSSM Choruses, is: 'Cleanse me from my sin Lord, Put Thy power within Lord, ...'." That was the chorus that had meant so much to him when he was converted as a student. His life was a testimony to God's answer to that prayer.

In the following years Joe was able to visit Switzerland for the 28th annual Revival Conference at Leysin, and Uganda for the 5th annual Kabale Convention in 1975.

Joe's greatest preoccupation, however, was the revision of *Every Man a Bible Student* and the publication of his *Quest for the Highest*. "For four years at Little Shelford," he wrote in 1977, "I have concentrated on the publishing of *Every Man a Bible Student* because I believe that individual study and understanding of the Bible, with the help of the Holy Spirit, is the basis of new life and purpose coming back to our country. It is more important than my Revival memoirs manuscript."

In 1977, Joe was able to welcome his very close friend, Yosiya Kinuka, who visited England in 1977 for medical treatment. A special bed was made up for him in his study. "This helps me do the nursing necessary, and for us to have talks and laughs over the past."

Joe's health deteriorated slowly over the following years. He was tended by Decie who remained mentally very alert. Towards the end she often spoke for him in conversations with people when he was unable to articulate what he wanted to say. Joe's nod would indicate that her words were also his.

Joe died on 29 September 1989 aged 90, and Decie followed him on 30 March 1991 aged 86.

Joe and Decie have gone to receive the "Well done, good and faithful servants' from the Master they served for the whole of their lives. Those who knew Joe would add that he was a man who lived his life for THE HIGHEST - God's *highest* for him in every aspect of his life.

Chapter 3

William and Sala Nagenda

The early years

William Nagenda was born on 1 September 1912, one of eight children. His father, Festo Manyangenda, was a well respected Muganda chief who lived, with his large family, on the slopes of Namirembe, one of Kampala's 'seven-hills' and on which stands the Church of Uganda Cathedral.

After junior school in Kampala, Nagenda attended King's College, Budo where he did well and went on to study at Makerere College. As a University College, Makerere had not yet been granted full university status, so Nagenda was awarded a diploma and not a degree. He gained a very good knowledge of English and he was made a clerk in the Governor's office at Entebbe. On occasions he acted as interpreter to government officials.

Successful, as he was in his work, his way of life gave concern to his father and mother who were devout Christians. They prayed that God would bring Nagenda to Himself and save him from a dissolute life.

"I was brought up in a Christian home," Nagenda said, in giving his testimony, "I thought that I knew a lot about Christianity. When I was about sixteen, I thought that I was going to be a missionary and go to the Congo to preach the Gospel, but I had never found Christ as a person. Christianity was nothing really real to me.

"When I was about seventeen or eighteen, I found that, deep down in my heart, there were things that made it difficult for me to walk with God. These were things mostly in my thought life. People were saying that I was a very good Christian, but deep down in my heart I knew that I was not a Christian, not because I committed adultery, nor because I was a drunkard—I did not do that sort of thing. I thought that I was very good but there were things that made me sad and I knew that, if I could not get victory over those things, there was no difference for me between Christianity and any other religion.

"When I was twenty-one, I gave up the idea. I thought that it was better for me to enjoy what other people were doing—enjoy the world, go and commit all the sins there are and then deserve my punishment. It was then, when I was beginning to go downhill and there was no hope of anything happening in my heart, that Jesus sent four Africans to the town where I was. I looked into their faces which were so full of joy and peace. I said to myself, 'I wish I had such a face.' I asked them what made the difference. They said, 'We have not done one thing to become different. The Lord Jesus did it all for us at the cross of Calvary.' I couldn't believe it. That, to me, was a new Gospel."

Things became worse for Nagenda. Despite his salary as a government employee, he became deeper and deeper in debt but he refused to call that 'sin'. "That is not sin," he said to himself, "I haven't stolen money. I have simply borrowed it and I intend to pay it back." The logic of his reasoning did not, however, satisfy him.

One weekend, Simeoni Nsibambi and two or three friends cycled to Entebbe from Kampala to preach in the open air. It so happened that Nagenda and some of his friends were walking along the road where Nsibambi and his team were preaching. They stopped and listened to the preachers. "I do not know what you are talking about!" William shouted at them scornfully. Simeoni recognised William and, to his surprise called to him by name and said, "O, William, I wish you did!"

That Saturday night and early the next morning, the words of Nsibambi rang in Nagenda's mind and kept him from sleep. "It was a Sunday morning," recalled Nagenda, "when Jesus came and convicted me of one thing after another. 'That is stealing,' he said, 'Lord, I haven't stolen, I borrowed that money.' Jesus said, 'That is stealing.' I had to bow my neck and say, 'Yes, Lord, I am a thief.' Then Jesus said, 'You are an adulterer. You have committed adultery.' I said, 'No, Lord, I have not.' But there were certain thoughts and habits which Jesus said was adultery. So Jesus went on pointing out sin. In the end I said 'Yes' to them all. That Sunday morning I came to the end of myself. I knew there was no hope for me. I want to praise God that I saw the Lord Jesus Christ—on the cross for me. Somehow I heard Him saying, 'This has been done for you. All your sins have been carried away from you through the death of Jesus'."

That morning, Nagenda went to where he knew Simeoni Nsibambi was staying and found him and his friends still praying. He knocked on the door and went in to those who were praying. He told them of what had happened and how he had been very troubled by Nsibambi's words. "I have come to tell you that I have been saved," he said. He was welcomed with great praise.

"It was a wonderful thing when I came to the Lord," William testified years later. "I did not know how to praise Him. I did not know how to thank Him. I looked round to see where was the burden of my sins. I could not find it any longer. I knew that I was a new man. Deep down in my heart there was something I could not keep quiet about. It was a burning fire. I went out and found myself talking to people about the Lord Jesus Christ. Some people thought I was mad but I knew I was all right. Something had happened and I wanted to tell the whole world about it."

Nagenda was a man of action. He went to Bishop Cyril Stuart, Bishop of Uganda, to offer himself for full-time service in the church. The Bishop recognised the potential in Nagenda and planned for him to be trained for ordination.

Nsibambi's younger brother, Blasio Kigozi, arrived at Gahini in 1929, to work with Joe Church, Yosiya Kinuka and others. Blasio died after a brief illness. His death had a profound effect on William Nagenda, his future brother-in-law. He felt that this was a very real call to him to offer and take his place although he had no training.

Bishop Cyril Stuart recorded that "ten clerks at Entebbe have banded themselves together to resist sin and to spend whole weekends preaching around the countryside. Four of them have come to me saying they want to read for ordination." William Nagenda was one of these.

The Bishop was, at that time, preparing to visit Rwanda and promised that he would try to find a place where Nagenda could learn some pastoral work and do some teaching before going to Mukono Theological College for ordination. When, in a diocesan committee, Bishop Stuart asked which of the Rwandan mission centres would receive him as a helper, Joe Church immediately requested him as he knew him to be a convert of Simeoni Nsibambi. William arrived with Sala at Gahini at the end of 1936 to take over the running of the Evangelists' Training School.

Family life

As the son of a chief and with his associations with Nsibambi, it was natural that he should know the Bakaluba family well. The eldest daughter of that family was Eva, Nsibambi's wife. Another daughter, Katharine, was married to Blasio Kigozi. Nagenda married a third sister, Sala. When Nagenda was invited to work at Gahini, he and Sala were already married .

With her sisters, Sala shared a father who was concerned for the education of all his children. The elder daughters, Eva, Katherine and Sala attended Gayaza High School. The two youngest went to Budo, a co-educational school—an unusual course of action in those days. So it was that Sala grew up in a very stimulating atmosphere. In the years that followed, the Nagenda family proved to be very caring, and Jesus-centred.

Stephen Nagenda writes very appreciatively of his parents and of the home in which he was brought up. "The first thing that comes to my mind when I think of my parents is that they were always very happy together. We never saw them quarrel. There was hardly ever a cross word. I am sure they had their disagreements but overriding it all was the fact that they were very happy together. What also struck me was the fact that they shared together everything they did. June, my wife, brought this up when we were having a difficulty in our marriage and she said, 'We ought to do what your father and mother did and talk to each other and discuss things.' Over the years this lesson has helped so much in difficult situations and we have shared our thoughts together.

"Another thing I noticed about my parents was that, when any of us asked if we could do something, they would say, 'Let me first consult my wife (or husband),' So this sharing or 'walking in the light' meant that each person knew what the other one was thinking. They were my parents but they also became my friends. Of course I 'got it' from my father when I misbehaved badly. My mother was, however, my closer friend. I found I could talk to her about my triumphs, failures and my trials. One also has to remember that my father travelled a lot and was often not at home, and I was frequently away studying. It was, therefore, our mother to whom we usually went.

"My father was a very strong person, but he was also very, very humble. In my own life, I find that is where I often fail. I want to show the other side, that I am right. I do not think I have the humility that I admire in my father. My mother was very friendly to a lot of people. Both my parents were very outgoing and I think that is one of the reasons they reached so many people.

"We had people from many places to our home, not just from Buganda, but from all tribes. No matter what time of the day or the night they arrived they were welcomed, and people from overseas came as well. You could tell that they had something in common which they shared, not only between my mother and my father but between the other visitors who used to come, and I think that the thing they had in common was a real love for Christ.

"We loved welcoming father home from his visits overseas because we knew he would come with some goodies for us! We missed him when he was gone but we were tremendously excited when we knew he was coming back. I suppose the thing I missed was being able to get closer to my father as a person and getting guidance from him in my Christian life, and there I think we missed out. Although my mother was more available, there are certain things that a growing boy needs to share with his father. They gave of themselves very much, and as we grew older we realised that to have had so much time for us as they did was very fine and really something.

"His laughter was very genuine. There was nothing forced about it. It was definitely from the heart! And he often saw the funny side of things. There was a time for instance when we were playing cricket in our front garden, and he said he would join us. We were sceptical about this, but we found that he could play; then he suggested we should run round the house. We thought the poor old man would not be able to run fast and he roared with laughter when he beat us. He also used to laugh at the Swiss cows which seemed to have shorter legs at the front than the back so that they could climb the hills!

"Both my parents came from fairly important families in Buganda and both of them knew the Kabaka. My father went to see him to tell him about Jesus. Sometimes he went to see him before an overseas visit and then again on his return. But they always felt very comfortable with people from completely different backgrounds. I noticed how well my father dressed, but he was not at all fussy, he was very free and comfortable wherever he went.

"On the gender issue, one thing I remember noticing amongst the brethren was that there was such equality of the sexes. I noticed this particularly in the way they consulted and respected each other.

"I had a lot of opportunity to talk with my father in the days when he was ill. At the time I did not take much notice and I would think that you repent of your sins and that is it, but now I have seen that I need to come back often. I recall how he used to talk to me, and I would describe all the commitments I had, and he would say, 'Yes, but does what you *do* ever allow you to have a quiet word with God?' and I would say, 'Yes, of course!' This 'Not I, but Christ' is the hardest question. There is always that desire to do what 'I' want. Many of these truths mean much more to me now as I look back and see."

"As a child I found my parents 'walked in the light,' therefore we did not have any dark secrets," added John Nagenda. "Although they were very firm Christians themselves they gave us quite a lot of freedom, and therefore when I stopped being a *mulokole* (a revived one) myself I told them and of course they did not like it, but they accepted it. We still went to church every Sunday, and had daily prayers, but what I remember is how remarkably liberal they were towards their children. We were always great friends. Looking back on my upbringing I do not remember any disadvantages. To this day I am not a Christian but there were certain things which became part of us, and so throughout my life I have been very conscious of how my parents have regarded this and that although I myself am not a Christian, I might term myself a humanist. Another thing for which I am eternally grateful to them is that they did not have any racism, or tribalism. My mother spoke perfect Kinyarwanda. We grew up without any problem about the different tribes, and to this day I am happy with all different tribes and races. They were also extremely strict on the matter of us respecting people older than ourselves, even if that person was working for us."

For those who visited the Nagenda home, there was always a loving welcome, from whatever race or class. Enoch Rukare remembers: "When I was in the upper classes at Mwiri, two of William and Sala's boys, John and Stephen, joined the school, and they asked me to look after the pocket money for the two boys! I found Sala to be such a loving person. She treated me like the older brother of her sons. Even when I had finished studying I would go to Namutamba, and she would give me a room and look after me as if I was one of them. I always asked myself why Sala bothered with me. I was not from her natural ethnic group, but that was Sala, she was different."

Robina Kalega remembers the testimony of a 'brother' who was "on a journey and went to call in on William and Sala at Namutamba. They arrived at about 11.00 in the morning. William asked Sala if the visitors could be given some lunch, even though it was not yet lunch time. So Sala brought out the lunch that was for the family! They had chicken which is a delicacy in that area. That was typical of their generosity. Whenever he was given any clothes he would give away what he had. He did not do this publicly but as it says in Scripture: 'Do not let your left hand know what your right hand is doing.'

"We are so grateful to William for what we have learned of the Lord through him. One of the reasons the Lord used them so much was because William and Sala appreciated each other so much, and they saw that they could learn a lot from each other. We saw that they complemented each other. They were wonderful models for us. There is no perfect team, but they were, for us, close to perfection."

Canon and Mrs Bunyenyezi were neighbours of the Nagenda family at Namutamba. Mrs Bunyenyezi said, "I learned from the lives and wisdom of William and Sala. They showed us how to be disciples of Jesus in our lives, in our homes and in our villages. Sala taught us so freely and so lovingly that I not only grasped what she said, but I shall never forget her teaching. It is part of my life and I passed it on to others. In their home and in their lives you really saw the glory of God."

The characteristic of the William and Sala Nagenda family which all who were near them noticed, was 'consistency'. They were in their individual lives, in their home and in the community what they proclaimed from the public platform.

Ministry in Revival

Soon after William began work at Gahini he was conscious that he was following in the footsteps of his brother-in-law, Blasio Kigozi, and he felt that people would expect him to live up to his high spiritual standards. He decided to visit Nsibambi, share his fears and concerns and ask his advice. "Don't try to 'do' things, William," Nsibambi counselled him. He urged him to repent of trying to copy Blasio, and simply to be what he was as William. Nsibambi quoted from Paul's letter to Timothy, "Study to show yourself approved to God." Then he went on to say, "If you are right with God, revival will never stop."

At Gahini, William noted some unusual happenings at the church centre, in the district around and over the border around Kabale, Uganda. He was perplexed by physical signs of powerful spiritual convictions—people weeping, falling down and crying out under waves of conviction of sin, people spending hours in prayer and singing, sometimes through the night. He saw these things happening but he did not then feel part of them.

In July 1937, William wrote to Joe Church, then on leave in England. "Three weeks ago, I had a week quiet with God. It is wonderful because God showed me a great number of sins in me which can stop the blessing: (1) looking for self-glory, (2) not knowing God, (3) lack of love, (4) bad thoughts which creep in. You see these are the sins of the heart; wanting people to think that you are a very strong Christian. We do not know of any saint who looked for his own glory. God has shown me that He has always been a friend of every true seeker. I want to long for people to be saved. There must be a vision of people perishing."

A later letter showed how William was progressing spiritually. "Pray that many may go through a Pentecostal experience. God has been showing me millions on their way to hell. How many cry about things today? How can one help weeping and crying when we see this. I feel very sorry for Jesus, having died for the salvation of His people, to see so many going to hell. He is crying!"

Then God began to work in powerful ways through his ministry. "On Whit Sunday, at Gahini, I preached in the church," he wrote. "A man stood up and began confessing his sin, so we asked all those who were convicted to stay behind, and about three hundred remained."

"Team work helped William to develop spiritually, and it brought out his gifts of leadership," wrote Joe Church. "Team exposition—a method of expounding the Scriptures— developed amongst us. One would come prepared with a message as a Bible Reading and then the team would follow on expounding it further, and illustrating each point by personal testimony. Often William would come in at the end with a costly repentance and a searching appeal. People would begin to stand up while we were speaking and pour out their hearts to God. Sometimes meetings were held up by many weeping.

"In the midst of all the extraordinary happenings of that time, William had a wonderful gift of going right in with them but bringing them back all the time to Jesus Himself."

Dora Skipper was in charge of a girls' boarding school at Gahini. She wrote of some amazing events at Gahini Church during Easter 1937. "Ten or more at once were praying with deeply convicted hearts . . . no excitement or hysteria, deep sincerity . . . the walls of Jericho came down ... William and Yosiya were almost brutal in refusing anyone to confess who was not to the point ... helping each one to see his or her sin and Jesus as Saviour." [9144]

Following those events, a half-term holiday was given to the Evangelists' Training School at Gahini and a team set off for Shyira which included William Nagenda, Yosiya Kinuka and Gideoni Kabano. As they spoke, there were remarkable scenes of physical manifestations. Dora Skipper wrote that "many people physically fell to the ground ..." The team took little note of the outward manifestations, but what God was doing in people's lives gave them great joy. "Everywhere they went," continued Dora Skipper, "they found people prepared and waiting to be saved.

William was given wisdom. When they found people rather 'keyed up' they left off speaking about sin and preached the mercy of God. But there was always a cost to be paid. One senior person, who had been helping a missionary in translating the Bible, had threatened to beat anyone who confessed his sins. He was in tears as he, with his wife, produced charms and confessed to practising witchcraft" [9144] The team returned to Gahini with great joy and immediately set off for Kabale, Uganda, to tell of what God had been doing.

In 1938, a difficult situation arose at a church centre in Buhiga, in Burundi, when Joe Church's brother, Bill, was in charge of the hospital. Bill had been at a missionary conference in Gisenyi when 'Revival came to Buhiga' in his absence. He described how, on returning to Buhiga, "three evangelists came from Gahini to hold meetings. During a conversation with me they stated that in their opinion I was not born again. To my surprise four of the leading Christians at Buhiga supported them." The situation was shared with the team at Gahini, and Joe Church wrote, "William and the others seem to agree now that there is some confusion in terms; 'being saved' is muddled up with 'being sanctified' ... We asked God to heal this thing that had caused so much trouble and to help us to learn from it." [9156]

William was one of the team at the African 'Keswick' at the Alliance High School, Kenya, in September 1938. After some difficulties, "A break came on Wednesday after preaching about the Cross," wrote Joe Church, "and many began praying all over the church at the same time. William and Yosiya pleaded with people to get right with God. William speaking on the words, 'Jesus wept' and 'Jesus died'. God seemed to tell us clearly to stress sin and repentance, centring it all around the Blood of Jesus. I have never known the messages go home with such tremendous force. We decided to avoid all holding up of hands so as to leave the results entirely to God. This was a big decision, pressed by the wise counsel of William and the African team members who felt that at this stage we should check emotionalism, and even make it difficult. But one or two Europeans on the team, who had been praying much for a definite outpouring of God's Spirit, were very grieved and felt that we were wrong in this." Q157-158 Incidents such as this countered the accusation of some that the Europeans were encouraging African emotionalism.

William was one of the team that visited the mission centres of the Africa Inland Mission in March 1939. There had been 'stirrings of revival' in four of the AIM mission centres in aastern Congo. An opposition to what was understood to be over-enthusiasm in Revival had begun when "an African boy who was very ill sat up in bed and stretched out his finger at one person present, pointing out his specific sin, and then dramatically lay down and died. The African leaders there had taken this to be the voice of God, and it was practised in preaching and from the pulpit. William and I (Joe Church) had to listen to a fervent and convincing 'exposition' by a young missionary of Revelation 12:10, 'the accuser of the brethren is cast down', suggesting that this was of the devil. William especially pleaded with the missionaries present to be patient and not to quench the Spirit. ... After this we continued south through the tall tropical forests of eastern Congo to enter Uganda again near the Rwenzori Mountains, reaching Kabale on April 4, after being away for two weeks and having covered 1,700 miles. Some of the time we spent in reading Charles Finney's 'Revivals of Religion', William reading it to us from the back seat of the car as we drove along." Q166

In the following year, January 1940, William left Gahini to attend the Theological College at Mukono, Uganda, for training for ordination. He joined a group of about 40 who shared his enthusiasm for what God was doing in Revival.

In August of that year, a convention was held at Namirembe, Kampala. It was the first to which all the *balokole* (revived ones) were invited. William felt that it was important to hold a convention at some central point to bring together, for encouragement and further teaching, those who had been touched by Revival.

This convention was remarkable in many ways, not least in the fact that the speaking was entrusted to a team which included all the pioneers in the East African Revival whose lives are recorded here: Simeoni Nsibambi, Joe Church, William Nagenda, Lawrence Barham, Yosiya Kinuka and Erica Sabiti.

William Nagenda returned to his studies at Mukono Theological College but a letter to Joe Church, received in November 1940, revealed that he was having problems: "Mukono is such a difficult place in every way. One can easily get cold," he wrote. "We are trying to go out preaching as much as possible on Sundays. One Sunday we preached from morning till sunset, and even then people were still urging us to preach to them the Word of God. They wouldn't even allow us to sing hymns. We went on preaching till 8 pm." [9][180]

In what became known as the 'Mukono incident', William was one of 26 students—ten ordinands and the remainder church teachers in training, and some reading for the Primary Teachers' Certificate—who were dismissed from the college. The situation arose from the restrictions imposed on the students which made it difficult for them to find opportunities to meet for prayer together and to preach. The *balokole* students were never put on the rota to preach in the chapel.

"On October 22nd, 1941," wrote Joe Church, "the Warden addressed the College, mentioning the outbreak of thieving, disobedience and disputes that had been taking place, and announcing that a new timetable was going up at once. No one was to leave his cubicle before 6 am and there was to be silence from 6 to 7 am. The meeting for prayer and meditation at 4 am was to cease forthwith." A group of students pleaded with the Warden to allow them to continue the early morning prayer meetings. This was refused.

"At 4 am, the next morning, 26 students, together with the African chaplain, met as usual. The Chaplain and the students who had disobeyed the instructions were then informed that they were being dismissed from the college.

"The ten ordinands were allowed to remain over the weekend and then, on the Monday, they were given a 'last chance'
to sign a document in which they promised amongst other
things that they would not preach or take part in any meeting in the College without the permission of the Warden.
They all refused this so were ordered to leave immediately."

One of the students, Yohana Bunyenyezi, wrote afterwards, "When we got back (from a student tour of Rwanda
and Burundi) to College at Mukono, God said to us, 'Don't
think about when you will go back to where you've been,
but rather, I have 'sent' you to the College.' Because at
College the Bible teaching was not good, a quite wrong way
of interpreting the Word of God. We talked to the principal
of the College that it was not right. There were with us
some older clergy who had come for a refresher course,
some theological students, some teacher trainees, and all
of them denied the possibility of being 'saved'. But God
told us, 'Speak with them.' We said, 'What shall we do,
because the timetable is full?' So we decided to meet to
pray in the Chapel at 4 am. At the stroke of 4.0 we would
throw off the blanket, and if we delayed we would feel convicted! And at six when we had prayed we would go outside and sing and say a few words, and tell the students
the Word of God.

"The students objected to what we said, and the Principal too, because we were critical of his teaching, began to
be against us. He wrote to Bishop Stuart that he ought to
send the Archdeacon to give us rules. They said we must
not go on teaching others, or to get up at 4 am to pray. If we
agreed we must sign. If not they would expel us. We said to
him, 'We cannot stop speaking of Jesus and we cannot leave
off praying.' They said, 'Since you don't agree, we give you
half-an hour to pack up your things.' I don't think we were
given even an hour. Everyone of us went to our dormitory
and collected our things.

"So we got up and went. We went to Kampala to Nsibambi
to tell him what had happened. He said, 'What! You have
left College? What riches do you have? He asked each of

us what we had, and none of us had anything. A few had houses, but I had nothing. William had nothing, though his father was a chief. There were about 30 of us who were expelled. They thought we would leave our Church (of Uganda) but we refused, saying we would stay in our Church and preach the Word of God. Afterwards Bill Butler and Benoni Lwanga, the Chaplain, were transferred elsewhere. Everywhere we went God worked."

William wrote to Joe Church from Namirembe that Monday evening. "I feel this has come to show me that I may not become a clergyman. There is a big work to be done by free evangelists. I must lay down my life for my friends and for the Revival." Joe replied urging him "not to fall into the trap of being turned out on the grounds of disobedience to rules". Q185

Commenting later on what had happened, Joe Church wrote, "Though outwardly correct from worldly standards, the Warden seemed to have set a trap while the Bishop was out of the country, from which there was virtually no escape, for the twenty-six believed implicitly that they were being led by God to call the College to repentance before term ended. If the Warden could have managed to unbend and enter into their burden for Uganda, all this might have ended very differently. If only they could have waited for the Bishop to return from Zanzibar! ..."

William admitted that he had disobeyed the new rules of the Warden, "but," he added, "in doing so I had the assurance that I obeyed God ... The Warden rebuked us for the Gospel we preach. ... I do not blame him at all for having discharged us, but I blame him for having made such rules, and I believe he made them knowing that they were going to be disobeyed ... You will understand that many of us had one month only to go and we would finish at Mukono. There is quite enough work in the Church of Uganda for free evangelists who can go round and round ... We are out to glorify the Cross of our Lord Jesus Christ that in the end He may see of the travail of His soul and be satisfied. Do pray for us and for the leaders of the church and for all the Church of Uganda, that all of us may be kept humble to receive what God longs to give us. We are leaving the future in His hands and trust Him for our need." ⁹¹⁸⁵⁻¹⁸⁶

As soon as Bishop Stuart returned to Kampala, he rushed out a statement supporting the action of the Warden and adding: "There have been faults on both sides. In my opinion it was unwise to ask them to sign rules, for Africans hate signing their names to papers."

William, with eight others—Elieza Mugimba, Yona Mondo, John Musoke, Erasito Kato, Edwardi Kakudidi, Mika Mwavu, Erisa Wakabi and Mesulamu Waiswa—far from being daunted by what had happened, saw in it the call of God to "step out in faith as free evangelists to Uganda".

A meeting of ten Ugandans, including William Nagenda, Simeoni Nsibambi, Erica Sabiti and Yosiya Kinuka, met with thirteen Europeans, including Joe Church, Lawrence Barham, Godfrey Hindley, Leslie Lea-Wilson, Bill Butler and Algie Stanley-Smith, to discuss what had happened. They reported: "We are unanimously convinced that the 'Mukono incident' was unwisely handled, and that the students were not in any true sense 'rebels'." ⁹¹⁸⁶ The meeting recommended that the Church rules be modified so as not to hinder Revival in the Uganda Diocese.

Although not expelled from the College, as the students were, a young missionary on the staff was also 'located elsewhere' because of his sympathies with the expelled students. Due to a number of unexpected events, Bill Butler, although a relatively new CMS missionary, was ordained by Bishop Stuart, on 30th November 1940 "to kill two birds with one stone—ordain me and fill an essential gap at the Bishop Tucker Theological College, at Mukono".

This was, for the now Revd Bill Butler, a very abrupt and puzzling introduction to liberal theology. While, without previous theological training, Bill was not fully equipped to withstand the prevailing theological ideas, William Nagenda, with a number of the students, "had resisted these ideas fiercely and potently, and was bitterly resented by the staff because of that".

"William   was at Mukono a bit before me," wrote Bill Butler, "He had been there six months or so before me. When eventually I met him, I found him a bit abrasive, frightening, challenging, and I loathed him!

"I was teaching theology, which was really funny because I had never read theology. The impact of liberal theology on me was absolutely shattering and it was William and a few others who were radiantly walking with the Lord who held me firm and who challenged me when they saw me going astray."

A challenge from a 'lady missionary from Rwanda' made Bill realise that the blame for his resentment at the joy of the *balokole* students was not the fault of the students, nor of the College, but was in himself. "You know," the lady missionary said to him, "I wonder if you have been broken?" Then, with blazing clarity, he wrote, "I saw myself as Jesus saw me, as I *really* was ... my pride, my rebellion, my unwillingness to let go the failures and secret sins that for years had held me, that mask behind which I had been trying with so little success to hide."

Bill returned to Mukono 'in a daze', wondering how it was all going to work out. Of one thing he was sure. He had to get things right with the 'brethren' among the students. "If ever there was a brother with whom I needed to be reconciled, and whose forgiveness I needed to ask, it was William Nagenda. He, like Yokana and one or two others, had been aware of my growing coldness, my compromise with liberal theology, and general spiritual malaise, and had lovingly expressed concern from time to time; even, to my chagrin, assuring me that he was praying for me! William had been especially anxious about me, a fact which in my wretched pride I had bitterly resented and shown in many ways."

As it was during a vacation, William was at home and Bill decided to drive the 35 miles there. "I'll never forget that journey," he wrote, "It was as if there were two passengers in the car: one reminding me of 'the loss of face' and prestige that was bound to ensue, the other that this, in a

very practical and specific way, was what 'dying to self' was
all about. As I drew up at the small house where William
and Sala were spending their holiday, and tooted the horn,
they came running out. Before I could say a word, William
took one look at my face, and with an indescribable look of
joy greeted me, 'Praise the Lord, brother!' My prepared
speech, like that of the penitent prodigal, was brushed aside,
as William hugged me as I had never been hugged before,
in an African embrace.

"For the first time in two years I knew myself one with
an African! That faltering step was the first of many. Never
before had I known such readiness to forgive or such warmth
of love—God's love, Calvary love—as met me then. It was
just like coming home. I found myself immediately part of a
warm praising fellowship I had never dreamed of, or experienced, in which I was safe; accepted without any need for
pretence, but a fellowship which would challenge fearlessly,
ruthlessly, yet with amazing grace anything less than 'the
highest'!

"Nor, in their wisdom and love, did the Africans deal with
me as so many would have done in England. When some-
body is converted or blessed, or takes a new step forward
spiritually, our tendency is to say, 'Splendid, now we can
leave them to it." But not so with these Spirit-taught men.
Indeed their reaction was, 'Praise God, Bill's had a blessing, now we can really get to work on him!' And that, with
remarkable insight and grace, is just what they did. Those
'wretched *balokole*' whom I had so resented and feared became, overnight, my brethren to whom, under God, I owe
an immense debt of love."

After his expulsion from Mukono, William spent a short
time in Kampala with Simeoni Nsibambi. He was offered a
house at Namutamba, the tea-estate owned by Leslie Lea-
Wilson, where he was able to receive many visitors.

William's involvement in the 'Mukono incident' left him
free to work increasingly with other leaders in the Revival,
but he was restricted by the fact that the Bishop had removed his licence to preach in the churches of Uganda.

In February 1943, William was asked to address the first
Advisory Church Council of the Ruanda Mission, at Buye,
in Burundi. "He led us through the Bible to see how light,
God's Holy Spirit, penetrated the story of man in the Old
Testament and New Testament, sweeping away darkness,"
recorded Joe Church, "and he ended with Pentecost and
his own testimony of recently being filled anew. We can't
work in this land full of darkness unless we are filled with
the Holy Spirit, but if we let our eyes dwell too much on our
troubles and problems, we will lose the vision of the world's
need." 9198

An event in 1944 was notable for the absence of William
Nagenda. Joe Church was invited to take a team to South
Africa. The Bishop reluctantly gave permission for William
to go as it was felt that a 'black and white' team was essential. Sadly, the South African authorities, then in the days
of *apartheid*, refused permission for both William and Yosiya.

In 1945, William Nagenda and Yosiya Kinuka went
through a spiritual crisis, sometimes referred to as the 'Crucifying-the-old-man' controversy. In the Authorised Version,
Romans 6:6 reads: "Knowing this, that our old man is crucified with him, that the body of sin might be destroyed,
that henceforth we should not serve sin." The term 'old
man' is the translation of the Greek word which means
'flesh'. Here it means 'what we are naturally, before God
makes us new, when we are born again into His family'.
Then, to use a similar term we become a 'new man'.

William and Yosiya Kinuka had heard a preacher ex-
pound this 'crucifying the old man' as something they had
to do. In order that they should 'crucify the old man' once
and for all, the two went to a place in the Rwenzori Mountains where Simeoni Nsibambi had been in the past for
quiet meditation and prayer.

Joe Church records what happened: "The Tooro brethren brought them food while they spent several days in a
small hut on the mountain side. They came down refreshed
but still looking for a mysterious 'something'. Many times
we have heard them tell the story of how in the days that

followed they became strained and irritable in their homes
and hard on the children, but giving their testimony to this
new experience. Till one day William went to see Nsibambi
who greeted him and said, 'What is the matter, William?'
The reply came, 'Oh, I am really seeking to "crucify the old
man" in these days.' Nsibambi then looked at him sadly
and said, 'Don't you know, William, that your old man was
crucified for you, long ago, at Calvary! Go home and rest,
brother, rest in the finished work of Calvary.' The light came.
William went home to repent of striving, and entered into
that rest which had seemed so elusive. This testimony began to go forth far and wide, through preaching tours and
to many parts of the world. God saved the Revival from
what could have become a dangerous 'Jesus plus'." Q215

Towards the end of 1946, Joe Church and others felt
that as, while on leave to the UK , they would be invited to
tell of what God was doing in Revival in East Africa, it was
essential that William Nagenda and Yosiya Kinuka accompany them. The country was recovering from World War II
and, at first, the finances were difficult, but these were resolved and both William and Yosiya flew to England.

Their first engagement was a prayer meeting with members of the Cambridge Inter-Collegiate Christian Union
(CICCU) in the Henry Martyn Hall. William and Yosiya were
shown the 'roll of honour' of past Cambridge missionaries
inscribed on its panelled walls. This was followed by a garden party where, recorded Joe Church, "I told the story of
how the African brothers had come to England. Then William
stood up and began something like this: 'Today I saw the
name of George Pilkington on the walls of the Henry Martyn
Hall, the man who brought the Gospel of the Lord Jesus to
my country, Uganda, and who gave his life. Now I have
come to thank you and to tell you that we too have found
the living Lord Jesus and we've come to talk about Him.'
This was the first of many appealing messages that so en-
deared William and Yosiya to the hearts of people in England on this and more than a dozen future visits to this
country." Q227

One of the students who saw William and Yosiya on that occasion in the Henry Martyn Hall was David Thomson, who later became a lecturer in Physics at Makerere University College. "I was reading Natural Sciences at the time." he wrote, "but after 51 years I can still remember one or two things that impressed me. My first recollection is of the cheerfulness and ease with which William, Yosiya and Joe related to each other. Joe spoke about living for the 'highest', and about repentance and particularly brokenness. In the 'achievement' culture of Cambridge and of Cambridge Christianity, these were things we needed to learn."

It is typical of William that, later, he used the air flight from Africa to England as an illustration of the Gospel they preached: "It was paid for by someone else as our salvation is paid for by Jesus." It wasn't only the journey that was paid for, but also everything they needed on the way, for their food. And when they arrived at a hotel they found that their names were known and a room reserved for them.

William and Yosiya were invited, with Joe, to an IVF Conference of some 150 theological students, arranged by Dr. Martyn Lloyd Jones, of London. This led to a number of visits to Westminster Chapel and a special invitation to them to visit him whenever they were in London.

The team returned to Africa at the end of 1947, William to his family on the tea-plantation at Namutamba. He was able to share in the leadership of four conventions in 1948: Kampala in Uganda, Matana in Burundi, Kumbya on Lake Kivu in Rwanda and one at Gahini.

Between 1949 and 1959, William Nagenda and Joe Church visited a number of countries with the 'message of Revival': 1949 - France, Germany and Switzerland; 1951 - Malawi, then named Nyasaland; 1952 - Angola; 1953 - the United States of America.

Incidents in these tours remain in people's memories. On one occasion in 1949, during the visit to France and Switzerland, as they were being driven by car to Strasbourg in Alsace, France, recorded Joe Church, "William and I were sitting in front with the driver, and two German deaconesses from Marburg were behind. William and I laughed and chatted and there were one or two things to be put right between us. At Strasbourg one of the deaconesses made the remark: 'I was listening to you two talking and putting things right on the way. I want to tell you that I learned more about fellowship on that journey than in all the meetings.'"

During their visit to Malawi, in November 1951,William and Joe found some opposition. "Church after church was filled with silent rows of black-suited elders and pastors and their wives and families," wrote Joe Church, "Some were critical as many new sects had come into Nyasaland. William and I looked at those rows of lined faces and puckered brows, and wondered what they were thinking. 'What are we to do?' I said to William as we sank on to our beds. 'There is nothing to do but to cry to God,' William replied. So we did and He began to answer at once.

"William spoke about his home life and about being open about money with Sala, his wife, about his children, and about his debts that had to be paid back to the Government when he was saved. He talked about Jesus and we preached about the Cross. The first thing that changed was their eyes. They began to soften. They loved William and they crowded round after the meetings just to look at him and listen. A missionary slipped up to William and said, 'God told me to ask your forgiveness for not wanting to carry your bag at the airport because you are an African.'"

During the tour to the United States of America in 1953, Joe wrote, "We were warned that we might not be allowed to stay in one of the hotels at one of these places with William, but we were surprised later to find a special gift of fruit, brought by the hand of a janitor—a thank offering from the manageress for spiritual help she had received from William in a private talk."

In 1957, William visited England where he linked up with Bishop Festo Kivengere. They found themselves together again in 1962, when both received invitations independently, to visit the United States of America. The first meeting which they addressed together at the Calvary Baptist Church in New York was described by the Pastor, the Revd Dr Stephen Olford: "These two dear servants of God approached the pulpit together, and in tandem fashion taught and testified concerning the work of the Holy Spirit in Revival, illustrating lucidly what was taking place in Rwanda and Uganda. The power of the Holy Spirit was so evident in the hour that followed that there was hardly a dry eye in the congregation, as the great themes of brokenness, confession of sin, walking in the light, being filled with the Spirit, and living out the glories of the blessed Saviour were emphasised and applied. My own heart was deeply moved in repentance and response to the call of Christ to another quality of life."

After a short interval, "Festo and William came to the pulpit once again, and for nearly another hour they opened their hearts to our people. There was a spirit of Revival pervading the entire church and lives were touched and transformed in a living and lasting manner. That is a memory I will always treasure."

The biographer of Bishop Festo Kivengere continues from this quotation: "This was just one of dozens of similar meetings held in churches throughout America that spring. Throughout the tour, and indeed many times in the years to come, Festo and Nagenda preached together. They were 'like brothers' and 'made a great team' a friend recalls. Festo was supremely the evangelist, while William had some of the quieter, pastoral gifts that Festo lacked.' Nagenda was quiet and often described as 'intense' whereas Festo was warm, 'bubbling' and outgoing. Nagenda was a man 'with an open heart' when sharing a lesson he had learned— even when it meant 'humiliating himself to the dust'" [K217]

This willingness of William to 'open his heart' in testimony, even, or even especially, when it meant humbling himself to do so, influenced Festo as he described: "One day we were together on a mission. I had a burden on my soul and wanted to share it, but I was afraid to share it with William. While I was refusing to open my mouth,

William came and shared with me exactly the same temptations which had defiled his heart—and shared them
openly. The Lord used that to cut my chains of pride as
with a knife. William was absolutely in love with Jesus
Christ." [FK218]

As William and Festo continued working together, the
success of William as an evangelist, although outwardly
praised by Festo, was secretly resented. "I became jealous
of the success of my brother," he wrote. "I became critical
of everything that he said. Each sentence was wrong, or
ungrammatical or unscriptural. His gestures were hypo-
critical. Everything about him was wrong, wrong, wrong.
The more I criticised, the colder I became. I was icy, lonely
and homesick. Then the Holy Spirit intervened. I didn't
invite Him, but He has a lovely way of coming anyhow. He
said quietly, 'Festo, you are suffering.'

'No, no. It is his fault. I had worked out carefully how to
defend my case and expose my brother. But he turned the
whole thing around, saying to me, '*You* are right!"

"When Festo finally admitted his sin, he next found that
God was saying, 'Go tell your brother why you were so cold.'
Festo hesitated and hesitated, but when he finally approached Nagenda and admitted his jealousy, 'That dear
brother got up and hugged me and we both shed tears of
reconciliation. My heart was warm, and when he preached,
the message spoke to me deeply. One thing he said was, 'St
Paul didn't think that to admit failure was a blot on the
gospel.'" [FKK219]

There are few records of William Nagenda's addresses.
Those given at the Grace Abounding Conference in London
in March 1963, were recorded. In one of these talks, he
spoke of his spiritual experience 27 years previously and of
the way God opened his eyes to 'see Jesus'.

He read Acts 1:8-9, where it is recorded that, just before
Jesus ascended into a cloud, He promised that the Holy
Spirit would come on His disciples and they would be His
witnesses to the world. William went on: "This was a very
confusing time for the Apostles. When the Lord Jesus went

to the Cross, they never expected Him to come alive again, but after three days Jesus was seen by many. To Him, it didn't mean anything if people closed the doors and locked them. He could come right into the midst of those who were gathering, as He is here tonight. ...

"The apostles had heard that Jesus would go back to heaven to prepare a place for them but all those things meant nothing to them. ... They all looked at Him when, all of a sudden, it happened. His feet lifted, they didn't know what to do. They couldn't talk any more. And while He was still there, the cloud came and took Him out of their sight. Can't you see the confusion? ...

"It brought the disciples to the end of themselves, so much so that they went up in the 'upper room' to sit and pray. I don't know what they expected to see at the end of their prayers. It seemed all that they had loved so much in Jesus had come to nothing. It seemed now as if Peter must go and do his job again. They had no power. Peter had repented when he had denied his Lord, but had no power. He needed something. What did he need to see? What is it that we all need to see today? It is the same old teaching— the Holy Spirit must come. ...

"I remember some 27 years ago, when I was in darkness and I didn't know where to turn, I heard that voice: 'Let there be light!' And there was light in my heart and I began to feel for the first time that I was a great sinner. In fact, that I was the greatest sinner. ...

"Now the day of Pentecost came. What a wonderful day! There was the wind accompanied by the flames of fire. It was not only that, but people started speaking in other tongues. ... There was confusion among them, and they started talking, almost laughing at what had happened. And Peter went on to say: 'You men of Israel, hear these words: Jesus of Nazareth, a man approved of God. ... Him being delivered by the determinate counsel and foreknowledge of God, you have taken and, by wicked hands, have crucified and slain, whom God has raised up, having loosed the pains of death.'

"This is what I understand. This is what I believe. From the day the Lord Jesus had been taken up, it seemed that there was a dark cloud among them. They couldn't see clearly, they needed someone to help them. We are help-less without the help of the Holy Spirit. The Bible becomes just a book; it has no meaning. If we are to understand what we are reading, the Bible must be illuminated by the Holy Spirit. It is as if we are blind. I put on these glasses because I can't see what I am going to read. If I want to read properly, I have got to wear my glasses and when I put them on, where I didn't see anything, I see lovely words.

"I believe this is what happened on the day of Pentecost. Jesus had gone! Where had He gone? The Bible tells us He was at the right hand of God the Father. The disciples did not know that. The day of Pentecost means this: that day the curtain was lifted; the cloud was removed, and what did the disciples see? I can almost see Peter saying, 'Look! There is someone like Jesus sitting on the right hand of God the Father. I can almost hear John saying: 'Yes! I see Him. Yes! He is the very Jesus whom we know.' ... They were encouraged when they saw the One whom they knew so well; the Man who carried the Cross; the Man who had seemed so poor; the One who was treated as if He was noth-ing. Yes! The man of sorrows. Jesus of Nazareth.

"Now Peter sees something. The cloud is removed. I be-lieve that in the hearts of all those who love the Lord this cloud, which seems to be between us and God, needs to be removed. It may be that this cloud is a cloud of sin; it may be of sorrow, it may be of fear. When that curtain is re-moved, you begin to talk, you begin to shout round to others and tell them. Any man in history who has ever seen this vision is brought right down to his knees—when he sees that splendour, that greatness, that glory of God. He sees Jesus standing, as it were, at God the Father's right hand. ... What a wonderful thing that we are Christians at all; that man can look away from man and look and see heaven opened and see the cloud removed. ... This is what the Holy Spirit does, He removed the cloud. If that is not fullness, then I say I don't know what fullness can be. And I am telling you my own experience, what I have seen, which may not be, perhaps, as clear as you see it. But I believe that when we come into the presence of God and we see, away at the right hand of God the Father, the Man who grew up in Nazareth, the Man who died and rose again and is now in heaven in my place and your place, then we can talk with heaven in language that can be understood. ...

"It is the Lord Jesus who gives meaning to all that we believe as Christians, but the Holy Spirit must interpret it to us. This has brought such rest to me. There was a time when I was worried and I was looking for the fullness in myself. I didn't realise that all the fullness that God has is in Jesus Christ: Jesus, the Man of Nazareth. And from that day 27 years ago when I saw the Lord and the Holy Spirit opened my eyes, I knew in my heart that God was calling me to tell the world that Jesus is a wonderful Saviour. In our country, that is what has been happening for the last 35 years. Men and women have come to look at Jesus through the power of the Holy Spirit, and they have found themselves transformed, made new creatures.

"Our prayer to God at this time here is that, as we go back we shall pray that God will open our eyes to see Jesus through His Holy Spirit. ... It is Jesus we need to preach and the Holy Spirit will glorify the Lord Jesus all the time ... What a Gospel to preach! There are so many people, even tonight in this great building, who may be feeling there is something that the Holy Spirit does. The Holy Spirit wants to reveal Jesus, but there is that cloud. Let Him remove it. The Lord has promised that when we cry to Him, He will never go away and leave us.

"The Gospel that needs to be preached today in this country and in this world, is the Gospel of the Lord Jesus, in simplicity, by the Holy Spirit. I pray that, as we go from here, and things are difficult, we shall know that we go out, not alone but with Jesus. He is at the right hand of God the Father, in that place of power, to carry our sins, our battles, our burdens and our sicknesses."

As others saw them

What of William and Sala as people? First impressions are often important. Zak Kalega speaks of the time when he was still at school: "In November 1957, after I had come to the Lord, I was staying at Buloba and some of the breth-ren there at that time suggested that 'this young man should go and spend a few days in Namutamba, as it would be good for him'. So when school days had ended arrange-ments were made for me to go there. ... We arrived at Namutamba just as the morning service was ending. In those days brethren would stand together after a service and talk about the message, and share together their testi-mony of what the Lord had said to them during the service. They had just started to stand round like that, and I stood there, not knowing anyone at Namutamba at all. I had never even met William. When they saw me someone called out, 'Oh, here is the brother from Kampala, newly saved.' And I found myself surrounded by those happy men.

"They said, 'Now tell us who you are.' I cannot remem-ber clearly what I said, but I expect I gave them my name and told them when I was saved. As I did this, a brother gently came to my arm and took my holdall from me. Then someone came up and spoke to me. I did not know who it was so I asked who it was that had talked to me and they explained that it was William himself. I was a simple vil-lage young boy but William took time to talk to me and he said, 'We are so glad to see you, you have found us here, we are very busy, I am going somewhere else, but when I get time we shall sit and talk.' He was always busy but he always had time for people.

"What do I remember about William?" Zak Kalega con-tinued: "The joy! To see a man with a shining face and a deep love for the Gospel. You could see that he could talk to people irrespective of their social status. He could mix well with the highly educated. He mixed well with the least educated, and he could mix well with the Europeans. He was well accepted and loved by all people, and he was well understood by anyone.

"When meeting with more senior people you can lose touch with the 'man in the street' but he never lost that touch. He had a great love for other people and longed to see them develop. He had such a big heart for everybody. He also loved and enjoyed sharing his faith with other people and preaching. If you wanted to see William at his best, then it was when he was talking to others about Christ. He was simple but not simplistic, and the message was always very clear, about the love of Christ and what He had done for us."

Robina Kalega adds: "For me, I did not know William as much as Zak did, but I always enjoyed his preaching, because he was a serious type, like me. He may have made us laugh at the beginning of a talk or sermon, but then as the sermon continued he liked to come to a climax, and really challenge people. His messages always demanded a response, and they were so touching that they brought people to tears. He brought many people to see their own sin, and to come to Jesus with it."

It was the first meeting which made a deep impression on Senoga (now Canon): "In 1941 I passed an examination so that I could go and train as a primary school teacher, and I had a place at Namutamba Teacher Training College. When I arrived there, I found that the preaching was very wonderful, we heard singing all over the place. ... I had heard by now about William Nagenda, and I knew he was saved, but I also knew that he was an educated man who had studied at Makerere University. When someone had been to Makerere we honoured them and respected them, and I found myself wanting to go to William's house to see this man who was educated but had accepted Jesus as his Saviour.

"I remember one Sunday afternoon, I went to his house to see him. I knocked on the door and a man opened it and offered me a seat in the sitting room. Soon William came out of his room to greet me. Immediately I realised that I was meeting someone who had the Holy Spirit. I saw it in his eyes. He was a humble man, and straight away I felt the love of Jesus through him. Straight away I was struck by him and his gracious ways, and I marvelled at this educated man. He asked me to tell him my name, I told him my name and explained that I had come to Namutamba to do my teacher training course, but that I had today come to see him so that I could know more about him. And so with a very humble voice he said, 'I am here, my name is William Nagenda, my wife is not here today but her name is Sala Nagenda, but we thank God because He saved us, especially me.'

"During that time he gave me his testimony, and that helped me. I began to take what he said very seriously. I was not saved on that day, but I went back to the college. From that day my thoughts went more and more towards considering Jesus, and I went on thinking about William and how he had been saved. I saw so clearly that I did not have the faith that he had." However, it was not long before Senoga saw his need of Jesus for himself and, as a result, his life was completely transformed.

Professor Wilfred Mlay, of Dar es Salaam, first met William Nagenda in February, 1965. "I do not remember the exact date. He had been invited to speak for a week to our Bible class group at Tabora Boys' School. I had just begun my 'A' levels at that school, one of the then prestigious schools in Tanzania. I had been a member of the Bible class group for many years, but despite my interest in the Bible Class, I had not yet committed my life to the Lord. Because of my formative missionary education I had come to enjoy greatly Bible stories and the class was an opportunity for expanding my knowledge of the Bible.

"It is almost thirty years since I met Mr. Nagenda. However, I can still remember vividly the first day he entered the room where the meeting was being held. He was dressed in a grey suit and tie, a somewhat stern gentleman, dark and short. I was captivated by his penetrating look and his quiet and yet authoritative manner of speech. Above all, I was absorbed by his complete confidence in what he was saying. When he talked about Jesus, it was like talking about Someone he had just been with, Someone he knew intimately. I believe he spoke for five days at the school on the same topic and the same verse; I never missed any of his talks. Yet at the end of each meeting when he asked students who wanted to ask questions to stay behind, I was the first out of the room.

"His text was Gal. 2:20. He asked one of the students to write the theme on the blackboard: 'Not I but Christ'. The 'I' was drawn in the form of a man standing erect and stiff; the 'C' of Christ was drawn as a man sitting with his legs stretched and head bowed forward in prayer. Obviously I cannot recall the exact words he said in those five days. Nevertheless the message that kept ringing in my ears in William Nagenda's quiet voice was that 'man in his pride thinks that his destiny is in his hands. But only when a man allows Christ to take over his life, forgive his sins, cleanse him by the Blood shed on Calvary, can he become all that God intended him to be'.

"I did not have an opportunity to talk to Mr. Nagenda for the first four days. As a matter of fact I had no desire to. What he had been saying had greatly disturbed me. Up to this time, I honestly thought I was as good a Christian as the next man. In fact, I secretly believed that I was better than most. I was disciplined and well behaved, so the teachers told me. I was never on the punishment list. I was always where I was expected to be and doing the right thing. Ah, but Nagenda spoke of pride. He spoke of a personal relationship with Christ! My confidence melted...

"The only time I came face to face with William Nagenda was on the last day of his visit. I remember it was on a Sunday. The meeting was held in the school dining hall and all the students had been invited to hear the visiting speaker after supper. Very many came out of curiosity. After the talk he gave his usual invitation of questions and most of the students started streaming out. I also made a move to go. But something held me back. And I found myself face to face with this quiet man of God. Some of the students that remained had specific questions to ask. When they

had been satisfied with his responses they left. Then he
came to me. I did not know why I had remained. I had no
questions to ask! He asked me if there was something I
wanted to know. I said no. So he asked if I wanted to receive Christ. I said yes! He put his hand on my head and
led me through a prayer of confession and I received Christ—
or should I say that Christ received me!

"I do not think that today William would be considered a
great preacher. He did not speak with the passion and the-
atrics of our current crusade leaders. He did not beat people into the Kingdom of God, nor did he trick people into
making decisions by the 'three step trap'. In fact he made
it quite difficult for someone to 'come forward'.

"Though I was in his presence only a few moments, he
left a very powerful impression on me. It was the intimacy
of his relationship with Christ which seemed to come from
his face and voice which captivated me. He was certainly
eloquent and spoke impeccable English. But it was the man
himself whose life communicated the love of Christ."

Mrs Pat Aldred, née Searle, was a single government
English nursing sister at Jinja, Entebbe and Gulu 1961 -
1963. "It was at Jinja, as a friend of Bill and Nancy Butler,
that I was invited, with others, to attend the Butere Convention in Kenya. From that moment my spiritual life took
a new turn from which I have never looked back. There I
heard William, Joe, Bill and others talk about repentance,
the shed Blood of Christ and walking in the light. To me,
William was one of the most beautiful people I have ever
met. His closeness to his Lord, his uncompromising preaching and the serene look on his face are things which I will
never forget."

Eileen Travis was one of many who heard William
Nagenda and others speak at a summer camp for girls at
Keswick, in England. "Each morning of that week," she
wrote, "William and Yosiya came into our camp to take our
morning prayers. I had been a Christian for ten years, but
that summer marked the beginning of many new things for
me. The message of revival which they shared with us was

so different and so vibrant, and the Holy Spirit used them in blessing to many of us."

Simeon Hurst, an American, was for 26 years a Pastor, then a Bishop of the Mennonite Church in Tanzania. In 1943, he wrote: "Having been touched by the Holy Spirit through the East Africa Revival, my wife and I visited Kampala and also the farm with the Lea-Wilsons and William Nagenda, for a week. Every afternoon, at about 5 pm, the workmen on the farm would gather in the Lea-Wilsons' house for a fellowship of 'walking in the light', where they shared and repented of their sins and praised Jesus for His cleansing Blood. They emphasised the need of living transparent lives with Jesus and with each other. We returned to Tanzania and shared this with our brethren and sisters there."

Bakiranze was one of those who, together with the students who had been expelled from Mukono, met regularly for fellowship and prayer. "It was during these times that William Nagenda suggested that I might consider joining the Mengo Nurses Training School at Namirembe, Kampala," he remembers, "so I applied and was accepted and started training as a Medical Assistant in 1943, some two years after being expelled from Mukono. William took a personal interest in me and my future. He was a man of prayer, he really loved his Bible, he loved Jesus and he loved people. I used to laugh at him as he used to pray as he went along in the car, but mercifully with his eyes open as he was the driver! He was a great preacher and seemed to be able to make a passage come alive when it meant nothing to me. He also had a great gift which is such a help to evangelists, and that was the gift of imagination. Scenes came to life as he spoke.

"He was a man with a great concern for others individually and he would go miles on journeys in order to see them. I remember that on one occasion William and I went to Jinja to see a man. When we got there, I thought that we would see this man and go back home. To my surprise after we had visited this home William said he knew of someone else at Mwiri who needed a visit so we continued on to see him. Such was his love and concern for people."

Sala's ministry was appreciated by many, as it complemented that of William. "Sala was extremely good at teaching the other women, hand sewing, machine sewing, making mats, looking after the home, cooking, and so on," wrote Martin Kasiriye. "In addition to the Christian meetings Sala would have meetings in the home. She organised the women as she organised her own children. She took it to be her responsibility to teach others how to banish flies and fleas from the homes. She had a tremendous care for other women. She would take people who were not educated, from any tribe, and teach them until they got to the standard in their homes of the very well educated. There was such a difference between the homes of those who were saved and those who were not. And then those who learned did all they could to pass it on to others. There were also fellowship meetings when she shared what the Lord was doing for her and some practical teaching came in as well."

Canon Max Warren, Sub-Dean of Westminster and General Secretary of the CMS, wrote: "I have a lovely memory of William, at our first meeting in Kampala in 1949, we sat together on the top of Namirembe Hill ... and he told me of his own experience of how the Revival Movement began ... My main memories are of a great lover of Jesus and a great seeker after many disciples."

John E Leatherman, a missionary from the USA, wrote in a letter to family and friends: "I had the privilege of labouring a bit with an African evangelist who has not been officially ordained, but whom God has filled with the Spirit and wonderfully blessed with a fruitful ministry. During one of his messages, he said he was often asked how one can know if he is filled with the Spirit. He answered in words that burned into our souls: 'You are filled with the Spirit when Christ is sweet and precious to you above all things. Didn't Christ say that the Spirit would testify of Him.'"

Later he wrote that "it was commonplace to suggest that the time will come when the Africans will be sending

missionaries to England and America to warn a dead orthodoxy and civilization. Well, this suggestion is in the first
stages of reality. For several months now, two Spirit-filled
Africans are making widespread contacts in England and
are witnessing with power to the perfect salvation of the
Lord Jesus. Their names are William Nagenda and Yosiya
Kinuka. Recently I read a letter from William in which he
wrote that the people of England would like to have Revival
but they are looking for something new and spectacular.'
They need to realize that revival is just Jesus.' To men of
this holy calibre Jesus is the living mighty Saviour, as the
Scriptures set Him forth, and they are free because they
are not bound by the fetters of a cold orthodoxy and intellectual theology. They have only the testimony of Jesus. ...

Don Widmark vividly recalled William's visit. "You cannot live with a man who is as transparent before the Lord
as William Nagenda is for sixteen days without coming to
know him intimately ... We were driving north from Los
Angeles to Fresno. The sun was just coming up and casting
long shadows from the hills over Bakersfield and the valley
below. William had just awakened from a snooze and was
looking around, when he said. 'Don, do you have any weak
brethren who know that they are weak?' I asked what he
meant. William went on to say, 'You Americans are wonderful people. You are so strong. You know how to do things,
get things done. You are organized so efficiently.' I was beginning to be really confused, 'You know how to do things
so well you really don't need Jesus too much. Don, do you
really have one person who is weak, who knows it, and so
in all things he can trust Him who alone is strength to do
for him all and in all?'

"The first day William began to repent as he looked at
the schedule as there were so many meetings and he was
so long away from his home. Tired in body, he just couldn't
see how the Lord could see him through it. He was repenting so much, and on such little matters, that I thought he
was carrying this matter of confession of sin and repenting
too far... I wondered as we went into the first meeting how

God could get enough of him together to bring glory to Jesus' name. Then, before the people, he stated how dry and cold he was in the first meeting. He added that he had taken this coldness and dryness to the Lord as sin for cleansing.

"The meeting was before the Women's Prayer Fellowship in Fresno. He spoke on John, fourth chapter, of the woman at the well. It was in such power, so fresh, as ear had never heard it before. Then the story about the mirror, how when we looked into it we not only see the mirror (Jesus) but we also see ourselves."

Dr J R Billinghurst came into contact with William in Oxford and when he was practising in Kampala. "William had an uncanny ability," he wrote, "an ability of the most extraordinary magnitude of being able to discern what was troubling the hearts of the people he met, whoever they might be. Using excellent English, he would speak quietly and rather slowly, so directly that the encounter could be disconcerting and by no means always welcome. ... In a very special way he could point his hearers to Jesus because he himself loved Him so wholeheartedly and walked with Him so humbly."

The Revd Y Musajakawa wrote: "William had the gift of love. He loved his Lord. He loved his wife, Sala, and he loved the brethren. He was a man of repentance and was always willing to forgive others. He loved preaching the Word of God. He longed to see the Lord in heaven and thank Him in a real 'Kiganda way' for saving him."

"He will always be remembered by his love for people," wrote Joe Church, "his hearty laugh, his infectious enthusiasm, his great gift of encouragement, his gift of discernment and penetrating challenge, his apparent victory over all colour-bar (he was very dark), his youthful vitality and love of children and beautiful things, his resonant voice and his flow of words of testimony to the Lord Jesus that melted people's hearts, and often left them unable to move from their seats after a meeting. ... He has left an indelible memory in Uganda and in many parts of the world where he travelled on his preaching tours." [12]

For many years, the names of William and Sala Nagenda were linked with the tea plantation at Namutamba owned by Leslie Lea-Wilson. "The first time William and I met," wrote Malcolm Lea-Wilson, "was when a car load of brethren returned to my father's farm from a multiple wedding in Kampala in December 1946. The light was fading but that made no difference to their joy. At one point they came over to me with open arms and gave me the warmest of hugs, and an even warmer welcome in English. William had taken the initiative and acted completely naturally, even towards a Flying Officer of the RAF who also happened to be the son of the owner of the farm.

"William was my Best Man at our wedding. He had given an open invitation to 'all the brethren'. And they came! About 700 gathered for the service in Namireme Cathedral and in the Archdeacon's house for the reception. William was completely at home as Best Man and Master of Ceremonies. When the reception was about to start an English missionary called out, 'William, we have not said 'grace'. Quick as a flash William replied, 'It's all right brother, we are "in grace"'. There was certainly evidence of the Lord's grace at work all that afternoon.

"William's testimony to the power of the Blood of Jesus to cleanse and set free from sin led to my own converesion and blessing. Previous to that, I had never known what to do with my failures.

"One result of William's travels world-wide was the number of visitors who came to stay with us for fellowship with William and Sala and the brethren. This was a constant blessing to all of us.

"I remember, too, the joy and praise that flooded over the hill whenever William returned from one of his many journeys. There was always so much to talk and pray about and learn about 'walking with Jesus' as he shared his experiences. He told us, however, that he and Sala never found his homecoming all plain sailing. Both longed for the day of his return but his testimony was that it never took the devil very long to try to spoil and fellowship and joy that they were both experiencing. Perhaps a shaft of impatience or of criticism would slip in when neither of them wanted it to. William said that the only cure was to come to Jesus once again, ask his forgiveness and cleansing and say 'sorry' to Sala.

"When William was at home, we knew that there would always be fresh ideas to think and pray about and plan for. These could be spiritual, but were also related to people's temporal well-being. He and Sala were always concerned to raise people's living standards. Their home showed that such advances were possible for anyone of any tribe, colour or social standing. William was equally at ease with the workman in the banana garden as with the Kabaka (King of Buganda) in his palace."

The later years

For some time William felt a call to go to England and work among students there. Sadly, he began to show signs of a mental illness. "We began to notice his final illness at the end of 1964," wrote Joe Church, "soon after the Mombasa Convention, but after getting the best treatment in London and, through kind friends, in Germany and Switzerland, and after much prayer, God allowed him to suffer patiently with us for several years more." [14]

As a near neighbour at Namutamba, Malcolm Lea-Wilson was able to note the change in William. "During the latter part of his time at Namutamba," he remembers, "William was not mentally ill, as we normally think of that illness, but he slowed down greatly. There was the *okuzukuka* (awakening) split among the brethren, which he could hardly believe and which nearly broke his heart. There was great distress with one of his own family members, and then, while Sala was in the USA, he was involved in a car accident as he was driving along the Mityana to Kampala road. As he was passing a stationary bus, a young woman stepped out from behind it. Other members of the public tried to stop her, but she continued to cross the road. William could do nothing to avoid the accident and the car knocked her

down. I think that she died before she arrived at the hospital. I do not think that William ever recovered from this.
After seeing the police he came home in a state of very great
shock, as is natural for someone who is so caring and responsible. From then on, he could not even manage to answer his mail. He asked me to read his letters and answer
them. I told him those which I could answer and I would
take his dictation for the others. He was not at ease until
Sala returned and it was not long after that they moved to
Kampala. I think that the appalling shocks of a split among
the brethren, family trouble and the tragedy of the car accident slowed William's brain down into low gear."

In early 1966, he and Sala started work in the Overseas
Hostel Association in Oxford, England. There they had
personal contact with many students from different parts
of the world. After three years in Oxford, they moved to
Witney, not far from Oxford.

In his talks, William seemed to know that he was going
to suffer in a terminal way. "William often ended a series of
meetings on the note of the need of brokenness as a pre-
requisite of Revival," wrote Joe Church, "He would say, 'Don't
be surprised if after all the blessing we've had at these meetings, you get some troubles and testings when you get home.
Satan always fights Revival. Run to Jesus every minute of
the day. Repent where you have been wrong, and go on
pressing on all the time for the Highest. Ask forgiveness of
someone if necessary and say you are sorry, and go on praising. Keep turning to the Blood of Jesus for cleansing. This
is Victory! The Holy Spirit will help you. There's no other
Revival. Remember, we are like tennis balls, the harder
you hit them the higher they go! Satan may be allowed to
buffet us to strengthen our character. Keep praising! The
harder he hits you the higher you go! One day Satan will
have such a big whack at me that I will bounce right up to
heaven—right to Jesus, and you will not see me any more!
Everyone will be going round saying, "Where is William?"
But you won't find me any more!' Here he would walk round
the platform, where he was preaching, holding up his arms

and looking up at the ceiling, and then he would turn to the congregation with a smile and say, 'I'll meet you up there!'" [L10]

In December 1971, it was suggested that William be referred to a hospital in Germany where there were specialists in Parkinson's Disease. After a brief improvement in his health he suffered a stroke and treatment was stopped. Later that month William and Sala flew back to Uganda leaving their sons in England.

Medical science could point to no definite cause of William's illness. Today it would probably be diagnosed as premature senility or Alzheimer's disease. There are those who saw a possible link to the distress that William felt at times at what he saw happening in Uganda. Zak Kalega pointed to the fact that William loved to work in a team "but when the 'reawakening' came in to split the team it could have been the beginning of William's being unwell. His love and concern were so deep, and the division brought great pain to him, but pre-eminently he loved the Lord."

Canon Senoga wrote of the last years of William's life: "He was very grieved when some of the brethren separated off, and when he was ill this was a great burden on his heart for, as he used to say, 'Jesus is one and cannot be separated.' One cannot mention William without bringing in the name of his wife, Sala. In fact, they were generally known as William-and-Sala. As the terminal disease, a type of Parkinson's Disease, progressed, they would preach one sermon together. The invalid chair would be wheeled into the chancel. There William would very slowly say a few sentences praising the Lord Jesus for being so near him, and then he would bend over to Sala who was standing behind him. She would take his hand in hers and go on where he left off, perhaps for another fifteen minutes."

William died on Monday, 8 January, 1973, at the age of sixty. The funeral service at Buloba was conducted by Archbishop Erica Sabiti. At the grave side, Bishop Festo Kivengere gave a moving appreciation: "My dear brethren, this is a wonderful day, and I want to praise the Lord that

God's people have asked me to say a few words about my dear brother. I'm not going to say much about my dear William, I'm going to tell you a little about his wonderful Saviour. I know why you are here. You will permit my tears. I can't speak about him without tears. They are not tears of hopelessness. There is no despair about William. People in Germany are rejoicing. People in Indonesia are rejoicing. People in New Zealand are rejoicing, because this son of Buganda, taking the Gospel which Mackay brought to Buganda, has preached it throughout the world, Oh! the world will never say 'thank you' enough. And I want to remind you Baganda that we thank you, that out of Buganda came a man like William Nagenda. You did not know what you had. Perhaps now you do. We know what you had. We know what he did; and so we praise Jesus. ...

"Do you know the reason why we are all here?—I think this is the reason why some of us are weeping—Because he loved us. He loved everyone. He ran round with one message. Oh! He encouraged those who were in despair; he encouraged the fallen sinners to come back. You could never be with William and feel that you were not wanted. Whenever he found you deep down in the dumps, he sat quietly by your side. He never gave you the impression that he was better; he always told you he was much worse. Then he took you by the hand and he led you to Calvary.

"He went round the world shouting, in tones of love, not making a noise. He shouted in tones of love. Sometimes he spoke very quietly, Oh! it was wonderful to hear him.

> "Oh, that the world might taste and see
> The riches of His grace!
> The arms of love that compass me,
> Would all mankind embrace.
>
> Happy, if with my latest breath
> I may but gasp His name;
> Preach Him to all, and cry in death,
> "Behold, behold the Lamb!"

"Those who were at Namirembe know that he gasped His name. Yes, in the last breath of William, he asked us to sing, 'How sweet the name of Jesus sounds'."

A message from William's widow, Sala, to their many friends from Kampala, written after the funeral, brings a note of victory. She wrote: "Now William is with the Lord. He left us on the 8th January, Monday at 6.25 pm, at the age of sixty and three months, after a long illness which he bore with much patience, longing to depart and be with the Lord. I was holding him, with our family around his bed ... William's two wishes were fulfilled. He had always told me some years ago that he wished to die in Mengo Hospital under the care of Dr Roy Billington . . . William also wished to be buried at a church where his many friends from over-seas might see his tomb ... Thousands from Uganda, Kenya and other places were present. The love and sympathy which were showered upon us ... the telegrams, letters, wreaths, messages of all kinds ... were uncountable."

Sala carried on with her work as warden of a girls' train-ing college, and tried to deal with her letters and the visi-tors that came daily to her home to offer help and comfort her, but it could never be the same again.

The Lord was very real to Sala, but before six months had elapsed, she was admitted to hospital with a mild heart attack. She seemed to have a premonition that she was going to meet William very soon. One who knew her at that time wrote: "She knew she was going to die. She died at about 1.00 pm but from about 10.00 am till then, she had been saying to nurses and the occasional visitor that she would be 'in heaven' that day, and would be with William. I asked how she seemed when she said that, sad or fright-ened, and they said, 'Not at all, in fact quite happy.' She was quite sure about it, and so much so that one of the nurses said, 'Well, when you get to heaven, please greet so-and-so for me.' Sala said quite seriously that she would."

For William and Sala, death was truly 'gain' but for those whom they left behind, the loss is still felt but also the com-mission to preach to all, "Behold the Lamb"."

Chapter 4

Lawrence and Julia Barham

The early years

Lawrence Barham was born in Balham, London, on 25 June 1901, the eldest child of Harold and Florence Barham. Harold Barham worked for Barclays Bank, in Wimbledon.

The Barham family attended Emmanuel Church, Wimbledon all through Lawrence's childhood. The vicar was the Revd E L Langston who brought to the church a keen interest in mission, and particularly in the Ruanda Mission of the Church Missionary Society. He was the first Chairman of the Ruanda Mission (CMS).

At primary school, Lawrence distinguished himself by gaining a scholarship to Merchant Taylors' School. On completing his secondary education there, he gained a second scholarship, this time to Cambridge University. He studied Classics at Gonville and Caius College. There he revealed his academic talents to the extent that, on graduating, he was invited to become a university don, specialising in Hebrew and Aramaic.

In 1913, through the ministry of Hudson Pope, a well-known children's evangelist, Lawrence, at the age of 12, came to a real experience of Jesus Christ as His Saviour.

While at Cambridge, Lawrence joined in the activities of the Cambridge Inter-Collegiate Christian Union (CICCU). He felt increasingly that God was calling him to missionary service overseas. This became focused, for him, on China. He offered for service there and was accepted. So convinced was he that this was God's will for him that he declined the invitation to the prestigious post of university don. Joe Church at Emmanuel College and Lawrence at Gonville and Caius College, were founder members, in 1922, of the Cambridge University Missionary Band.

With China firmly in his sights, he studied Oriental languages while at Cambridge. It is interesting to note that he not only studied classics at Gonville and Caius College but was a cox for the College's Rowing Club. A prize Jug still bears witness to Lawrence's prowess in this field. Lawrence also enjoyed playing tennis and walking, and two other activities which were of a more passive nature: reading Hebrew and listening to the marching music of brass bands. These latter enjoyments he was to carry into his missionary service.

Lawrence, as the Stewart of Rannoch Hebrew scholar, gained First Class honours in 1920, going on to Second Class honours in the Oriental Languages Tripos in 1923. He was convinced that God's call for him was not only to serve Him overseas, but he was to do that as an ordained minister of the Church of England. To that end, he studied theology at Ridley Hall, Cambridge, after which he was ordained deacon in 1925. After ordination, he served a curacy at St James Church, Hatcham, London.

Julia Leakey was born in Kenya, to Canon Harry and Mrs Mary Leakey, missionaries of the Church Missionary Society. She was a sister of the famous archeologist Louis S B Leakey. She attended school in Bournemouth and then returned to Kenya where she helped her sister Gladys to found one of the first intermediate level girls' schools in that country.

At the end of the First World War, she returned to England. For two years she took a course in parish work at

Bristol. In 1924, she applied for and was accepted for missionary service with the CMS in Kenya, the land of her birth.
It was necessary first, however, for her to complete her training as a teacher. For this she attended Goldsmiths' College
of London University, New Cross, London. This was at the
time that Lawrence was serving his curacy at the nearby
St. James Church. Lawrence's duties as curate took him
into Goldsmiths' College, and it was there that Lawrence
and Julia met. On completing her training, Julia returned
to Kenya. As Lawrence believed that God was calling him
to work in China, it seemed that their paths were unlikely
to cross again.

In 1926, Lawrence offered to the CMS for work in China,
preferably West China. When that country temporarily
closed its doors to foreigners, that included Lawrence. However, he did not take this to mean that his call by God to
serve Him as a missionary overseas was revoked. As he
thought and prayed about his future, he was invited by
Canon Stather Hunt to consider working with the recently
formed Ruanda Mission in Uganda and he and Mrs Hunt
promised to provide key support for him as the Ruanda
Mission was not the financial responsibility of the CMS. An
ordained Bible teacher was urgently needed at Kabale, a
newly established church centre in south-west Uganda, and
Lawrence was accepted to fill this post.

In April 1928 Lawrence set sail for Africa. At Nairobi
station he was met by Canon Harry Leakey who undertook
to teach him Swahili. Julia was then headmistress of the
Girls' School at Kabete. Lawrence found, to his delight, that
he was to be staying with Julia's family. It is not difficult to
imagine her surprise when he walked into the house unan-
nounced, while she was playing the organ. He had proposed marriage to her several times. This time, she had
peace that this was God's will for her. CMS regulations
prevented them being married immediately, so Lawrence
went on alone to Uganda.

In 1924, the pioneers of the Ruanda Mission (CMS), Dr
Len Sharp and Dr Algie Stanley-Smith, had established the

first Evangelists' Training School at Kabale and then the Kigezi High School for boys. It was to this mission church centre that Lawrence was called, and to which he was posted in 1928.

The year that Lawrence arrived at Kabale was a crucial one for missionary activity in that area in several ways. The previous year had provided a great encouragement. At a gathering of some 75 teachers from the churches of Kigezi, the need was expressed for teachers to go as missionaries to Rwanda. Although Rwanda was just over the border from Uganda, the cultural differences were such that this was a call to sacrificial service. Thirty men offered to go. Overall, however, "the rising tide of success in Kigezi showed signs of superficiality. One after another, evangelists and leading Christians fell away into sin. The bondage of drink, the corruption of sexual vice, the deep strong roots of witchcraft, and the allure of the world began to take their toll." [RR49]

So disheartening had this fact been that the missionary leading the church work at Kabale in 1927, the Revd Jack Warren wrote, "Unless help comes soon, the last state of Kigezi will be worse than the first." He pleaded for a 'Week of Prayer and Humiliation' before God to be observed there and at home in the UK, "Then we know," he wrote, "that we may indeed expect a wonderful outpouring of God the Holy Spirit, an outpouring that will not be limited to Kigezi, but in its flood will reach the uttermost parts of Ruanda in the days to come." The call to prayer was taken up in the UK by the growing number of supporters of the Ruanda Mission. Many, "both at home and in the field, were pleading for an outpouring of the Holy Spirit." [RR37]

As happened many times in the story of God's working, the events which immediately followed did not appear to be the expected answers to prayer. In February 1928, Jack Warren suffered a recurrence of tuberculosis which resulted in his departure for the UK at Easter and death the following January. It appeared to be a sad blow to the growing church in Kigezi. It also meant that there was no experienced clergyman at Kabale to welcome and guide Lawrence.

Despite his lack of experience, Lawrence was appointed as the headmaster of Kigezi High School, and, at the same time, he was given charge of the Church development in the Kigezi area. "It is interesting work," he wrote in 1929, "and in our four schools there is splendid material for producing first-rate Christian leaders, but it ought to have a constant and careful supervision by a European. With nearly 300 churches to visit and look after, I find it impossible to give more than an hour or two a week in the High School. ... I hate to see things, that I know could be better, going on as they are for lack of someone to give more supervision to this side of the work."

It was while in the headship of this school that Lawrence introduced the Boys' Brigade. The band, which formed an important part of it, was to play a notable role in the development of the youth of Kigezi and beyond. One of those whom Lawrence taught to play the side-drums was a schoolboy named Festo Kivengere.

The following year, 1930, the school work was taken over by a new missionary, the Revd Jim Brazier, (later Bishop), thus releasing Lawrence to concentrate on the church work.

A very able African pastor, the Revd Ezekieri Balaba, from Buganda, had been invited to share the responsibility of the Evangelists' Training School with the Doctors Len Sharp and Algie Stanley Smith, whose main endeavours were in medical safaris and the building of Kabale Hospital. Ezekieri Balaba joined Lawrence in the leadership of the Evangelists' School.

In November 1928, Joe Church and Lawrence Barham, already friends from student days at Cambridge, were able to get to know each other in rather unusual circumstances. Joe recorded in his diary, "My jiggers (burrowing fleas) began to gain on me a bit so Algie (Dr Stanley Smith) sent me to Kabale for a rest and I shared a tent in the Sharps' garden with Lawrence Barham with my temperature up to 102 degrees. He also was ill so we had long talks from our beds. God used these times to bring us into deeper fellowship as we both were seeking and praying for Revival." [946]

Lawrence wrote of that time: "I followed Dr. Joe Church six months after him. I remember talking to him when I got there, and I felt there was something that he was talking about, that I didn't know anything about. I had been a curate for two years and I had gone out as a missionary. I would not have said I was a proud man. I didn't think I was, but somehow I really did not know much about what he was talking about. And unfortunately he was only a doctor and I was a parson, and I felt a bit sorry for him!"

Another event in 1928 underlined the satanic source of much that was proving to be so disheartening to the missionaries. In January of that year, a sorceress in a remote village of Kigezi had a dream in which she claimed to have heard God instructing her to call people to worship Him. So powerful was her presentation of that call and so clearly was its source supernatural that crowds thronged 'to the worship of God'.

Very soon after the end of Jack Warren's 'Week of Prayer', reports began to come to Kabale of increased attendances at the village churches. One of the African clergy was visiting his churches and on two consecutive Sundays found over 1,000 people at the Sunday morning services. The rudimentary church buildings were quite incapable of holding such crowds and people gathered in the open-air.

In March, as the mass movement of inexplicably large church attendances increased in the Kigezi district, a witch-doctor incited a crowd to attack and destroy a government post. This was only foiled by "the courageous action of a young Christian chief, who surprised the ringleader, and a few followers very early in the morning, and led him unresisting with a rope round his neck to the government post at Kabale". [RR38]

Was this Revival? There was an air of expectancy as missionaries saw what was happening. Certainly this was a mass movement in the name of God. "Thousands flocked to the village churches," wrote Dr Algie Stanley Smith, "so that there was no room to contain them. Safaris undertaken at that time revealed a truly amazing desire for the

Word of God, not only among the young, but equally among the old men and women. Special volunteers were enlisted to meet this emergency, and pilgrim preachers set out every weekend to all churches within reach to assist the local teachers in shepherding and teaching the way of salvation to the hungry crowds. These preachers were specially prepared with a message for each Sunday which would make clear even to the simplest soul the Way of Life through trust in Christ. We were at this time joined by the Revd E L Barham, whose sunny nature was indeed a fresh breath of encouragement and cheer to hard pressed workers, and who, owing to his quick mastery of the language, was soon able to take charge of the hundreds of churches in Kigezi.

"The mass movement lasted about a year and then it died away with no significant results. There was, however, in 1929, a strong resurgence of the power of witchcraft so that the whole area of religion came into disrepute. Even the government authorities were fearful of its threat to law and order."

It was into this storm of powerful spiritual activity that Lawrence was thrust. It was undeniable that supernatural powers were at work among the people, but it was not always clear which were of God and which were satanic.

Lawrence and Julia were married on 21 October 1931 at Limuru Church, Kenya, by Canon Harry Leakey, Julia's father. At the Kabale Theological College, a happy and fruitful partnership grew up between Lawrence and Julia Barham, and Ezekieri and Losira Balaba. Academically, miles apart, but spiritually one, they were a living testimony to the power of the Gospel to save from the divisive power of racial discrimination and to the unifying power of God's grace when those concerned all live 'at the foot of the Cross' together.

However, the spiritual state of the Church which they were working to build was disappointing. Lawrence wrote in Ruanda Notes in August 1931: "The work here in Kigezi is in a very sleepy spiritual condition. We need reviving very desperately, and possibly we are holding up the blessing from others. The pull of animism all around is very great, and we ask you to make a special point of praying for a reviving by the Holy Spirit at Kabale and in the district. I have been hearing lately of quite a number of Church teachers who are living in fear of witchcraft." Then in the November issue he wrote: "We believe that 'blessed are they that hunger and thirst after righteousness'. God has put this hunger in us. We believe that God is going to give us a big new blessing and an enthusiasm for His Word. Do not be surprised to hear of a new wave of blessing coming over the church in Kigezi."

If a problem with jiggers for Joe Church and illness for Lawrence Barham had brought the two men together again soon after Lawrence's arrival at Kabale, an even stranger circumstance brought the two men together in August, 1933. "My wife and I were going for a little tour round the stations before we came home on furlough," related Lawrence, "and we had to go past his (Joe Church's) station (Gahini in Rwanda). We were going to stay one night and then hurry on. Unfortunately I caught chicken pox and had ten days in his house. Well, with all the spots and the red beard that I developed, God did a work in my heart, perhaps in his too, that knitted us together, I believe for eternity. Wonderful, isn't it, how God can use even chicken pox in his purposes!"

On his return to Kabale, Lawrence arranged for all the church teachers of the Kigezi district to meet at Kabale from 8 - 11 September 1933, He invited Dr Algie Stanley Smith and Kosiya Shalita to be the speakers. There was little in the way of visible results of this mini-convention but later Lawrence wrote of it: "Spiritually, I believe it was a greater success than we thought at the time." Joe Church added the comment that, "this was, historically, the first of the teaching conventions that were to become so much a feature of the Revival throughout Rwanda, Uganda and other parts of East Africa." [995]

In that same month, September 1933, a 'Keswick' convention was organised at Kabale. For those unused to the name, this was one of many conventions supported by the 'Keswick Convention' held annually at Keswick, in Cumbria, England. The Revd A St John Thorpe and the Revd W A Pitt-Pitts formed a delegation from the home 'Keswick Convention' in England to the Church in Kigezi. It proved to be a time of great heart-searching for the missionaries, including Joe and Decie Church and Lawrence and Julia Barham. These shared in a deep conviction of failure in evangelistic enterprise, in relationships between the missionaries and in personal spiritual barrenness.

In the early years of the work of the Ruanda Mission in south-west Uganda, centring on Kabale, and in north-east Rwanda, with Gahini as its base, there were very encouraging indications of numerical growth and a desire for schools and churches to be built. There was not, however, in general, a deep spiritual conversion, and this worried the missionaries. It appeared all too easy for those who outwardly accepted the signs and symbols of the Christian faith to revert to animistic practices when faced with problems such as illness which the doctors could not cure, or marriage customs which the church could not accommodate. Conversion to Christianity often did not include release from the domination of animistic powers.

A cause of friction between the missionaries was labelled the 'parson-layman' controversy and related to the leadership role which the Church of England traditionally gave its clergy. The founders of the Mission were laymen with very clear evangelical convictions and a strong call to evangelise and so lead converts to baptism and the formation of churches. They were more concerned with the Biblical basis and reality of the emerging churches than with the forms of their structures and services. The supporters of the Mission, however, were Anglican, and missionaries were compelled, therefore, in principle, at least, to introduce Anglican forms of worship and practice. The clergy whom God called to work in the Mission were also Anglican and it was natural that they should adhere to their Anglican roots and follow the pattern of their sending churches.

The Anglican roots were, however, in the Church of England of the 1920's and 1930's, which was strongly in the grip of 'clericalism' where clergy authority was supreme.

Furthermore, it was a regulation of the Church Missionary Society that, where an ordained man was posted to a mission station, he would be the head of the station, however junior he was to other missionaries. The early lay missionaries found it difficult to accept this imposition of clerical authority. They also disapproved of some forms of Anglican services and regulations which they believed to be untrue to the Scriptures, or of secondary importance.

This controversy could have caused a barrier between the Revd Lawrence Barham and Dr Joe Church. However, if there were differences in terms of church forms of service and structures, there was unity on the spiritual principles underlying them.

After his initial high hopes, this first tour of service proved a great disappointment to Lawrence. He had worked hard, preached and taught the biblical truths which were very real to him, but the results were far below his expectations, and there was not that unity among the missionaries which he had expected. He returned to England feeling that he had influenced no one and that his efforts had been largely in vain.

Returning from leave, in 1934, Lawrence returned to Kabale to raise the level of evangelist training and found what is now the Bishop Barham Divinity College. In addition to his teaching in the Bible School and Church work in the district, he supervised the first of the new blocks which still form part of the more modern buildings.

"The spiritual battle is fiercer than in any year I have known," he wrote a year later, in early 1935, "The preaching of the need of a second birth and a clear cut from sin and surrender to the Holy Spirit, have produced a wave of spiritual opposition. ... Kabale is passing through what may be the most difficult period of its history so far ... but the signs are not wanting that the prayer for revival is within sight of being answered." [9][112]

Family life

Kabale became not only the centre of the leader training and church building work, in which Lawrence Barham and Ezekieri Balaba were engaged, but it was also home to Barbara and Ken, the first two Barham children. "My parents had a happy marriage," testifies Ken, the eldest son, now Bishop of Cyangugu, Rwanda, "and all five children have very happy memories of our homes. None of us could ever remember any time when our parents quarrelled. I believe the lessons learned from those early days of Revival went very deep. Dad's greatest friend was Joe Church."

Peter, the second son, was born in England, but his early memories are of Buye. "Our house was an open house, our outside doors were never shut," he wrote "when we went out for a picnic or walk it was almost inevitable to return to find the sitting room full of people wanting to talk to Dad.

"As children living out there, one memory we all have is of the 'missions' on the station. We used to go to bed with the sound of *Tukutendereza* breaking out first in one place and then in another. We heard the mission lorry going off on yet another mission, laden with people singing. We went to school in Kabale and the conventions there were incredible; the speakers at the bottom of the hill speaking with interpreters to a throng splayed out across the hill.

"In his youth, Dad played tennis as a hobby and loved walking. His other leisure activity (if it may be called that), was reading Greek and Hebrew. He had no real contact with the Boys' Brigade before going to Africa, but he thought that it would be a good way of attracting boys, especially when he saw the African love of drums. Our first Boys' Brigade band at Buye had home made drums, and bugles made out of bamboo.

"Dad had a great knowledge of how things could be done—carpentry, building, etc. although he himself could not hammer a nail in properly! Buye Cathedral was built with Dad as the only supervisor of the work. He reckoned that every part of that building was pulled down and rebuilt at least six times!

"One incident I remember very well. Dad found that tools were disappearing from the carpentry shop. Of course, everyone denied any knowledge of where they were. Then one night we had a thunderstorm and one house near the Cathedral was hit by lightning and burnt to the ground killing the couple inside. The charred remains of the missing tools were found in the wreckage. It had a tremendous impact on the community at the time.

"Life in the home with Mum and Dad was a true reflection of their outward lives. I have never met a couple who lived with such peace and serenity. We never had any money but neither did we ever lack for anything that was really needed. I can remember a time of open prayer in the little hut at Buye. A missionary repented of jealousy of Mum because she always seemed so peaceful and seemed to have everything. Then Mum repented of jealousy of *her* because she had more money then *they* had. Then the two ladies stood up and hugged one another, brought together at the Cross. Mum had to sell her engagement ring to buy us proper shoes so that we could go to school. We did not have any before that.

"Another memory we have is, when we left Kabale in 1946, the car was surrounded with people beating time on the car as they sang a hymn. We still remember the words of that hymn which mean, 'We will meet again in heaven'.

The education of missionaries' children always posed problems because it was necessary for them to be at school and away from home, at least during term time. Commenting on this, Ken Barham wrote: "Most of the missionary families sent their children to the UK for secondary school. We opted to stay in Kenya and get home for holidays. This probably contributed to the total lack of any sense of hurt over the separation."

A testimony to the Barham family life from outside the family came from Irene Gregory-Smith. "I lived with Julia and Lawrence for the first three years of my missionary service, and it was a home of peace and light. It was a home always open to Africans and missionaries alike."

Ministry in Revival

In his second tour of service, and with increasing intensity, there grew in Lawrence the strong realisation that his preaching and teaching, albeit evangelical according to their deepest convictions - as indeed those of all his missionary and African colleagues - would only have superficial effects, unless God intervened.

On returning to Kabale, Lawrence learned that some of those he had taught had, in fact, turned to Christ in repentance and faith while he was away. This encouraged him spiritually, but it also made him aware that conversion to Christ was God's work - not *his* alone.

Lawrence was then challenged by his own students: " I went to a station," he said years later, "and I had to teach people—it was a Theological College, if you can give it that grand title. All the time I was conscious that there was something that I did not have. God made me very hungry for it. I had read books about the fullness of the Spirit and sanctification, and I became more and more hungry.

"Then two of the students came to me. I must tell you if you are a student, especially a theological student, for goodness sake do not go to your Principal and say what these men said to me, unless you do it with the same grace and humility that they did it with. They had a great burden for me and they said, 'May we talk to you?'

"I said, 'Yes.'

"They said, 'May we tell you about what we think?'

"I said, 'Yes.'

"'Well,' they said, 'we see a missionary who could be quite a good missionary, he might even be a bishop one day.' Actually the same thought had occurred to me! They went on, 'You know, pride is a terrible thing, so is ambition.'

"While they were talking, I had a picture of myself standing in a great pulpit with a surplice on, preaching down to everybody that they were sinners, which was absolutely true. I was saved as a boy and I knew it, and I was preaching the Gospel, but I was preaching it right up there somehow. I had a picture of the Lord Jesus, who was the Holy Son of

God, who humbled Himself to be of no reputation, and took upon Himself the form of a slave and became obedient unto death, even the death of the Cross. And there was the Lord Jesus, right down there and I was up here. If I wanted to follow Him it did not mean being right up there. I thought being filled with the Spirit would make me a great man, right up there somewhere. Everyone would look up at me and say what a saintly fellow I was. And the Lord Jesus had gone all the way down. He had become sin for me so as to lift me out of the pit of destruction and save me.

"I wanted to run away. They said, 'No! Stay. You are just beginning to be useful now.' God showed me then that if I really was to follow the Lamb of God, it was to be following Him down there at the Cross."

Although life changed for Lawrence internally, externally his preaching and teaching ministry appeared to go on as before. But there was a difference and people saw it. Preaching the Cross became central to his work, with less emphasis on building the structures of the church. He met considerable opposition. "Some of the church authorities and mission authorities were not, as I thought, very helpful." He wrote, "A missionary said to me, 'You know, Lawrence, if you go on like this, you will lose your dog-collar!' I replied that the devil had told me that several times. But I knew that if I followed the Lamb wherever He goes, I would be safe. I have only to follow the Lamb. He will not let me go into anything which will be wrong. All I have to do is to follow Him and I'm safe.

"People came to me and said, 'You've lost your way, you've messed things up by going this way.' I would like to give my feeble testimony now that I feel it is all gain. The Lord Jesus became so precious to me as a result that I would not go back to the other thing for anything. It seems to me that the Lord Jesus began to be real to me. He became a living daily Saviour. I used to say that I was saved in 1913, which I was, and somehow the challenge came: 'Well, that's all right, but are you being saved now? Are you praising today?' It all began to be so real and so worthwhile."

Despite the difficulties and some opposition, the situation changed at Kabale. For Lawrence this centred on the Kabale Theological School.

"For the last three years," wrote Lawrence, "Revd Ezekieri Balaba and I have been concentrating more especially on teaching the meaning and implications of the Gospel, studying it particularly from the typology of the Old Testament, with the evangelists in training. Of course, we have been doing it for years, but latterly more time for teaching and a better knowledge of the language have intensified this work. In our preparation and in discussing these things with the men, we ourselves have learned far more than we taught, and our hearts have burned as we have realised more and more the wonder of the Gospel, our utter hopelessness because of sin, and the free grace whereby we are 'accepted in the Beloved'.

"I believe more than ever that the Gospel is the power of God unto Salvation, and I believe that God has used this teaching as a basis for a Revival. All last year we had been burdened with the need of Revival, and had prayed much for it, and in that year, the spirit of opposition to the claims of the Lord to full consecration increased, till in the September holidays, conviction of sin came on a number of men separately in their own homes. One and another came back in fear and trembling, because they knew they must testify to the others, only to find that others were the same! They, then, received (quite independently of any help from any of us) a burden of prayer, and met every night for prayer."

To his pastoral and teaching roles was added, in 1935, the work of Acting Field Secretary of the Ruanda Mission. "The result", he commented, "is that most of my teaching in the Boys' School and Evangelists' College has gone by the board, and this at a critical time when careful Bible teaching is absolutely vital, and when the spiritual battle is fiercer than in any year I have known here. The preaching of the need of second birth, and a clear cut from sin, and surrender to the Holy Spirit, have produced a wave of spiritual opposition, yet we feel hampered, by unavoidable pressure of 'serving tables', from giving due time to prayer and teaching. We have prayed much for more clergymen recruits, and we see the work apparently suffering very considerably because of the lack of adequate supervision." [RN54.9]

Nevertheless, the growing signs of spiritual life were encouraging, so much so that Ezekieri Balaba and he, in 1935, "sent off post haste to Dr Church to come with a band of workers to bring the Word of the Lord".

It was in response to this letter that a team from Gahini in Rwanda joined a team in Kabale, Uganda, with Simeoni Nsibambi from Kampala, for the Kabale Convention at the end of September 1935.

"It was a memorable convention," wrote Lawrence, "The prayer of the chorus, 'Spirit of the living God, fall afresh on me ... break me, mould me, fill me,' was sung repeatedly. And God answered that prayer in reviving power. Hundreds were convicted of sin. In a congregation of about 2,000 it seemed as if a wave of conviction went over them. Many of them were weeping quietly. Others cried out as they realised, perhaps for the first time, what sin was—rebellion against a Holy God, with its inevitable punishment of eternal separation from Him. The Holy Spirit then revealed to them something of what the Cross really meant—that Christ bore our sins in His own Body on the Tree, and redeemed us by His most precious Blood. The joy that filled those who had come into this new-found liberty was expressed in exuberant hymn singing, but it also sent men and women out all over the country to tell others of what the Lord had done for them. So the blessing spread from district to district, and on into other countries in East Africa."

In Ruanda Notes, the magazine of the Ruanda Mission, Lawrence wrote: "This Convention was greatly blessed, as its simple teaching and definite testimony met the hearers' needs, and we saw clear evidence of the working of the Spirit. Confession of sin, restitution, apologies followed; many had dreams, sometimes receiving strong impressions to read certain verses of the Bible which led them to put away some sin, beer drinking for example. Preaching bands have gone all through the District, and very many are stirred. The result is that in some cases, with Satan ever active to deceive, some have been inclined to go astray a little. Ezekieri and I with a car-load of helpers have, therefore, been going out for the last few Sundays to various centres of Revival. ... There is naturally a good deal of opposition and a certain amount of persecution, but we believe that, with much supporting prayer, the blessing will spread and deepen, and make the young Church a real force for God in this country". [RN56.12]

The following year, Lawrence wrote, "It is very refreshing to see people being transformed and their whole outlook being transfigured, yet so many are still untouched. Here, on this Kabale station, we are conscious that some who profess and call themselves Christians seem to be cold and untouched. Last year the blessing started in the Training College, and those men went back to their village churches carrying a fire which is still burning and spreading. Now we have a new set of men in training, and we long for a fresh outpouring on them and more zeal and boldness among us all." [RN57.8]

Lawrence Barham and Ezekieri Balaba travelled many miles and spent many hours in teaching and counselling those who were perplexed by strange new experiences. There were some physical manifestations which were difficult to understand. Some people were healed of diseases in one area, but not in another. There were some manifestations which were seen to be spurious—psychological or satanic.

"Often teams were asked to hold large meetings," wrote Lawrence, "and as many as 15,000 gathered for several days of convention. Among those who were in such gatherings, there was a fellowship of spirit which transcended colour, tribe and language. Indeed there were many who met at these conventions (where the addresses might have to be translated into two or three languages) unable to speak each other's language; all they could say to each other might be: *Tukutendereza Yesu* (We praise You, Jesus). This is the first line of a chorus in Luganda, the English version being:

'Glory, glory, Hallelujah! Glory, glory to the Lamb! For the cleansing Blood has reached me, Glory, glory to the Lamb!'

"It must not be thought that this began without opposition. There were some in the Church who had misgivings about what was happening; some even opposed it. No doubt there were mistakes and sometimes excesses, and later apologies had to be made, but through the years more and more have come to realise that this was indeed the work of the Holy Spirit. Nor must it be thought that the whole Church was revived. Even today it is only a comparative handful in each community who would include themselves in the Revival movement."

Within the Ruanda Mission itself there were tensions. Most missionaries recognised that there was a powerful working of God's Holy Spirit over the whole region in which they were working. Some were less sure of the spiritual sources of what they saw happening around them. Some were openly critical if not antagonistic.

At a specially convened Missionaries' Conference at Gahini, thirty-five missionaries were joined by Bishop Cyril Stuart, Bishop of the Diocese of Uganda and Ruanda-Urundi, and representatives from outside the area. It was the strong testimony of Lawrence Barham to the power and reality of God's working in the Kigezi area which convinced most of those in that conference that this was truly God at work, while, at the same time, being warned of the satanic influences which were seeking to oppose genuine Revival.

For the next two years, Lawrence was fully occupied with the effects of Revival in the Kigezi district. Teams, led by Lawrence Barham and Ezekieri Balaba, spent a lot of time, particularly in North Kigezi, teaching and preaching among those who had recently come to faith. The preaching of the saving Gospel of Jesus Christ was very powerful at this time, but needed to be followed up by Biblical teaching in order to establish Christians in their faith, and to enable them to discern and withstand satanic counter-attacks and psychological counterfeits. Lawrence was also invited to join teams further afield in Uganda, Rwanda and Burundi.

Lawrence's love of marching music had led him to introduce the Boys' Brigade to Kabale and the Kigezi district.
There had been a good response to its activities, particularly that of leading marches with its bands. Now the Boys'
Brigades felt the impact of Revival. Lawrence described the
annual camp of 1938. "It was really an evangelistic cam-
paign with the Company and Band as a magnet. Almost
our sole activity was to march to a different centre each
day for an open-air meeting. We had two Boys' Brigade
officers, augmented by several other men, as speakers. Four
or five spoke at each meeting, the talks being so arranged
that the subjects led on from one to another. As I sat at the
back, praying, my heart was bursting with praise, for these
men had not been converted very long, yet here they were
preaching with great humility, but complete assurance that
Christ can save from the guilt and power of sin, and supporting it by their own testimony.

"These men had come to Ruzumbura at their own request, sacrificing their much prized holiday, because they
felt that Ruzumbura needed what they had got. Before we
went down there we could not point to one in all the
churches there who had definitely consecrated his life to
Christ, and some were openly scoffing at the need for it.
But the word was faithfully preached, while some of us met
in little huts nearby to pray, and we began to see that a few
were being convicted, and at the last meeting two evangelists got up and said they had been hiding sin in their life.
One, the head evangelist of Ruzumbura, said he had been
convicted in the Mission last September, but he wanted to
say that, the day before, he had restored money stolen by
him up to ten years before, and he likened himself to Achan,
holding up the blessing of Revival from coming to his district; it isn't easy to say that before your juniors, who may
be scoffing, but after the Boys' Brigade had left, we had
quite a number of men and women coming to us throughout the following week, restoring money, wanting advice
about their bad temper, or convicted of sin, but still not
understanding the way of Salvation. We are praying and

expecting that the Boys' Brigade leader's action may prepare the way for others to enter into the same experience,
but the heathenism in this place can almost be felt, but we
pray that the power of Christ may break through.

"Most of the preaching and personal work is directed at
the readers and Christians these days, and it was most
thrilling to see, at the close of each meeting, people sitting
about in twos on the grass as speakers tackled their friends.
But you must not think that the heathen are not being
preached to as well; in two meetings, groups of 20 or 30
heathen who had come to hear the band, when they found
the speakers were talking rather a lot about sin and its
consequences, got up in a body and went noisily away. In
one place, a thrill went through the crowd when it was announced that someone had brought an *ekisingo* (a leather
'crown' with cowrie shells, used in witchcraft), signifying
that she had broken away from her lifelong fear of 'familiar
spirits'. We have had two brought to us, amid the great
rejoicings of the Christians, who realise what it means to
be in the bondage of fear, and to be given liberty." [RN58.12]

On a visit to a relatively inaccessible area of Kigezi, Lawrence was accompanied by Dr Jack Symonds. "We had been
praying specially for that particular *saza* (sub-district) for
some time, as it was the only one to be still untouched by
the spiritual awakening. We had prayed specially for the
saza evangelist, Daudi, who had seemed to be untouched
spiritually. We prayed that he might be convicted of sin
even before we got there. To our great joy, on the first night
of our visit, he came to me and returned money wrongfully
taken out of Church funds nine years ago, and told me of
other things he must put right, which had been preventing
him from praying for some time. We knew then that God
had answered our prayers, and was going to work during
this week; we left the preachers at the *saza* centre, and
went on to see the other Churches. When we returned, they
told us of about twenty who had been convicted of sin, and
on Sunday, Daudi and several others gave very good testimonies. Now will come the battle for them...

"I have been away several times lately, twice to Ruzumbura ... The day before we left for this safari, a gardener came to me and, with great beads of perspiration standing out on his forehead, told me of a few small things he had stolen from me. I should have been inclined to think them of no importance, but he told me of how he had lost all peace, and had had to face up to going to prison for theft if he confessed.   I realised afresh that even what we would call petty pilfering is sin. This 'small sin' was giving this man agonies of shame and distress of mind. This is not emotionalism: it is stern conviction of sin by the Holy Spirit, and it fills us with awe." RN59.16

Lawrence was, at times, able to use illustrations drawn from local customs. Once, when he was visiting a Church to question candidates for baptism and confirmation, he was discussing, with the local leaders, a native custom. "They produced a word new to me, *Ekarabu*. The meaning of this word is something as follows: If a man commits a crime against a member of another tribe and the injured party doesn't want to take vengeance, he can tell the man to bring an *ekarabu*. The man will bring a lamb, kill it, sprinkle the blood, then wash his hands in the blood with the injured party. Then they eat the lamb together and peace is made. What better picture could you have of such phrases as 'the blood of sprinkling ...', 'washed in the blood of the Lamb'? My greatest joy was to hear an evangelist in training use this illustration the following week to a heathen audience in the open air." RN47.16

The missionary work of the Ruanda Mission in the country of Ruanda-Urundi, as it was then, had developed rapidly, and it was felt important to establish a central training centre for church teachers and clergy ordinands. In 1938, Julia and Lawrence Barham were posted from Kabale, Uganda, to Buye, in Burundi, to build and establish a Bible School there. The geographical distance between the two places was accentuated by the fact that while Uganda was under a British, English-speaking adminstration, that of Burundi was Belgian and French-speaking.

The Bible School at Buye opened in early 1939. Five men were accepted for the first course for ordinands. The first three to be ordained were Shem Ndimbirwe, Erenesti Nyabagabo and Yosiya Kinuka.

For the next eight years, until 1946, the work of Lawrence and Julia was centred on training men and women for ministry and passing on to them the great truths which had been and still were being so clearly highlighted by Revival manifestations.

Lawrence supervised the construction of what was then known as the Canon Warner Theological College at Buye, a memorial to a previous chairman of the Ruanda Council. He also built All Saints Church at Buye, completing it in 1951. This later became the Cathedral church for the diocese of Burundi.

When Lawrence and Julia first arrived at Buye and began the work of constructing buildings, "the local inhabitants listened and looked on with mixed feelings of suspicion and curiosity," wrote Canon Alan Lindsay, who succeeded Lawrence at the Bible College. "Then one day a typical thunderstorm blew up and a sudden flash of lightning claimed the life of one of the builders from Rwanda. 'We told you so,' claimed the Barundi, and it certainly looked as if the first round had gone to Satan. A row of houses was built so that the students could bring their wives with them, as the training of clergy wives was regarded as of equal importance with that of the clergy themselves. Many of those who have passed through the College testified to the blessing received—the wives as well as the men."

In a letter written in March 1939, Lawrence wrote, "We were away last week-end, and when we returned, we found that the Holy Spirit had begun a work among the members of the ordination class and their wives ... People who had remained hard and unmoved for years were coming under conviction of sin and were being saved." And so it continued. As God had worked in Revival among the ordinands and other students at the Kabale Evangelists' School, so God was working among the students at Buye.

It was to Buye, the central church centre of the Ruanda Mission, that an urgent meeting was called in 1939 to face a serious problem which had arisen, first at Gahini, in the north of Rwanda, but was spreading elsewhere. There was a sad rift growing between 'revived' Christians, known as the *Abaka* (the 'on-fire' ones) and the others. There were, among the *Abaka*, some who appeared to be aggressively harsh to all who did not see things their way. They had been privileged to 'see the light' of what was sin and to know the forgiveness which God gives through the Cross. They felt very sensitive to what they saw as 'sin' in the lives of others. They challenged this, often, with little grace. In the other group were those who considered themselves to be Christians, but did not accept or experience the Revival. There were those who resented this 'challenge'—some would call it 'attack'—on their integrity both by Africans and some-times by their fellow-missionaries.

Lawrence Barham and Joe Church were able to bring to the conference a combination of Biblical truth and personal experience of ministry in Revival. It was a Devil's tactic to divide those who were 'one in Christ'. The form or expres-sion of 'inner revival' in any individual depends on person-ality as well as on obedience to the truth revealed. Grace in relationships is as essential as maintaining Biblical truth. The two founders of the Ruanda Mission—both present—commented on this conference: Dr Leonard Sharp, "We all felt deeply thankful to God for bringing us into a new unity," and Dr Algie Stanley Smith, "We never want to go back to the old complacency."

At the centre of the church work and the training of ordinands and church teachers in the then Ruanda-Urundi, the influence of Lawrence and Julia was quiet, gentle and very persuasive. Revival in these countries was securely founded on God's word and not limited to any church de-nomination or ethnic group. During the years at Buye, Law-rence was invited on missions to places in Rwanda and Burundi, but college responsibilities limited his freedom to travel far elsewhere.

In 1945, a team of leaders in Revival was invited to visit South Africa. All efforts to obtain permits for William Nagenda and Yosiya Kinuka to enter that country failed. It was during the period of Apartheid. So it was that three missionaries—Lawrence Barham, Godfrey Hindley and Joe Church—formed the team that accepted the invitation to address meetings in Pretoria, Cape Town, Johannesburg and then on to Port Elizabeth.

It was at Port Elizabeth that Lawrence Barham received a letter from the Bishop of Grahamstown "serving him with an 'inhibition' (a forbidding to exercise an ecclesiastical function) for taking part in a united Communion service at Cape Town". This was taken, not as a reprimand, but as an honour—a recognition of the unifying power of the Gospel, even where the state imposed disunity. *Apartheid* was then very strong in South Africa in general, and also in the church.

In that same year, having returned from South Africa, Lawrence recorded, "While on holiday in Kenya, I was invited to go to a convention in Tanganyika, on the slopes of Mount Kilimanjaro, to find that as two speakers had failed to come I was to take a share in the speaking. It was thrilling to meet representatives of three other missions, and to see how the Lord's message, given to us in Rwanda, is being given to so many others in East Africa: the message of our union with Christ in crucifixion and resurrection, and the power of the blood of Christ to cleanse from sin as we walk in the light."

The home leaves of Joe and Decie Church and Lawrence and Julia Barham coincided in 1946, largely due to the cessation of hostilities in Europe the previous year. This provided an occasion when Lawrence and Joe were able to meet the home Council of the Ruanda Mission (CMS) face to face.

There had been so many stories circulating—some true but mostly false—about excesses and irregularities which had occurred in the Revival events, of the past few years that the Council was genuinely concerned as to which direction things were going. Were the events about which they had heard so much, truly 'Revival'? A meeting of the Council to answer these questions was, therefore, planned for October where Lawrence Barham and Joe Church would be present.

The Barham and Church families arrived in the UK in July and both Lawrence and Joe were invited to speak of their experiences in Africa at meetings, including the Roy Hession Holiday Conference at Southwold in August and at the Missionary Conference at Elfinsward in September. Such was the response to their ministry at these meetings that the October Council Meeting was attended in a spirit of acceptance and praise. It was also a time for the confession of wrong attitudes and actions on the side of both the missionaries in Africa and of the Council members. And there was mutual forgiveness, because God had forgiven. Thus the meeting, which had promised to resemble a court room, turned into a fellowship meeting.

On returning to Africa after leave, Lawrence was nominated to be the first Bishop of the then joint countries of Ruanda-Urundi. The Bishop of Uganda refused to allow this "because Canon Barham was too involved with the *balokole*". This happened, remembers Ken, the eldest son, "when all five of us children were at home and we knelt together and praised the Lord for that honour!"

At Buye, Lawrence and Julia continued their training and church supervisory work until 1956. Lawrence summarised the eighteen years at Buye as "starting on a treeless hilltop, with long grass waving above our heads, and watching it gradually develop to become the central station of the Ruanda Mission; beginning the training of African pastors and senior catechists, and training the first twenty-seven of them, with Julia teaching their wives. This was a period of newness of life in the African Church and, to many of us missionaries, of new discoveries of our own sinfulness and of the need for repentance in our daily walk with the Lord, if we were to know the continual cleansing of His Blood and daily victory."

In 1957, Lawrence returned to Kabale for two years as the Archdeacon of Ankole-Kigezi, while Julia stayed in England for one year to make a base for their five children

The years at Kabale gave Lawrence a great opportunity of "cooperating as Archdeacon with Bishop Kosiya Shalita, and the tremendous privilege of ministering the Word of Life among the million people of Ankole and Kigezi, meeting the thousands of saved men and women who have contributed to making this area one of the most progressive in Uganda, and still walking with the Lord. We praise God for the large crowds that we continually meet as we move round the churches in both Ankole and Kigezi."

It was particularly encouraging to Lawrence to see the progress of the boys' organisation he had introduced many years previously. "Two Sundays ago the Boys' Brigade had an evangelistic weekend, finishing with a gathering of about 3,000 on the Sunday morning. The sun shone strongly, and the plain football pitch we were meeting on looked as though it had suddenly sprouted bushes as many people had plucked branches to act as sunshades. ... It is a wonderful privilege to be able to present 'the Lamb of God that taketh away the sin of the world', and people are saved at these gatherings, and it is of course a strengthening of the considerable number who are already saved. Naturally, Satan is active, trying to take away the seed, and our hearts are saddened by those who resist Christ's claims."

In November 1958, Lawrence added: "It was a great thrill to me to attend the Silver Jubilee of the 1st Kigezi Company of the Boys' Brigade, which Warren Orpwood and I started in 1933. There are now two officially registered Companies, and a number of embryo ones, and on the Saturday, we held a Band Contest and a Display, followed on the Sunday morning by a Church Parade, which also included Scouts and Guides. It was a fine sight to see our big Kabale church packed with young people. We finished the day with a large open-air meeting as people were attracted by the massed bands some ninety strong, which marched through the Kabale valley."

Lawrence also commented on Uganda's move into democratic self-government: "The first General Election of representatives of Uganda's Legislative Council has been held recently, and with the general excitement of this, and of progress in general, the vision of souls perishing tends to get blurred, yet what a comparatively very small proportion of Ankole-Kigezi's million people are saved, and how great the need is for a vital preaching of Christ crucified, before the Day of Grace comes to an end, and 'this same Jesus' returns again!"

An incident in that year impressed Lawrence. On a journey from Kampala to Kabale, "we had a puncture and, as we were struggling to change the wheel with a broken jack, a party of Indians in a lorry stopped to help us. After a while they said to the three Africans who were with me:

'Are you saved people?'

'Yes,' they replied,

'And is the Bwana saved too?'

'Yes. What makes you say that?'

'You seem to be different!'

"I marvelled at the grace of God that could bear an unconscious testimony to the Lord Jesus before people to whom we had not actually spoken." [RN140]

In 1958, on his retirement from Africa, Lawrence with Julia returned to the UK where, for five years, he was the General Secretary of the Ruanda Mission (CMS).

Lawrence was one of those who spoke at the Grace Abounding Convention in London in 1963. One of his addresses summarised the truths which he found to be at the heart of Revival as he experienced it in his own life and as it was experienced in the lives of thousands to whom he ministered in East Africa:

"Here, in John 1:14 we have the testimony of two men named 'John'. 'The Word was made flesh and dwelt among us and we beheld His Glory, the Glory as of the only begotten of the Father, full of grace and truth." What a wonderful expression. You see, John saw that Glory on the Mount of Transfiguration and he would never forget it. ...

"Then John the Baptist came along. John bare witness of Him and cried saying, 'This to the One I was speaking about and of His fullness have we all received and grace upon grace.' 'Grace upon grace.' Grace piled upon grace! You might almost say: ' Grace abounding.' Then he went on to say another thing about what this Glory meant: 'The next day John seeth Jesus coming unto him and sayeth' - not look at the Glory, but 'Look at the Lamb of God.' 'Behold the Lamb of God which taketh away the sin of the world.' That was his Glory—the Lamb of God which taketh away the sin of the world.' We are asking the Holy Spirit this evening to do just that for us, to enable us to 'behold the Lamb of God which taketh away'- my sin, your sin, not just the guilt of it but cleansing us day by day.

"Do you think that John the Baptist saw a picture when he saw the Lord Jesus walking along? We read of him that he was to be filled with the Holy Spirit from his mother's womb. What a wonderful thing to be that man. And don't you think that the Holy Spirit in him was teaching him these things. Nobody else can teach us these things except the Holy Spirit.

"From a small boy, John was filled with the Holy Spirit and the Holy Spirit was lighting up God's truth to him. When he saw Jesus, I think that the whole of the Old Testament flashed before his mind, the whole meaning of the Old Testament flashed before him.

"I think that his mind went right back to the first family, to Abel. Abel offered a better sacrifice than Cain, we are told. It was better because it was the shed blood of a victim, of an animal. Cain offered his produce of the garden and God didn't have respect for it. But Abel offered a lamb, an animal, killed it and offered it up. God accepted it, and He accepted Abel and he was counted righteous. It was by faith he did it.

"You go on, and Cain's family grew worse until God said, 'I shall have to destroy them all except the family of Noah.' When Noah and his family came out of the ark, after that terrible destruction, what was the first thing he did? Well!

He built an altar and offered up a sacrifice as much as to say, 'God has delivered us, but we are still sinners. We did not deliver ourselves. God did it! ... And it's true, the Lord smelled a sweet savour, and the Lord said in His heart, 'I won't curse them again like that.'

"Go on to Abraham. He was told to leave the comfort of Ur of the Chaldees and go to a place he did not know where. And what was the first thing that he did: 'the Lord appeared to Abraham and said to him: 'Unto thy seed will I give this land' and there he built an altar unto the Lord who appeared to him. Once again Abraham said, 'I am a sinner chosen by God in His grace, but I am a sinner. It is not my goodness that caused Him to choose me. I deserve to die, but I am trusting in the blood of this animal that I am killing.' And God accepted Him.

"Go right on to Moses appearing before the King of Egypt. He delivered God's message ... 'Every house must choose a lamb and kill it and sprinkle the blood upon the doorposts of the houses where you are.' If I may dare to say it, it is a silly thing to do from a human reasoning point of view. How could that help to deliver people from a strong nation like Egypt? Hopeless! And some people said that. ... So the Israelites took the lamb and killed it and took its blood and sprinkled it on the doorposts, and, in the morning, the first-born was alive! 'When I see the blood,' God had said, 'I will pass over you.'

"There is such a thing as judgment. Whatever we may think about it, the word of God makes that very clear. And God says: 'When I see the blood, I will pass over you.' That was God's way of setting those Israelites free, set free by the blood of the lamb. And when they reached the wilderness, God met with them on Mount Sinai and He ordered them to offer a sacrifice. And they did. God made a covenant with them—a covenant of blood. Moses sprinkled blood on the people and on the book of the covenant and said: 'This is the blood of the covenant which I have made with you. You will be my people and I will lead you into the promised land. And they said: 'We will keep it.' But they didn't! ... And God gave them all the wonderful sacrificial system. Detailed descriptions of it go on for chapter after chapter in the book of Moses. All pointed to the fact that these people, though redeemed, were still sinful people. They had not become perfect. They still needed those daily sacrifices, morning and evening all through the year, as much as to say there is never a time when you don't need atoning for by blood. You are that bad! And so they had this system. It was all picture language pointing forwards. ...

"And they had the great Day of Atonement once a year when the High Priest was told to take the blood of an animal, of a goat, and go into the Holy of Holies and sprinkle the blood on the mercy seat, within the veil. ... Then there was the other goat. When he put his hand on the head of the animal and confessed all the sins of the people, and the goat was taken right away into the wilderness bearing their sins in its own body, so to speak. These were pictures—divinely given pictures—and they meant something.

"If you go further on into the Prophets, there are many references, but I only want to bring you that one in Isaiah 53. It is the most wonderful chapter in Isaiah. 'The Lord hath laid on Him the iniquity of us all. He was led as a lamb to the slaughter and as the sheep before her shearers is dumb, so opened He not His mouth. All we like sheep have gone astray. We have turned every one to his own way, but the Lord hath laid on Him the iniquity of us all. He was wounded for our transgressions. The chastisement of our peace was upon Him and with His stripes we are healed.' Who could that have referred to but our Lord Jesus.

"Zechariah, another prophet, said: 'They shall look on Him whom they have pierced and they shall mourn for Him and there shall be opened a fountain for sin and uncleanness.' What is in the fountain? It is the Blood of Jesus. What other fountain could there be?

"So I go quickly through these little cameos in the Old Testament, some of the things which the Holy Spirit shone into the heart of John the Baptist when he said, 'Look! There is the Lamb of God.' ...

"The Lord Jesus Himself, spoke about His own Blood. 'This is the New Testament in my blood which is shed for the remission of sins.' He said it Himself before He had actually shed it.

"The Apostle John was at the Crucifixion when the death of the Lamb of God actually took place. He saw a soldier come and pierce His side. He did not do it to the others, but he did it to the Lord Jesus because He was already dead. John saw that there came out blood and water. 'I saw it and I bear witness to it,' he said. He saw a spiritual significance in it. There was the Blood of the Lamb of God actually being shed in his presence and he saw it. ... The life-blood of Jesus. The very life of Jesus—the perfect Holy life of the Son of God—was poured out on the Cross for us.

"You go to the Epistles and the various writers all refer to it. Paul says to the Romans: 'All have sinned and come short of the Glory of God; being justified freely by His grace through the redemption that is in Christ Jesus, whom God hath set forth to be a propitiation through faith'—what in? 'In His Blood—to declare His righteousness for the remission of sins that are past.' (Romans 3:23-25)

"Where else shall we go—I am only going quickly through these things so that we may see that the Blood of Jesus is not an isolated matter, but runs right through the Bible. It is the kernel of the whole plan of God for our redemption.

"What about Ephesians? 'In Christ Jesus you Gentiles who once were far off are made nigh'—how?—'by the Blood of Christ.' ... And in Colossians. 'Having made peace'—how did He do it—'through the Blood of His Cross.' No other way. But He did it. Peace was made by the Blood of the Cross. Hebrews! There is a lot about it there. Christ became a High Priest of good things to come, by a greater and more perfect tabernacle not made with hands, neither by the blood of goats and calves, but by His own blood. He entered into the Holy Place having obtained eternal redemption for us. Not a 'once a year' business: it is done for ever. He offered His own Blood, His perfect life, once for ever. We are sanctified by the Blood of Jesus, set apart, cleansed, purified, made able to stay in His presence and live with Him in fellowship. There is no other way. It is as clear as a pikestaff, isn't it?

"Peter was another of those people who saw the Glory of the Lord on the Mount of Transfiguration and Peter no doubt saw the Lamb of God actually being killed on the Cross. He said, 'You are not redeemed with corruptible things as silver and gold but with the precious Blood of Christ, as of a lamb without blemish and without spot.' Peter saw the meaning of that Blood he saw shed.

"John, in his epistle, said, 'If we walk in the light as He is in the light, we have fellowship one with another and the Blood of Jesus Christ, His Son, cleanses us from all sin'— it goes on cleansing us from all sin, keeping us cleansed as we walk in the light with Him.

"When you get to the Revelation you find that the Lamb is the favourite title, of the Lord Jesus. If you go to Heaven— as you will if you are trusting in the Blood of the Lord Jesus—you will find them all talking about the Lamb of God who shed His Blood for them and redeemed them. And they think: 'We would not be here but for Him. ... However did we get here, if it wasn't that we have been cleansed by that precious Blood of Jesus.' And they sing: 'Worthy is the Lamb that was slain, for He has redeemed us by His blood out of every tribe and nation and country.'

"May I ask you a question? Do you know the Blood of Jesus?   Do you know the power of the Blood of Jesus in your life? First of all do you know Him as your Passover Lamb? You may be in bondage. We have all been in bondage. You may never have come out of the bondage of sin and Satan. You may not be saved and the Angel of Judgment is, so to speak, hovering over you with the Sword of Judgment. If you haven't trusted in the Lord Jesus, that is what is happening. Do you know Him as the Lamb of God that takes away your sin, the guilt of it, the penalty of it, the fear of it. And do you know that cleansing in the Blood of Jesus day by day? ... It doesn't make us wonderful people, but it makes the Lord Jesus very wonderful. He becomes precious and we begin to understand about the precious Blood of Jesus. And there is victory. 'They overcame him, that is the devil, by the Blood of the Lamb and by the word of their testimony, and they loved not their lives unto death. (Revelation 12:11) When the Blood of Christ is being applied to our hearts, how can the devil get there. He is a defeated foe. There is victory there.

"God is offering us, in His beloved Son, a fullness of life that we may enjoy Him and serve Him. He is offering it to us. We can say, 'No! I cannot accept it.' Or we can say, 'Lord, I am willing. I am a sinful person. I am a failing person, but I believe the Lord Jesus is not a failure.' May God open our eyes to see the Blood of Jesus and allow the Holy Spirit to reveal it to us day by day and make us willing to say, 'Yes, Lord', to Jesus."

The first bishop of Rwanda and Burundi, Bishop Jim Brazier, retired in 1964. Although Lawrence Barham was in England as General Secretary of the Ruanda Mission, it was recognised that he was the only possible choice to replace Jim Brazier, for he was "the one man available who possessed the confidence of clergy and people," as he set about the task of dividing the diocese and appointing assistant bishops. Archdeacon Lawrence Barham returned to Africa from England and was consecrated Bishop in Namirembe Cathedral. His major task was to be responsible for the new diocese of Ruanda-Urundi until African Assistant Bishops could be trained and consecrated for the two dioceses that would be formed, following the granting of independence to Rwanda and Burundi which had taken place in 1962.

The two years as Bishop of Rwanda and Burundi proved to be very strenuous and demanding for Lawrence. Ethnic tensions between *Hutu* and *Tutsi* were strong in Rwanda where violence had claimed many lives and resulted in many refugees fleeing to countries beyond its borders. The selection of bishops was fraught with difficulties as the church faced the implications of the ethnic pressures. "It nearly killed him," wrote Ken, his son, "He had his first heart attack at Kabale where he was attending a missionaries' conference. His life was saved because all the missionary doctors were there for the conference."

In 1965, Lawrence was able to see the newly elected bishops into office—Adoniya Sebununguri, Bishop of Rwanda, and Yohana Nkunzumwami, Bishop of Burundi—and the new independent Diocesan Councils inaugurated.

The following year, Lawrence retired from Africa a second time, to become the Vicar of Emmanuel Church, Wimbledon, England, where he was brought up. Strictly speaking, the title 'Vicar' was incorrect because that Church had no parish and was not supported by the Church of England. However, the Trustees of the Church gave Lawrence five years in which to see an improvement in the situation. In those five years the congregation grew and they were able to open a 'daughter-church'.

In addition to his duties as Vicar of this church, he was also appointed an Assistant Bishop of Southwark. Under Bishop Mervyn Stockwood, he was given the oversight of the evangelical churches in the diocese.

"When he (Lawrence) went to be licensed by the Bishop of Southwark," remembered his son, Ken, "the Bishop asked him if he would wear cope and mitre as a condition of being an Assistant Bishop. He said, 'No! I would rather just do the Wimbledon job.' The Bishop then said, 'If I let you wear Convocation robes will you do it?' Dad agreed. The Bishop wrote to all his clergy telling them that Bishop Barham would be an Assistant Bishop; and would only wear chimere, rochet and scarf. There were several big occasions when all the bishops were co-celebrating and were asked to wear cope and mitre, but Dad stuck to his guns and stayed with the same robes in which he was consecrated."

It was while acting as both Vicar of Emmanuel Church, Wimbledon and Assistant Bishop of Southwark that Lawrence suffered his second heart attack and was taken to St George's Hospital, Tooting, London. Despite being advised to 'slow down' in his activities he rarely took a day off and took every opportunity to preach.

As others saw them

Canon Ian Leakey, a missionary in Rwanda and Burundi, wrote: "Lawrence was one of the group that spoke at the University Christian Union at Cambridge in 1947, sharing the extraordinary story of revival in East Africa. He was quiet, unspectacular, self-effacing, with a whimsical smile which usually had something to do with puncturing his own pride.

"In an unassuming way, concealing his scholarship, the power of Jesus was present through careful Bible teaching, backed by quiet personal testimony about things like envy, pride, competitiveness among leaders, purity, 'bossyness'—areas not often mentioned in my experience. Very central to all this was the place of the Blood of Jesus, shed at the Cross, but also available today to make and keep repenting Christians clean and effective. I was soon to discover that this kind of openness was not always popular in some evangelical church circles.

"A little later, when considering service overseas with the Ruanda Mission, I was much impressed by this man whose heart was so peaceful and single-minded, and lifestyle so simple.

"In the mid 1960's, Lawrence found himself unexpectedly appointed Bishop of Rwanda and Burundi. He had the difficult task of installing the first national bishop in each country. By then the 'wind of change' was blowing strongly, with pressure to hasten these moves with insufficient personnel, preparation and finance. The pressure was increased by the constant influence of the dominant Roman Catholic Church, with its powerful hierarchy and impressive buildings. It would have saddened Lawrence to see how his own minimal concessions, as a convinced evangelical, to Anglican vesture and ceremony were overtaken by an urge to copy other more popular Anglican models. He would have longed, too, that all the training and example which he gave would have created a servant leadership style in the Church, strong enough to overcome other patterns, inherited and learned. But with his love of youth, seen in his passion for the Boys' Brigade, sadly suppressed in those difficult times as a 'military organisation', he would surely have foreseen some of the exciting growth of younger Christian leadership in that land today."

Canon Alan Lindsay, who succeeded Lawrence at the Buye Theological College, wrote, "Many of those who have passed through the College have testified to the blessing received—the wives as well as the men. One wife of an ordinand remained silent and apparently unmoved until, one day in class, she suddenly seemed to wake up and, with an expression of evident joy, she said, 'Since I came here I have been as one asleep; but now for the first time I have begun to realise what Jesus has done, and what He can mean to *me*'. As the light dawned in her heart, that class became transformed from an academic time of instruction into a time of spiritual power.

"The fact that families of differing tribal backgrounds came to spend two years living together in close proximity is in itself a practical training; there is a sense of being members of a community. At the end of one of the ordination courses, a student gave testimony to the grace of God which had enabled ten families of different tribes to live together in fellowship and harmony. 'But for the Blood of Jesus,' he said, 'it would not have been possible'."

For some younger missionaries, Lawrence and Julia became 'parent figures'—acting as human and spiritual parents to those who were new to Africa and relatively young in their Christian experience.

Pat Brooks was one of these: "My memories of Lawrence and Julia", he wrote, "are an unmixed blessing. They were both totally peaceful people and it was a joy to be a guest in their home. Ready as they were to confess their own shortcomings they never laid any burden on me, and somehow made me feel that their life was exhilarating and 'a great ride'. I found my spirits lifting when, as a bachelor, I knew I would be spending a night with them. Ahead of time, I sensed there would be something to smile about when I was with them. Lawrence shared his tastes and personal pleasures—you knew that he was keen on military bands and traditional ceremony, not to mention the drums and bugles of the Boys' Brigade. He was a fan of Churchill and once gave an appreciation of him at the Bujumbura Athénée (Secondary School) early in 1965.

"The years before Bishop Yohana Nkunzumwami (first bishop of the Burundi diocese) must have been ones of stress for him, and he came under fire from some missionary colleagues, but he never showed to us younger missionaries anything but a cheerful, positive exterior—a true reflection of the man inside. Julia, known as *mushiki wa Yesu* (sister of Jesus), was a very hard worker but gave no impression of being driven, nor of driving others. She particularly counselled me at a difficult time in my relationship with someone else. She shared her concern for her own brother, an unbeliever, and said to me, 'The four men brought their friend on a stretcher to Jesus. I bring my brother to Jesus but what if he refuses to get on the stretcher and be carried?'

"Their sense of humour, often dry, heartened me. Lawrence used to read 'Daily Light' before meals. One evening he read the verse heading: 'Walk in love.' The door opened suddenly and the house girl came in. 'That's right', he said, 'Walk in, love!'

"I enjoyed being with a linguistics expert, although Lawrence never pushed his learning on anyone. He stimulated your appetite to do better in the language.

"Lawrence and Julia had a constant testimony to the power of the Blood of Jesus. I couldn't always relate to it, but I always enjoyed being with them. I never felt threatened by them although I was often challenged by them.

"Lawrence's insights on African brethren steadied me a great deal when I was tempted to have a jaundiced view on some of them. I appreciated the fact that they came to the Kumbya Missionaries' Conference. I enjoyed his ministry in 1958 on the Old Testament sacrifices. He is the only man I've been with in a car who said, 'What awful driving!'—referring to himself and not to the other driver."

Decie Church said of Julia, "She was always involved with food"—she welcomed whoever came to their home whether in Africa or later in Herne Hill, England, and cheer-fully set about providing food. She was a home-maker, where their home was 'home' to whoever came to them. Together Lawrence and Julia were a source of counsel and strength to many—Africans and fellow-missionaries alike.

"Julia had a great gift as a speaker," commented Bishop Dick Lyth, "and right into her eighties she was in constant demand at women's meetings. Younger people found her to be someone in whom they could confide and trust. She was a true 'Mother in Israel' and reflected her nick-name given in Burundi of 'Little sister of Jesus.'"

Later years

Lawrence and Julia retired to Bexhill, Sussex, and it was there that Lawrence died in 1973. As he had been involved in St. Leonard's Parish church, it was there that his funeral took place. Active right to the end, preaching engagements booked up to two years ahead had to be can-celled.

At a memorial service in All Souls, Langham Place, Festo Kivengere preached a moving tribute to Lawrence. "That man was my Father," he said, recalling the days of his child-hood and the interest that Lawrence and Julia had taken in him.

Julia went on to serve their family and fulfil speaking engagements for a further twelve years. She died on 27 March 1985.

Many thousands of men and women—many of them lead-ers in the church and country— mainly in the Kigezi and Ankole districts of Uganda and in Rwanda and Burundi, owed their spiritual 'birth and nurture' to the faithfulness of Lawrence and Julia in preaching, teaching, counselling and example. 'Revival' became, for Lawrence and Julia, a normal way of life. The truths they proclaimed were those which gave their lives meaning, and their testimony, by word and life, drew many to share in that reality.

Chapter 5

Yosiya and Dorokasi Kinuka

The early years

Yosiya Kinuka was born in 1905 at Bwera in Katookye, near Bweranyangi, Igara, Ankole, Uganda. His father, Kabari Rushate Rwigimba, a chief, died while Yosiya was very young. He was brought up by his mother and aunts. Later his brother, Rurema, took him to Kajara in Ankole. Yosiya never had the opportunity to attend a school and so was not taught in his youth to read or write.

"When I was a boy," Yosiya wrote later, "I looked after my father's cows in Ankole. I heard people talking about the Christian gospel, but I paid no attention to it because I thought it was for the poorer people."

While in Kajara, Yosiya caught the disease of yaws—foul-smelling ulcers on his legs. In 1923, on one of his medical safaris, Dr Len Sharp visited that area, and although Yosiya did not see the missionary doctor he learned that he could be treated at Kabale, in neighbouring Kigezi. "I borrowed 18 shillings," said Yosiya, "to buy food on the way. When I reached Kabale, I was afraid because that was the first time I had seen a white man!"

In the hospital, the treatment was successful and Yosiya's legs recovered very slowly. During this time, Yosiya attended the morning prayers, which were held every day, and he listened to the Bible teaching with interest.

Yosiya also learned to read and write. He attended baptism classes and was baptised. Yosiya's remarkable abilities to learn and take responsibility were noted by Dr Len Sharp and he was invited, when the symptoms had disappeared, to continue as a trainee medical assistant . "I refused," said Yosiya later, "because I thought that that kind of work did not suit me. I went to say Good-bye to Dr Stanley Smith and he encouraged me to remember the words of God that I had heard in the hospital. I did not understand what he was talking about and so I went home. After four months, the sores reappeared and so I returned to Kabale. I was warmly welcomed. After a further year's treatment, I was completely healed."

Yosiya resumed the help he was able to give to the hospital workers in their nursing tasks and, in 1925, he became a hospital assistant. Later he was sent to the CMS Mengo Hospital in Kampala to be trained as a Medical Orderly.

Looking back on those days, Yosiya said, "On the 30th November 1924, I was baptised, although I was still an *umupagani* (literally, a 'pagan', meaning an 'unsaved Christian'). I went ahead in helping sick people."

Miss Constance Hornby was an educational missionary stationed at Kabale. She was known all over the hilly district of Kigezi, southwest Uganda, as the woman who travelled indefatigably, mainly on foot, visiting homes and persuading parents to allow their daughters to go to the Kabale Girls' Primary School. This was a boarding school which required the girls to leave their homes during term time and, hence, the household responsibilities which were an important part of their family life. Letting their daughters go and trusting them to Constance Hornby was no mean sacrifice for many parents. One success was a girl named Dorokasi. Her father, Nyamahinja, and her mother died while she was young but she continued to live in the Bufumbira region of south west of Kigezi, near Rwanda. In fact the people there spoke the language of Rwanda. She was encouraged to go with Constance Hornby by Abraham Rwatsika, a maternal uncle, and father of Dr Norman Kanyarutokye. Constance Hornby accompanied Dorokasi on foot the long mountainous path from Bufumbira to Kabale where Dorokasi received her primary education. During this time she met Yosiya Kinuka and they were married on the 28 May 1928.

That same year, Joe Church came to Kabale with a view to recruiting some workers for the hospital he was building at Gahini, over the border in Rwanda. "We were having a week of prayer and Bible study on the subject of the missionary call," Joe wrote in his diary, "in the hope that a team of African volunteers would be truly called by God to go to Rwanda to work in the hospital and to start village churches. There was a splendid response and about twenty evangelists and eight hospital workers offered to go to what was to them a foreign country. Amongst them was Yosiya Kinuka, who was to be my head hospital assistant and eventually my closest friend in the Revival."

This offer from Yosiya was surprising because, although baptised, he was not 'saved'. In June, 1928, Yosiya Kinuka arrived at Gahini with his wife, Dorokasi, from Kabale, to be head hospital assistant.

In 1929, a severe famine struck north Rwanda. Despite desperate pleas to the Belgian government for help, none was forthcoming immediately although some was given later. Joe Church decided to go to Kampala to look for help, and left the hospital in charge of Yosiya Kinuka, supported by a non-medical missionary, Bert Jackson. Yosiya ably carried out this responsibility.

Joe Church was not an eloquent speaker in English and even less so in Kinyarwanda, the language of Rwanda. This led him to seek out a close cooperation with an African who understood English and could translate for him into Kinyarwanda. He turned to Yosiya Kinuka. Although he was not then a committed Christian, Yosiya understood what Joe was trying to do, and between them they worked out a method of Bible teaching which was followed for many years. "It was", Joe explained, "basically letting the Bible speak for itself and it grew out of our own inability to speak the language well. It was clear that there was no possibility of me trusting in any preaching eloquence of my own.

"This was the method that evolved. We would both stand up side by side. After a prayer and a simple hymn I would read, perhaps from Mark 4:3 (we only had Mark's Gospel at that time). 'Hearken: behold there went out a sower to sow ...' I would read it very slowly in their language, then all the crowd, often several hundred, would repeat it, line by line, several times. I followed that by a few short simple sentences of explanation. Then—a very important part— Yosiya would explain to them what I had said, in his own words, and I would listen carefully to see how I should have said it! ... So the teaching developed and I began to see the power of the Holy Spirit that resides in the words of Scripture. Yosiya would hasten to say that at that time he himself had not yet found that place at the foot of the Cross." Despite the efficiency with which Yosiya translated and explained Joe's teaching, it made no impression on him.

During the hot dry season of 1929, with disease and famine all around, the staff at Gahini Hospital found that they were being strained to the limits. They were not given the food, living quarters or time off they would have liked in the prevailing conditions. Some of the staff also resented that they were considered to be not only hospital workers but evangelists, as were the teachers, and the teachers were better paid than they were!

In early 1931, Joe recorded that "the routine Bible teaching went on day by day at Gahini but with a new sense of urgency. We had staff prayers every morning in the hospital, which was a time of Bible teaching. ... Later we started a new time of fellowship with the hospital staff after supper on a few evenings in the week in our dining room, when we tried to understand one another better. But there was still

no spark of new life yet, and Yosiya still sat at the back
keeping out of my way. Blasio Kigozi used to come and help
me, and he was especially praying for Yosiya for he knew
that he was thinking of leaving to become a chief in his
home country of Ankole. I shared all those problems with
Blasio and the thought came to us as a last chance to send
Yosiya to Kampala to see Nsibambi." [978]

Yosiya wrote about that momentous visit: "Dr. Church
taught us a lot in those days about the question of being
truly born again. I did not understand. He was always trying to make us work like the church teachers, but we
thought it was 'not done' to work like the poorly paid evangelists. There were many troubles in the hospital then.

"About that time a Muganda Christian named Blasio
Kigozi came to Gahini to work, but I did not like him.
I wanted to go to Uganda, so I asked him to take me and he
agreed. Dr Church wanted me to go and paid my fare.
I arrived at Kampala and lodged with Simeoni Nsibambi,
the elder brother of Blasio. I had never seen such a fervent
Christian before. We kept talking about the subject of being born again. Simeoni had heard that the spirit of the
hospital was bad and he asked me the reason. When I began to tell him, he turned to me and said that it was because of sin in my own heart, and that was the reason why
the others on the staff were bad. I agreed with him that I
was not right, and he taught me many more things, but my
heart was still unchanged.

"In the motor lorry on the road back to Gahini I kept
pondering over these things, and before I got back I was
deeply convicted. My sins became like a burden upon my
back, and I yielded to Christ."

Yosiya brought to his new-found faith in Christ all the
zeal and abilities which he now demonstrated in the other
aspects of his life—hospital, church activities, evangelistic
team-work and his home.

"Yosiya's conversion was a turning point," wrote Joe
Church. "We were still wondering what to do about the hospital staff. None was truly saved. Would it be best to

dismiss some of them and start again? Then a sense of the
power and love of God gripped us. We decided not to sack
even one of them but rather to claim in faith that every one
would be saved." [979] A few weeks later, a smiling Yosiya
brought to Joe a member of staff who had been causing
much trouble—Paulo Gahunde, who said that he had seen
what sin really was, and he had repented.

Family life

It is not known when Dorokasi shared the new life which
was transforming Yosiya, but the reality of that change in
both of them was felt by the children.

One of Yosiya's daughters, Joy Kinuka, wife of Phineas
Nyenda, wrote: "At home he was a gentle father. He loved
praying and talking and telling stories, and people would
come from near and far in order to talk and pray with him.
His words helped people whether they were saved, unsaved,
or spiritually cold. He had a great love for wild life, and
each morning he would wait for the blackbirds to come
down and would feed them from his own hands."

"In 1954, Phineas Nyenda brought Yosiya on his bicycle to my home," said Mr Lugimbirwa, "where he stayed for
a whole month, basing himself there while going to visit
brethren. He was my best man when I was married and I
loved him as I saw him to be a man of God who conducted
himself in a godly way, and I felt he could help me."

Yosiya's concern for the family was reflected in an incident recorded by Canon Kituna: "I had given a testimony
as to how upset I was that my child had gone off the rails,
and how much this had upset me, and how Jesus was helping me. After I had finished speaking he drew me aside
and told me that he thought it was good that I had shared
what Jesus had done for me, but he went on to say that a
testimony of that nature can hurt other members of the
family, especially the children, and so he cautioned me to
be careful and to understand how my words would affect
the family. He said the most important thing about a testimony is to tell others what Jesus has done for you."

Archdeacon and Mrs Bamutungire relate how, on one
occasion, "we visited his home when he was sick, and he
told us how it was raining one day and how they could not
get the fire to light so that they could cook some food. Then
Yosiya went with Dorokasi to the kitchen and they worked
on it together until finally the fire was lit and they could
eat. That in our culture is unusual, for a man does not
usually help out in such things, but he and his wife worked
together and it brought them even closer together. This
helped me to learn not only about helping my wife in the
home but all about the riches that come from a broken
spirit. From then on my wife, Tophas, and I have done a lot
together. I have helped her to do the washing and we have
done other things together and it has really built up our
marriage.

"Yosiya also helped us in the matter of bringing up our
children. He said when they are saved they will understand
and change, but do not try to force them into changing
their ways. And if they do not come to Jesus, you go on
walking with Jesus. Do not let the children stop you from
walking with Jesus."

"I enjoyed seeing Yosiya with his wife, for he often thanked
her for her work, and even though she was a very quiet
person he never seemed to want to make her into a different person. He was content to let her be herself. Now that
was very different from me, for I would want Tophas to be
saved the way I was, and I would want her to do the things
in the home the way I wanted, and try and push her into
my mould. He really showed me what a difference it makes
to relax and be yourself and to let other people be themselves too. He would often go out preaching, but Dorokasi
rarely if ever went with him. They had peace with each other
to do what they wanted. You can find that, in a home, one
of the couple becomes the 'boss', but in their home they
were a team together, and a living witness to others as to
what a Christian home should be like."

Yosiya could be very strict and firm. "On one occasion
one of his sons, George, was learning to ride a bicycle

belonging to a friend. Maybe that young man was proud or showing off, for he fell off the bicycle and spoilt it! Some said the young son was drunk, and others defended him and said he was just playing. Yosiya was away at the time, and when he came home that evening he asked what had happened. None of the children liked to be asked to go to his small office or study. To be asked to sit on the verandah for a cup of tea and biscuits or cake and to talk sitting there looking over beautiful Lake Muhazi was one thing... but to be called to his study was quite different.

"On this occasion the son was asked to go to the office, and despite protests of innocence he was soundly beaten by his father, a beating he will never forget. Later on, Yosiya came to know the truth, that he, George, had been playing but he was not drunk. He again called his son, and this time he apologised to him for not understanding properly and for wrongly beating him.

"Yosiya and Dorokasi were great lovers of their family. However, Yosiya was often away for his church work or on evangelistic outreach and Dorokasi was busy in her fields, making sure there was adequate food for the children. Some of the years at Gahini were years of famine, but thanks to Dorokasi's hard work the family never once went hungry. God also provided for them in another way. A girl, named Flora, who lived about 12 miles from Gahini, had been abandoned by her family and had come to hospital as a very sick person. When she recovered she stayed in the Kinuka family, and was completely accepted by the whole family. Neighbours would ask where Yosiya was. Flora would know. When would Dorokasi be back? Flora would know.

"As Yosiya and Dorokasi were not wealthy and had no land it was difficult for them to know where the school fees would come from, but God provided for each of them. A cousin of Yosiya, named Mugimba, asked if he could be responsible for paying the fees of one of the family. The boys all went across the border into Uganda for their education, and when the holidays were only short they would stay with Christian friends. When the long holidays came the parents would send someone from Gahini to Kabale to collect them and they would walk with the escort the three- or four-day journey back home. Food was provided in the form of sweet potatoes and other food that would keep, and father advised them to sleep near a church, or if there was no church then to go to the Chief's house, but because of the fear of tick fever they were advised to sleep in the open air, and not in houses, as ticks did not attack those who were in the open air.

"For many years Yosiya had no transport of his own, and so he walked from village to village and church to church, covering a vast area of land. Then came the days when he had a bicycle, and later he acquired a motor cycle. The first was a 'James' and that was followed by a much more powerful 'Ariel'. On one occasion he took his son George from Kabale to Gahini as the pillion passenger. On the way they came to a part where local people had been burning the grass, and they were met by billowing smoke.

"Yosiya thought they would soon be out the other side but to his horror the smoke was thick and long. They started choking in the smoke and Yosiya's face was scorched by the flames. Mercifully they did not meet another vehicle in the fire, nor did they fall off the edge of the road. The hand of the Lord had protected them, and they came out the other side. When they found the fire was behind them, Yosiya stopped the motor cycle and said, 'Forgive me, I am sorry, I should have stopped before going into the smoke to see how long it lasted, but that was my male pride, and my stubbornness, please forgive me'. They not only realised that God had looked after them, but Yosiya was quick to repent of what he saw to be sin in his own action."

Mrs Kaburame was one of those who were able to see the Kinuka family frequently. "The thing that helped me the most about Yosiya and Dorokasi was their witness as a couple, and especially the way they supported and helped each other in the home as husband and wife. When Yosiya came back from the hospital he would take time to tell Dorokasi what he had been doing during the day, and she would tell him how she had been getting on. Because my husband and I were able as a young married couple to see first hand how they lived we were able to learn a tremendous amount that helped us in our own home. They became to us remarkable parents. One thing we particularly learned was that they never spoke of each other behind each other's back.

"They were not only open and honest in their life as a married couple but also in their work in the church. When in later life they worked amongst the Rwandan refugees in Uganda, the Red Cross trusted Yosiya completely with the supplies that were coming from overseas. Yosiya did not even take the parcels into his home but distributed everything from outside his own house on the verandah. This showed us that a man of God is not only transparent and trustworthy in his dealings, but also does not want to grab things for himself, but to share whatever he has with other people."

Ministry in Revival

While Blasio Kigozi was alive, he and Yosiya became a particularly effective team. They, with William Nagenda, Joe Church, and others, took part in medical safaris and teams of witness to the district around Gahini. On these there was Bible teaching, preaching the Gospel and testimony.

One morning, as they were praying, recorded Joe Church, "Yosiya could not open his mouth or pray. Then just as we were finishing he repented and said, 'O God, I could not pray because there was unconfessed sin in my life'." [982] Such was the oneness with each other and sensitivity to God the Holy Spirit in their personal and team lives.

An event occurred on Sunday, December 15th, 1935, which prompted Joe Church to write in his diary, "Blasio and Yosiya came to my house for one of those unhurried talks. There seemed to be more time in those days! They were looking at my books and magazines, and shared some of my letters. Then Yosiya said, 'I never thought that I should ever be allowed to read a white man's letters!'"

Whenever Joe Church was invited to take a Mission or lead a convention, he tried to take Yosiya with him. This was difficult sometimes as Yosiya could only with difficulty be spared from the hospital.

Yosiya was one of the team at the first Kako mission in February 1937. When, in May 1938, he and Joe Church were invited to hold missions, first at Kigeme, Rwanda, then at Buye, Burundi, they travelled by car to Kigeme. Joe was then able to go to Buye by car, but William and Yosiya walked from Kigeme, a journey of three days.

In August of that year, 1938, Yosiya was one of the team— with William Nagenda, Simeoni Nsibambi, Erenesti Nyabugabo, Ezekieri Balaba, Ezra Kikonyogo and Yusufu Byangwa—to lead the Kenya 'Keswick' Conventions. Mention has already been made of the way "William and Yosiya very effectively pleaded with people to get right with God".

In September, 1938, while Europe was in the throes of facing possible war, Joe Church conducted a mission at Kaloleni in Kenya while Yosiya Kinuka and William Nagenda joined David Symonds to take a mission at Kahuhia, also in Kenya. The following year, a similar arrangement of two teams visited Katoke and Ngara in Tanzania. Yosiya Kinuka and Lawrence Barham led the mission at Ngara, on the Rwanda border.

Yosiya was one of the team that took a leading role at the Namirembe Convention in August 1940. It was of this team—William Nagenda, Simeoni Nsibambi, Erica Sabiti, Yosiya Kinuka, Joe Church, Godfrey Hindley, Lawrence Barham, and Bill Butler—that Joe Church wrote: "This was a remarkable gathering with a large team of Africans and white leaders working in absolute oneness and trust." [9][180]

At Gahini, Yosiya found himself in demand not only in the hospital, for his expertise, especially in administering anaesthetics and in maintaining unity and vision among the staff, but also in evangelism and developing churches. He had been spared from the hospital to follow a course at the Bishop Tucker Theological College, Mukono, in Uganda, on the completion of which he was granted a lay-reader's certificate. When Lawrence Barham began the provision of theological training for ordinands at Buye in Burundi, in 1939, Yosiya was one of the first five to be accepted for training. He was ordained in February 1941. Yosiya was "located to Gahini," recorded Lawrence Barham, "where he has worked so long, and is now the only clergyman in charge of that big work and district."

Despite heavy church responsibilities "he would still come into the hospital if there was a special anaesthetic required." wrote Dr Harold Adeney. "He was so proficient that, if there was a tricky case, he would be called in."

In 1942, Yosiya Kinuka and Kosiya Shalita were the first two Africans to be members of the Ruanda Mission Executive Committee. This was an important step which expressed the Mission's concern to see a responsible African leadership in the growing churches, and it was a major step in removing the barriers between black and white. It was also a recognition of the special leadership qualities of these two men. They were to play a leading role in giving wise advice in the development of the growing churches.

In December 1942, a team—Yosiya Kinuka, William Nagenda, Erisa Wakabi and Joe Church—made a tour of many of the mission and church centres that had developed in Rwanda and Burundi. "We travelled 1,300 miles," wrote Joe Church, "and visited fourteen stations. Philippians 3:14 was our special message: 'I press toward the mark for the prize of the high calling of God in Christ Jesus'. Starting with Shyira, we did a long circular tour ending with Gahini, meeting especially with African leaders on all the stations, teaching and encouraging, strengthening and unifying each place, as they welcomed and strengthened us, spending most of our time in Bible study."

In 1943, moves were made in the Church of Uganda which appeared to threaten the Revival movement. Bishop Cyril Stuart, Bishop of Uganda, "continued with his plans for his convention in August, but it was organised almost entirely by those not connected with the Revival, if not actively opposed to it," noted Joe Church.

Yosiya was invited to take part in the convention, and to be part of the group—leaders in Revival—who shared their convictions with the Uganda Church leaders to bring peace to a very difficult situation. God honoured their efforts. Wherever leaders met to talk and pray about the people and issues involved, Yosiya was among them.

It was at this time that Yosiya and William went through a period of heart-searching as they wondered if they were missing something in their spiritual lives by not 'crucifying-the-old-man' as described in Romans 6:6. The answer to their problem was solved when Simeoni Nsibambi said to William, "Don't you know, William, that your old man was crucified for you, long ago, at Calvary! ... Go home and rest, brother, rest in the finished work of Calvary." Yosiya joined in this release from an unnecessary and unscriptural striving after something they already possessed.

In 1945 a startling event happened while Yosiya and others were preaching. A man was listening who was in the habit of standing up and ridiculing what was being said. "Don't listen to these people; they are speaking rubbish," he shouted. "My god is my cow Bugondo"—a brown and white spotted cow. So they stopped preaching and prayed for the man, "You see this man and his god, please show him that you are the true God." The man left to take his cows for watering and when he got there, lightning and thunder struck and both the man, the cow Bugondo and the calf were killed. It is not difficult to imagine the awe that such an event would create.

In 1946, despite the problems faced following the end of the Second World War the prevous year, the Council of the Ruanda Mission (CMS) invited Yosiya Kinuka, William Nagenda and Joe Church to visit leading evangelical societies, parishes, conferences and conventions in England. This tour, described in greater detail in the stories of William Nagenda and Joe Church, was signally blessed. One of the major sequels to this year of teamwork in the UK was the formation of a group of people who were able to witness there to the truths which Revival highlighted.

Back in Africa, Yosiya was a member of the team which led the second convention at Kako, in 1950. "Kako," wrote Dr Algie Stanley Smith, "a mission station in Uganda with a glorious panorama over Lake Victoria, was an ideal setting for the most remarkable gathering since the beginning of Revival."

The theme of the convention was that of the 'prisoner set free'. "Long after the first deliverance from the bondage of Satan at conversion," wrote Joe Church, "Christians find themselves bound by all sorts of inhibitions, frustrations, sins which in experience rob them of 'the liberty with which Christ has set us free'. There is the bondage of harmful habits, of the fear of man, of jealousy and rivalry, of the unforgiving spirit and the stiff neck of pride. ...

"On the Quiet Day, Yosiya and I had shared what God had been teaching us at Gahini about these verses, and the prison picture we had been using. All felt that this was God's message, so the next morning a blackboard was brought from the school and the Gahini team of two (Yosiya and Joe) began with the prayers of all behind them. ... Never before had representatives of so many tribes met together in East Africa for a convention." [9236] Even today, people who were there remember that amazing Kako Convention.

On one visit to Kenya, Yosiya was accompanied by Canon Zaribugire. "We had a great burden to preach about the depths of sin, and the results of sin in the life of a person," said the Canon, "Yosiya was usually the chairman at the meetings, introducing the speakers and winding up at the end. He usually preached, but only for a short time. Although Yosiya preached, he really loved taking the part of the coordinator or leader. We loved Yosiya's leading because he was sensitive to time, and would not let meetings run over their time. He would often end the meetings by inviting those who had been saved to come forward, but he would not press people, and always discouraged others from using their own personalities to produce results. He would only want to rest in what the Holy Spirit was doing. What shone through his life was his love for people."

There are few records of Yosiya's talks, but excerpts from
one of them gives an idea of his way of speaking:

"I want to talk to all of those of you who are here, those
of you who have already committed your lives to Christ and
those of you who have not yet done so. I know that what
has brought you here is hunger, and so I want the Lord to
touch your lives. Some of you have become familiar with
coming to Conventions and Christian meetings. Some of
you have given your money in order to help this gathering,
and others have done practical things to help get ready for
these meetings. Then you come to the meetings but you go
away empty, while others go away satisfied ... so today is
the day for you not to go away empty-handed, and what
you need to take with you is Jesus Christ.

"The time came in days of old when God was perplexed
by His people and the tremendous glory that shone from
Him—the glory that God had given to His church—began
to disappear from them, and so I want us to look in Ezekiel
Chapter 8 ... and may the Lord help our hearts this morning that they may be soft towards Him. ... I think that today
is the day when you are going to go away satisfied and full.
Many of you have been saved for a long time, and you had
great freedom, and were full of joy, but the time came when
these things went and you became resentful. You have tried
all you can to put on a good front, but it has not worked.

"The time came when Ezekiel was perplexed and worried as he saw the glory of the Lord departing, and he wanted
to know why this glory was going. In Ezekiel Chapter 8, we
see God explaining in a vision to Ezekiel why the glory had
left His people. God knew and understood why the glory
had left the church, and He knew what had brought division between Himself and His people, and He said, 'Let me
show you why the glory has gone.'

"In verses 3, 4 and 5, God showed him the reason that
His glory had gone ... it was called 'the image of jealousy'
(v.5) and God said to Ezekiel, 'Son of Man, do you see what
they are doing, the terrible things, the abominations that
are being carried out in the house of Israel?'

"Today we are not in Israel, but we are in Burunga in Ankole, and here today there are many saved people who have had their sins forgiven, people that God has visited and released from their bondage, people who have had a testimony in the past of God's saving grace. God brought Ezekiel and he was shown a vision of what these children of God had in their lives and in their homes. He saw and understood the darkness that was in their homes, things done by the husband, things done by the wife, things that your partner does not know about, but God knows about the things that are going on. These are things that contribute to the glory going and bring darkness in our lives, these are the things that (v.6) 'make me go far away from my sanctuary.'

"God's joy is to see men and women, boys and girls following Him, who are washed in His blood. That is what brings Him joy. But the problem is to see His redeemed, born again children, church-goers who sing His praises in church, but live double lives. Verse six continues, 'and you will see greater abominations than this'. Things that go on in our homes and on our farms that are shameful.

"I want to give you a little illustration of something that happened in the days when I was working in Rwanda. A European came to visit us, and as I know English, I was invited to accompany him as he went round some of the homes in the area. We arrived at the home of one family. They knew we were coming and so the wife had got the table ready, put on a nice tablecloth and some flowers in a vase, and everything was ready. But we were late arriving, and so the lady of the house decided that she would go and do something else a short distance away. Alas, when she was out of the house my visitor and I arrived. My visitor was thrilled with what he saw.

"Then he said, 'I am not satisfied, I would like to see her bedroom as well', and he said he would like to visit the children's room, and the kitchen as well. To his sorrow he found that apart from the sitting room all the other rooms were dirty and unkempt. Later on we met the lady, and she asked which rooms we had gone into, and when I told her she cried out, 'Oh! Gracious me!'

"That is a true story. Our Lord is not going to be satisfied with only going into the superficial lives we live. He is not satisfied with just singing praises or even going to religious gatherings. He wants to know how we are in the 'backroom' areas of our lives. Would you be like the lady that I met? Would you have to exclaim, 'Oh! Gracious me!' Or would you be able to welcome Him peacefully into every part of your life?

"So, let us return to the Lord. What do we have to do to return to Him? We need to face up to the things that have gone awry in our lives, in our homes, between husband and wife, in our financial affairs, on our farms. What about telling untruths. In these days we find that even God's people do not speak the truth. People no longer trust each other ... and now is the time to bring your life before Him.

"This passage in Ezekiel is amazing. As we look on we see the compassion in God's heart, which He was showing to Ezekiel (v.7-9). God showed Ezekiel a hole that was in the wall, and then He told him to go in through the hole so that he could see what was there. And there he found terrible things—people worshipping idols. And do we not find that today people worship their possessions, their animals, their cows, their money. Why has the glory gone? Why is there such coldness in our hearts? Come and see—see what is in the hearts and homes of God's people. We still greet each other as if all is peaceful inside whereas there are all sorts of idols that are being put first. Do you think that God is satisfied when He sees all this? No! He wants to come into the inner recesses of our lives. ...

"Praise the Lord for Jesus Christ. It is am amazing thing that Jesus is willing to enter those very dark and dead parts of our lives. Some of the things He finds in our hearts are embarrassing to us, others are disgraceful and we do not want to face them. But it is such a powerful thing that Jesus is willing to come into those very areas of darkness and death.

"Sometimes we go to the doctor and he asks us to sit or lie on a couch and then they put on the X-ray machine, and the things inside us are shown up on the screen. Today is the day for Jesus to act as our doctor and show up the things that are wrong on the screens of our lives. He wants us to have a thorough examination, and sometimes this is painful, just as it was painful to the woman who found that her visitor had gone into the unkempt areas of her home and she exclaimed, 'Oh! Gracious me!' That response was fitting for the situation she was in, and when I personally went into the other rooms with the visitor I found myself being ashamed on her behalf at the state of the rooms. I was sorry for her, and I did not want my visitor to go on seeing the shameful rooms of my friend. This reminds us that God took Ezekiel to look into all the rooms even though they were terrible, he opened the door and looked in and was shocked with what he found. ...

"So today God calls us, no matter who we are, He wants to clean out all our rooms. He wants to be that light like the X-ray that shines into our hearts. The one who looks into our lives is Jesus Christ Himself. Many of us are afraid of ourselves when we see what is in the darkness of our own hearts. What can we do? Are you going to go on with those dark rooms and those fears? Are you going to return home as you came? Are you going to go back empty-handed? I want to show you that Jesus Christ came into the world to save sinners. He calls sinners to Himself today, those of you who have never come to Christ in your lives, those of you who think that if you come to Christ you will lose out, those of you who fear that you cannot go on with your present life-style if you come to Christ, those of you who are afraid that you will not be able to put things right and apologise for the wrong in your lives: all those fears come from ignorance. If you come to Jesus and He enters your life, and your home, He will be the One who will take the 'abominations' out of your life, and you will find yourself praising Him for His shed Blood which cleanses from all sin."

Whether at Gahini, where he was Pastor after his ordination, in the many conventions in the leadership of which
he shared, in the small fellowship meetings or in his home,
Yosiya's message was the same. In one sense, he *was* the
message because what he was and what he said were in
perfect harmony.

Many are the stories that Yosiya told with such grace—
some drawn from Africa and some from elsewhere:

Taking another's punishment.

"There was a wild man who killed someone, but his
younger brother was a saved man, and the younger brother
knew that when the other came to court he would be given
the death sentence. So the younger brother clothed himself
in his brother's clothes. They were very alike and the
younger brother stood up in court and answered as if he
was the man who had committed the murder. So the younger
brother took on himself the punishment of the older brother,
just as Jesus has done for us. The older brother came to
Jesus through this, as his brother died instead of him."
And then Yosiya would end by saying, "I am what I am
because of the one who took my punishment."

The broken cup

One of his favourite stories was that of the little boy whom
he named Peter. "Peter had broken a cup when his parents
were not in the house. Peter was very afraid that they would
be angry with him when they returned. Consequently he
went and hid himself in a culvert so that they would not
know where he was. But the porter had seen him go, and
so when the parents came home he explained what had
happened and where Peter had gone to hide. His father
went out and called with a loving voice, 'Peter, Peter, please
come back home! You are more valuable than any cup.
Peter, Peter, I can get many more cups, so do not be afraid!'

"Eventually Peter came out of the culvert, and very fear-
fully went back to his father. When he saw him coming,
the father went out and hugged him, dirty as he was. The

father bathed him and welcomed him back." Then Yosiya would continue and say, "All of us have broken so much in our lives, but the Lord calls us by name and tells us that He loves us and that we are more valuable than anything we have broken. Our loving Heavenly Father welcomes us back with outstretched arms and washes us and cleans us up. Jesus loves us, calls us back and cleans us and pays the price for the broken cups in our lives."

The lorry on the dusty road.

When someone was going through a difficult situation he would remind them of journeys in Uganda on rough roads. "You can get stuck behind a lorry for miles and miles and give up hope that you will ever overtake it. But if you persevere you eventually find that the lorry and all it's dust are behind you. So it is in our spiritual journeys. Sometimes we despair when we are locked into an on-going difficult situation, maybe for years, and we despair of ever coming out the other side. But in God's good time the lorry and the dust of the situation are behind us."

The football match

There were always special celebrations to mark the birthday of the Kabaka (King of Buganda), and one of the activities was a football match. While Yosiya was a student at Mukono, one of the tutors, who had bought a ticket, could not go to a celebration match, so he gave his ticket to Yosiya. He was delighted and went to get ready. He did not have any special clothes but went quite simply dressed. So he went by car and when he got to the grounds they showed him which gate he should go through. The police looked at him and his clothes and saw that the ticket he had would take him into an area for which he was not well dressed, but he held on to the ticket and was taken to the seat that was prepared. To his surprise he found that he was given a seat right behind the Kabaka himself. So he sat in this wonderful seat and watched the match, and he watched the Kabaka hand out the cup to the winning team. Then later on there were instructions for those who had tickets like his, they were told where they should go to have refreshments!

"So it is with us," Yosiya would say, "Jesus has given us a ticket, and it takes us to a seat which is not fitting for us. We need to come to Jesus, and believe in Him, for He has the ticket that takes us unworthy people right into the Holiest place of all!"

The man with the luggage.

Sometimes people were not quite sure whether his story was of something that actually happened or whether it was a parable to illustrate his point. Such a story is that of "a man in Ankole who was going on a bus journey, and he carried a stick, and his luggage on his head. He got on the bus and still kept his luggage on his head. The people on the bus offered to help him to take it off his head, but the man refused the help and insisted on keeping it on his head all the way from Mbarara to Kampala, some 180 miles". Yosiya would then go on to say: "You have been saved, do not go on carrying your luggage, put it down and the Lord will take care of it."

The nail in the shoe.

"If you have a nail that is sticking up in your shoe you have to stop and get a hammer and bang the nail on a stone until it is level with the shoe," Yosiya would say to illustrate his point. "In the same way if you have a sin that is always popping up in your life and making your walk uncomfortable, if not impossible, then you must stop, look at the nail and remember that, at Calvary, the nail was not 'banged flat' but *taken out.* So bring the nails—the sins, to Jesus! He will take them out."

The thorn and the slow puncture.

After referring to the seeds which fell—some on the road side and others on thorns—Yosiya said, "You know, when we are saved there are many things that become thorns in

our sides, and they come to choke us. You know sometimes you can be riding a bicycle and you do not realise
that a thorn has pierced the tyre, and that you have a slow
puncture. The air comes out very slowly, and you do not
realise what is happening, but in time the tyre is completely
flat. Never allow the thorns to prick you because they can
slowly empty you and you can become like a flat tyre!"

Queen Victoria and her visit to a home.

One story he told came from England. "Queen Victoria
was walking to her home when it began to rain. As she was
not wearing a raincoat, she called into a house to ask if she
could borrow an umbrella. A woman answered the door
but she did not realise to whom she was talking. She disappeared into the house and returned with an old, worn
umbrella which she gave it to the Queen. After reaching
the palace, the Queen asked her footman to take it back to
the woman from whom she had borrowed it. With it was
the message: 'Queen Victoria thanks you very much for the
umbrella you lent her'. After a few days the Queen sent for
the lady, sending a horse and carriage to her home to pick
her up. The lady was afraid and wondered what the Queen
would say. But the Queen only welcomed her. If only we
knew when the King of Kings visits us. We give Him our old
umbrellas and our tatty things, and we fail to welcome Him
properly. Even so, like the Queen, He goes on loving us
and welcoming us."

The WAY OUT.

On one of his visits to England, Yosiya was in the London Underground when he lost his way. The winding cor-
ridors, sometimes going up and then down, were very confusing to him at first. "I soon learned," he said, "that everywhere I went, there was always one sign there. It said: 'WAY
OUT'. I praised God for that sign: 'WAY OUT'." Then Yosiya
would go on to explain the reality those words expressed—
there is always a WAY OUT: the Way of Repentance and the
Cross, from all failure and confusion.

"Do not play with God!"

An incident from the royal court of Rwanda provided a powerful warning against hypocrisy. "Ruhanamurindi was a man who was responsible for the King's cows. A believer went to his home and found drunkenness and all sorts of things going on. Afterwards, on the same day, he met Ruhanamurindi who called out *Tukutendereza* (Praise the Lord). The believer said, 'Wait a minute, I have just come from your home. How can you say "Praise the Lord" when there is so much that is wrong in your home?' Ruhanamurindi replied, 'I have asked the Lord to forgive me for all that.' The believer replied, 'Do not play with salvation, either come before the Lord and be saved, or choose the other way, but do not play with God.' At the end of a service, Yosiya would invite people to come in repentance to the Cross, then add, "Go to the Cross and *stay there!*"

The simplicity of these illustrations was typical of Yosiya's preaching. It was the way in which they lit up the truth he was proclaiming and the way God used them which was so outstanding.

As others saw them.

"The main thing we remember about Yosiya", said Archdeacon William and Mrs Tophas Bamutungire, "was that he gave the impression of someone who was at peace with himself. It is said that years ago in Rwanda he was given a cow, and although he was grateful for it, he found it troubled him and it took him away from his calling of showing Jesus, so after a while he sold the cow. Then when he moved to this area to retire he started a small dairy farm, but that too he found tiresome and so he decided to do without it but keeping his banana garden. He showed us that if he had money, that was fine and he would praise the Lord, but if he had none, he would still praise the Lord, for he knew that Jesus knew his needs and was his 'satisfier'.

"As a saved person Yosiya loved transparency—being 'in the light'," said the Archdeacon. "When I was thinking of getting married he talked with me. He saw that I found it hard to accept his advice, and so when he saw my hardness he told me very lovingly that I should go ahead with my plans. I knew he thought I was taking the wrong path, he spoke very frankly, but having spoken frankly he did not stand in my way. That attitude has helped me so much in my own life, to see how Yosiya handled the matter.

"He really understood me and said I had a lot of pride and hardness in my heart, and he was right. He saw how I had not wanted to listen to advice over my marriage, and the proud attitude I had to that. He also saw that I made much of my education, and gloried in that, and his insights and gracious frankness really helped me to ask the Lord to give me a broken spirit and a contrite heart.

"Another thing about Yosiya was the way he was quick to understand when people were going to excesses (obuhabe). On one occasion he found people striving after being filled with the Holy Spirit, and he gently showed them that the Holy Spirit of Jesus is always available to fill us, and we do not have to push Him to fill us. Then when Okuzukuka (Awakening) came he opposed the teaching that was being given. He always loved God's people and would often visit in our homes, but in addition he loved to be on his own and quietly study his Bible, or Oswald Chambers My Utmost for His Highest or Daily Light. One day during the war of Idi Amin he was sitting reading his Bible at his desk when a bullet came through the roof and landed not on him but on his open Bible and he was not touched at all!

"He was straight and faithful, and he gave us a living example of the way God's people should walk once they are saved. He showed us how to go on in the faith, how to keep going, and how to be satisfied with Jesus. He knew how to live at peace with God and man."

The Archdeacon's wife, Tophas, added, "I was saved, but there was one sin that kept mastering me, and that was chewing tobacco, and it really saddened the Lord's people. They would often come and stay in our home, and they would see that I had no up-to-date testimony, and some-times Yosiya would talk to me and ask me what was both-ering me, and why I did not seem to have a day by day testimony. But I would keep quiet. So one day he drew me aside and asked me again about what was troubling me and taking my peace and joy. He reminded me that I was saved, but could see there was an area of defeat, and he asked me what it was. I told him that chewing tobacco was something I really could not give up, even though I prayed about it. He said we shall pray for you and Jesus will do it for you, and give you freedom from it. He asked me if I had ever told William about it, and I told him that William knew and he understood my problem. So Yosiya advised me to tell William every time the temptation came so that we could pray together about it, but I had always been afraid to do that. Yosiya went away and prayed and the Lord really helped me to ask Him to forgive me, and I found I was no longer bound by that longing, and was no longer overcome by it, and I found great joy in myself. I began to share what Jesus had done for me, and I really thanked the Lord."

"Now I find I can quickly sense if someone is being trou-bled by that particular problem, and I can pray for them and sometimes talk to them as Yosiya talked to me. Some-times I find I can criticise such people, but Jesus reminds me that other people did not criticise me; they loved me into liberty! And Yosiya was so pleased when he saw I was free. It says that 'He who began a good work in you will bring it to completion in Jesus Christ', and that is what He has been doing in me, and I thank Him. Some of the Lord's people would come and be hard or critical but Yosiya was never hard, he was always truthful, but gentle."

Phineas Nyenda, son-in-law of Yosiya and Dorokasi noted, "His love and concern for others would often take him on long journeys.. When he heard that a brother was going through a period of spiritual dryness or was not walk-ing closely with the Lord he would go miles and miles to see him and help him. He would visit those who were strug-gling, and go to others just to see how they were.

"In later days he had a small car and would drive 50 miles from Rugando to Bweranyangi just to see how we were. 'I do not want a drink, and I do not want to stay long. I just want to know how you are!' After hearing how we were he would drive the 50 miles back to his home.

"He encourage young people to study the Bible and preach. He liked to take the final few minutes to bring the point of the message home to people. He never preached for very long, but his few words were greatly used of the Lord.

"When he was ill in later years, he would never speak about his illness, and never tell you how he really was feeling himself. He would only talk about Jesus. Sometimes he said, 'You people stop me from going to heaven', because people loved him so much that they would pray that he might get better and live on. Yosiya truly knew how to repent daily, and he hated arguments and disagreements. He would often share his testimony about his home and say that he would not go and preach if he had not first put everything right between himself and Dorokasi. He loved helping in the home, washing and wiping the dishes. He never wasted time, seeking to do everything as quickly as possible, making the best use of his time.

"At the end of his life, whilst in hospital in Kampala many brethren came to visit him from Rugando. He said, 'God has brought people to me that I cannot reach by other means'. Wherever he went he had a burden for other people. Not long before he died, when staying with his son Peter in Kampala, he asked to see the brethren in Kampala. He talked to them about Nehemiah and how Nehemiah wept to see the walls of Jerusalem broken down. As he shared this with the leaders, he wept himself.

"Sometimes he wept, and said, 'When I get to heaven and see the other people like William Nagenda and Simeoni Nsibambi what shall I tell them about your walk with Jesus?'. Even though he did not speak a lot, his life challenged one. He did not simply speak, his life was his testimony. His life and his words were one."

"In 1972, I joined Yosiya in a Mission to Rujumbura," recounted Yosiya Banyenzaki. "Yosiya especially loved to preach about the salvation for a sinner that comes from the Cross of Jesus. He especially loved talking about the Cross of Christ, saying that if any of you have been put in prison by the devil then come to Jesus. He is calling you with tones of love saying, 'Come, come'. His Gospel was full of the love of Jesus. He too, showed great grace and compassion.

"He used to love helping us in fellowship meetings, and would often say, 'Jesus satisfies', and so we should rest in Him and what He has done for us. He would often give his own testimony about everything that troubled him. Whether it was large or small he would talk to Jesus about it.

"Once he said, 'A few days ago, we really needed some meat to eat, but we had none, and we had no money to buy any, so I called Dorokasi and the children and we prayed to God, saying, "You see we have no money to buy meat, but we really need some, you see our need so would you please provide for us." My wife said, "We have no money and you ask God for meat!" But we had told the Lord, so we waited to see what God would do. After two days we saw a man coming with a leg of beef, and the man who brought it said, "This has come from your friend so and so."' Yosiya called his family together again and they thanked the Lord. At the fellowship meeting later, he said "We really should share all our needs with Jesus, for there is nothing that fails Him."'

"Sometimes he would talk about our walk with the Lord and our love for the things of this world. He would say, 'If you see people chasing after this and that at a speed of 50 mph then you lessen your speed to 20 or so. So go to Jesus about what you should do. Let others go at their speed but do not always do what they do. He loved talking about a broken spirit, using the life of Zaccheas as an example 'Come down, come down'.

"Yosiya had a great gift of illustrating what he wanted to tell people with a story which would remain in people's memories. He particularly encouraged people to keep in a close relationship with Jesus Christ. He would say, 'You have a lot of work I know in your office or on the farm, but you must keep the vision of Jesus clear. You young people, you cannot manage marriage, but stay near Jesus and He will hold your hand and lead you through.'"

"One of his favourite verses was Matthew 11:28: 'Come, all who are weary and heavy laden and I will give you rest.' He is near ... He is not far away ... call on Him and He will give you rest.' Then he would go on to say, 'Sometimes you think Jesus is far away, but all the time He is near you.'

"Another passage he particularly loved was Revelation 3:20: 'Behold, I stand at the door and knock, if anyone hears my voice and opens the door I will come to him and dine with him and he with me.' He called people to Jesus through this verse with such a gentle and loving voice."

"I once wrote to Yosiya when he was still working in Rwanda," remembered Zabulon Katombozi. "I was wondering what I should do. I was a policeman, and found that I did not have enough money to buy any land for myself. I was not educated and things ahead looked bleak. So I wrote to Yosiya, explaining my situation and asked him for his advice. His reply really comforted me then, and right up to now his words have never left me. He gave me the words from Isaiah 45:3: 'I will give you the treasures of darkness, and hidden riches of secret places that you may know that I the Lord who call you by name am the God of Israel.' He explained that God had treasures that He had stored up for me, but that at the moment they are hidden.

"'If you see that you need land, do not worry, for all that He has prepared or saved for you, He will give to you.' When I read those words peace came into my heart, and I knew that God would look after me. I wrote to thank Yosiya for his letter, and told him how the Lord had used it to help me, and I stopped worrying about the matter. Then, in an amazing way God gave me this piece of land where we are now. I did not have to pay anything for it! I remembered those words that the Lord would give me treasures that He had stored up for me!"

"One thing that many people remember about him", said Zak Kalega, "was that he was always keen to attend fellowship meetings. When he returned from any meetings, whether they were near or far in Africa, or from other parts of the world, he would never miss the fellowship meeting. It was part of his love and his life, and his commitment was very deep. He was very much a person who loved to work as part of a team, and whenever he went on missions he always went with other people. He enjoyed people and was never a 'pusher' or self-seeker. He never mentioned his own needs. He gave the impression that he had everything, because everything to him was Jesus.

"In those days the leaders of the fellowship meetings would always ask visitors if they had a 'word' to share. Yosiya always had a 'word'. It was always brief, never more than 10 or 15 minutes, and he would always be straight to the point and very clear. He was always a man of few words.

"Another thing about Yosiya was his love for people and his longing to help people to develop spiritually. I was much younger than he was, and I would not normally have been in his company very much, but to my amazement he kept calling and chatting with me. He had a deep concern for the Revival, and in later life when he was sick and staying with his son, he would call some of the brethren and share his concerns and anxieties about the way things were going. He said, 'I am sick and am going to be with the Lord, but how is the Revival?'

"We owe a tremendous debt to people like Yosiya, and when he went to be with the Lord we knew that he had faithfully done his part, he had 'fought a good fight' and deserved a rest. He has gone but he still speaks to us."

Rutanyohoko remembers that when he was very cold spiritually, he decided he should go and speak to someone, so he set out to see Erica Sabiti. Erica was away and so he went to see Yosiya. New things were coming into the church, politics, debts and tribalism, and even people he trusted were getting swept up in the most recent fad. He explained his worries to Yosiya who replied, "My child, I did not know you were confused like this. There will be many who will take other paths, and you should walk with them and love them. Jesus heard many things and He understood what was going on around Him, but they did not sway Him, and He did not enter into their ways. Jesus went on being Jesus, so what a strange man you are to be swayed by such things."

"From then on," Rutanyohoka added, "I was determined to walk with Jesus come what may. When I saw Yosiya later and told him that I thought of going to live in Nyabushozi—an area where there were at that time very few people and very few brethren, Yosiya doubted if it was right, and he wondered if I was going simply so as to have more land for my cows. He also wondered if my family and I would survive the pressure of life there, with no schools, no churches, and little food, but after talking he said, 'Yes, I am sorry, forgive me, you could find Jesus has a work for you there, and if He is telling you to go, then you should go'."

Peri Kabaza quoted an incident when Yosiya demonstrated the concern for others which was shown equally by Nagenda and other revived Christians: "What was amazing about those brethren was their love and understanding, and sympathy. They would enter into your situation. When I was married and had to go all the way to Mbarara to live, the brethren came with me from Kampala, but when they left I felt so bereft and was weeping. I rather expected someone to come and tell me that a person of God should not weep like that, but Yosiya came along and said, 'I understand your problem and am hearing'. My tears disappeared quickly.

Dr Harold Adeney, a missionary, remembers an early meeting with Yosiya. "For some 20 years I had to take journeys from Burundi and Rwanda to Kampala (Uganda) and back, either to take children of our missionary families to the train for their new terms at schools in Kenya, or to collect them off the train from Kenya at the end of the term. It was at one of these beginning of term trips that I had been asked, after saying goodbye to the children, to take Yosiya Kinuka back to his home at Gahini, in Rwanda. He had been having some treatment in Mengo Hospital. Gahini is 320 miles from Kampala, across the border where we had to complete immigration and customs formalities, and though the murram roads in Uganda were generally good, the last 80 miles to Gahini was a much slower road and in poorer condition. So naturally I was keen to make an early start for this long journey. The evening before, I went to see Yosiya in hospital to arrange the time to collect him in the morning, telling him that I wanted to leave in good time.

"The next day, when I collected him at about 8 am, he said, 'We must go into Kampala first as I have to pick up some clothes from the tailors.' Mengo Hospital is two or three miles out of the business district of Kampala in the opposite direction from the road to Rwanda. I was not best pleased! Then when in Kampala there were people to see and it was about 10 am when we finally turned the car out of the city to start on our long journey. The atmosphere in the car was icy, though it was a hot day. We travelled on in silence. After a good many miles I knew that I must repent of my self-pity and resentment and lack of love. I did so, and asked my brother Yosiya to forgive me. He roared with laughter! 'Yosiya, why are you laughing like that?' I asked. 'I've been in the wrong, you should have been sad about my sin!' 'No!' he said, 'I'm so happy, because now you are a repentant sinner.' The many miles passed quickly and smoothly as together we shared and talked of the love and grace of Jesus in cleansing repentant sinners in His blood. I thank God for the many times He spoke to me through my dear brother Yosiya."

Doreen Peck, was a missionary in Rwanda. She remembered with deep gratitude an early conversation she had with Yosiya. "It was at Shyogwe during my first months in Rwanda," she wrote, "walking along the road between the school and our house. Yosiya joined me as I walked and asked, 'Mademoiselle, do you know the power of the Blood of Jesus?' 'Oh, yes,' I replied, 'of course I do.' I was somewhat taken aback by his question, for this seemed to me a basic Christian truth that surely every born-again Christian knew. So often, in my Crusader Class and later, I had sung, 'There is power, power, wonder-working power, in the Blood of the Lamb,' so often. But he went on, 'Yes, as an article of faith, but do you really prove, in daily experience, the power of the Precious Blood to break the power of sin's hold on you—such things as wrong thoughts, jealousy, resentment, and the like? Once you have repented of a sin and brought it under the power of the Blood, it is gone, and you must not let the devil or other people bring it up again.'

"This practical awareness of the power of the Blood of Jesus to 'break the power of cancelled sin' helped me to understand why people sang and praised so much as they gave testimony to the cleansing power of Jesus' Blood. It was an everyday miraculous reality to them. As Yosiya was speaking with me I realised that I did not know, in personal experience, this releasing power of the Precious Blood. In fact, a situation came to my mind which I had tried to cope with in my own strength. It involved what I now saw as jealousy of another missionary who was praised for her attempts to speak Kinyarwanda—I could hear she made grammatical and agreement errors. I knew it was hindering my fellowship with her. That night I knelt down and brought the jealousy to the Lord, asked for cleansing and for the power of the Blood to break its hold on me. It is difficult to put into words what happened, but I 'felt' the hold of the jealousy broken, and joy and praise filled my heart."

Yosiya's nephew once asked someone, "Can you explain something I do not understand. I see that my uncle Yosiya is closer to people like Dr Church and others from other backgrounds than he is to people of his own background. I do not understand where this oneness comes from. But I know it is real, and very deep."

Archdeacon William Bamutungire saw Yosiya at work in the Church. He commented: "Yosiya faithfully attended Church Committee meetings, but he was known as someone who would not speak behind the back of people. On one occasion a certain man's name was put forward to go to be in charge of a parish. Yosiya said he was not happy about the choice, but rather than tell the committee his reasons he asked that the man concerned should be invited to the meeting so that they could talk openly with him. When he came Yosiya asked him if it was true that he had a mistress. He denied it, but Yosiya went on further and asked him about the rumours that he had heard that the man concerned had illegitimate children in some villages. In the end the man came to own up to the truth and ultimately left the church."

It is difficult to summarise the qualities of this exceptional man, Yosiya Kinuka, who was, at the same time, very ordinary. Had he been given in his youth better educational possibilities, he might well have reached academic heights.

He followed what he believed to be right even when that differed from what might culturally be expected of him. His adventurous spirit drove him to walk from his home in Ankole to Kigezi, when that was not accepted behaviour. He married a wife from a different area and tribal background when that was not socially acceptable. When he was invited to work in the hospital at Gahini, he was not afraid to leave Kabale and his home district of Ankole and identify himself with the Banyarwanda in Rwanda. His was a remarkable transformation from being an illiterate patient at Kabale Hospital to Head Hospital Assistant at Gahini, from being a simple clergyman in Rwanda to being an internationally respected speaker in Europe, Africa and elsewhere.

While Runyankole was his native language, he learned Kinyarwanda so that he became, linguistically, a Munyarwanda. He was also able to speak Luganda, and English.

After his ordination in 1941, Yosiya's pastoral ministry centred on Gahini and the churches in the districts to the north and east of Rwanda. The sight of Yosiya and Joe Church sitting on the verandah of Joe's house became a very familiar one. Although the immediate focus of their concerns were the church and hospital at Gahini, it was there that they discussed and prayed over the progress of Revival in East Africa and further afield. It was from there that Yosiya accepted invitations to visit elsewhere in Africa and in Europe.

The later years

In 1961 Joe and Decie Church were forced to leave Rwanda and the close collaboration between Joe and Yosiya was no longer possible. The political situation in Rwanda had become very tense from 1959 onwards. There was a great deal of violence as the leaders of the *Hutu* ethnic group rose against what they felt was the dominance of the *Tutsi* group. All around him, Yosiya saw the evicting of people from their homes, the burning of houses, destruction of crops and herds of cattle and the killing of thousands of innocent people.

Yosiya was a 'Munyankole'—from the Ankole district of Uganda, and not a 'Munyarwanda'. In July 1962, Rwanda became an independent Republic. It was natural, there-fore, that the leadership of the Rwandan Church should be drawn from its own people. Yosiya saw, in all this, a pasto-ral role for himself rather than in the higher levels of Church leadership. A few months after Joe and Decie left Gahini, the Rwandan Church committee responsible for caring for refugees from the violence in Rwanda, asked Yosiya and Dorokasi to return to Uganda to look after the refugees from Rwanda who had settled in the Orukinga Valley, near the Rwanda border. For six years, his ministry was largely to the refugees.

Of this period in the lives of Yosiya and Dorokasi, Dr J R Billinghurst wrote, "It has always struck me that Yosiya's decision to go and work amongst the thousands of Rwanda refugees, in that remote and previously sparsely inhabited area, was an act of the most extraordinary love and unself-ishness by such a capable and outstanding man."

In 1966, Yosiya retired to Rugando, about 11 miles from Mbarara along the Kabale Road. Although, due to age and, later, illness, his preaching ministry became increasingly limited during the remaining 14 years of his life, the influence of Yosiya and Dorokasi continued. There was a very powerful consistency in what Yosiya said and what he and Dorokasi were and did. Many are the testimonies of those who came to them for counsel and who experienced the reality of their faith.

Yosiya became ill in 1971 and received treatment locally, mostly in Mulago Hospital, the government hospital in Kampala. In 1975, he travelled to the UK for treatment. Later he was admitted to Mengo Hospital, Kampala.

While in Mulago Hospital, Yosiya received many visitors. He also wrote a duplicated letter from time to time to those for whom he had a special concern and who prayed for him. "This is my second letter since I came to Mulago," he wrote in one of them, "Satan has fought hard regarding my illness and it is nearly four years since we have been here at Mulago. Sometimes Satan attacks us with self-pity and exhaustion, but God helps us to repent. The other day I was going to have an operation but the doctor discovered that I had high blood pressure and said that the operation could not be performed. So to the illness I came with here has been added another one. Please remember Mrs Kinuka. She is tired but God's grace is upholding us. We are here in weakness and sickness, but we remember you in our prayers beseeching God to use this precious time for the preaching of the gospel, because we do not know how long the time is for in the world to preach the gospel. This is a short letter, but it is enough."

Those who visited Yosiya in his illness realised that he suffered a great deal but without complaining. He never ceased to praise God for His goodness to him, whatever happened. Often he would repent of self-pity and then would go on to rest in God's grace towards him. Dorokasi nursed him and shared his concern, never far from their minds, for those who were not yet 'in Christ'. He would encourage his visitors to 'preach the Gospel, for the time of opportunity is short'.

Many people continued to come to the home of Yosiya and Dorokasi for pastoral help—in their family and home situations, in their church relationships and in their business priorities. In all these, they showed a God-given discernment for the heart of the problems and they would encourage people to put Jesus first and things would work out for the best. That was their testimony.

Yohana Bunyenyezi visited him in hospital: "When, Yosiya, was ill in bed in Kampala he sent for me, and he said, 'Yohana, you see we are going to go, but the work of the church is huge, I want to ask you how you see *your* responsibility?' I understood that he knew that his work was finished and he was passing the work on to me. You know that when we bury someone we say 'He has completed his work!'"

Yosiya died in June 1981. Archbishop Erica Sabiti led the funeral service which was marked by many testimonies to the ways in which Yosiya had been used by God to bring salvation, peace and Revival to people of widely differing backgrounds.

During the next sixteen years, God gave Dorokasi good health and spiritual strength despite the loss of three of her children, Peter, James and Janet Nyenda, within a short space of time. Visitors from Uganda, Rwanda, Kenya, Tanzania and England continued to frequent her home in Rugando. Her's was a living, daily testimony to the grace of God right to the end of her earthly life.

Dorokasi passed away peacefully at her home on February 20th, 1998. The funeral service was led by the Bishop of East Ankole, Elisha Kyamugambi who gave great praise to God for her life and for the faithful support she gave to Yosiya in his great ministry.

Of Yosiya and Dorokasi, it can truly be said that "they faithfully completed the work God had given them".

No greater tribute can be given to any man or woman.

Chapter 6

Erica and Geraldine Sabiti

The early years

Erica Sabiti was born in the village of Rwebishuru, in Uganda, on a Sunday in 1903. In the language of Ankole 'Sabiti' means 'Sunday'. His father, a chief in Ankole, died while Erica was young and his 'first brother', in fact a step-brother, Ernest Katungi, became his guardian. Katungi had a good post in the government and there were others closely related to Sabiti who were in high positions in the country—an aunt was the mother of the Prime Minister, Noah Mbaguta. As many others of Sabiti's relations were well-educated, Katungi decided that Sabiti also should go to school and he paid the necessary fees.

As a child, Sabiti would tell people to 'go to church'. As a result, his mother gave him the nickname of *Makanisa*—'churches', in his language. This fitted in well with his name of *Sabiti*—meaning 'Sunday'.

At school, Sabiti worked well but there were times when his mind was elsewhere! "I was taken to school as a small boy," he said, "and after reading, first in a day school and then in a boarding school, my heart went back to the cattle kraal, and I used to run away from school to return to the cattle kraal to feed the cows and play with other small boys like me."

After his primary education, Sabiti attended secondary school at King's College, Budo. It was there that, at the age of 16, to quote his own words, "the Lord started His work in my life. Apart from Bible teaching and other Christian things, I was struck by the chapel windows. There was a small chapel where we met for prayer, and there was a coloured window with pictures. In one picture, on the right was the picture of the martyrs of Uganda being burned. In the middle was the picture of the Lord Jesus who was crucified on the Cross, and at the bottom of the picture were the words, 'I did all this for you, what have you done for me?' On the left was a picture of Canon Apolo Kivebulaya, the Mugandan evangelist who went to preach to the Pygmies in the Congo. I found I could not ignore those words at the foot of the picture of Jesus: 'I did all this for you, what have you done for me?'" There dawned within Erica a realisation of the person he really was—"wretched, perishing, sinful"—and a desire to do something in return for the Jesus who suffered so much for him on the Cross.

After two years of senior secondary school at King's College, Budo, Erica returned to Ankole. There he found that there were many opportunities to find a good, well-paid post, but his heart was set on "doing something for Jesus for what He did for me on the Cross". This, for Erica, meant working in the church, and that fitted in with his desire to teach. He was given a teaching post in a primary school and there he "started teaching and talking to boys about Jesus and His love and how He is asking every one of us that we should do something for Him for the love He showed us when He died".

In 1925, Erica began a teacher training course at Makerere University College. He was one of the first to gain a teaching diploma. At this time, he met and married his first wife, Georgina Kachanda. They were married for only a short time. Erica said of her, "I loved her very dearly, but God first called her to give her life to Him." Her death was probably caused by malaria. When Erica heard of her death, he set off to attend her funeral on his motorcycle. On his

way he had a serious accident and was taken to hospital
which prevented him from attending the funeral. The death
of his wife came as a serious blow to Erica. "If God is love,"
he reasoned, "how could He take my dear wife whom I loved
so much?" It was some time before he was able to accept
God's overruling hand in this.

In 1927, Erica attended the Jubilee celebrations in Kampala. Also there, were representatives from different parts
of the country. Among these was a company of Girl Guides
from the Tooro area. A member of that company was a girl
named Geraldine Kirunga.

Geraldine was born in May 1914. She was the fourth of
a large family of children. Her father, Yosiya Kamuhigi, had
worked for several years as the armed bodyguard of the
Omukama (King) of Tooro. Seeing great potential in Yosiya,
although he had had no formal schooling, the Omukama
asked the missionary doctor in charge of Kabarole Hospital
to train him as a hospital worker. From there he progressed
sufficiently to train for ordination at Mukono Theological
College. He was the clergyman in charge of the Church at
Fort Portal when Geraldine was born.

Geraldine's mother, Zipporah, died suddenly in 1928.
She was greatly missed in the church in Tooro as she had
been very active in the formation of the Mother's Union
there. As did all Yosiya Kamuhigi's children, Geraldine
attended Kindergarten, then Tooro Girls' Primary School,
later to become Kyebambe Girls' School.

As a keen member of the Girl Guides, she attended the
Jubilee Celebrations in Kampala in 1927. Erica Sabiti saw
her there and he immediately felt that she was someone
whom he would think of marrying, but he said nothing to
her. Geraldine did not remember seeing him at the celebrations. However, Geraldine struck up a strong friendship
with a fellow Girl Guide named Euniya Katungi, Erica's
niece.

Geraldine began a two-year teacher training course at
Gayaza High School in 1931, in the same year that Erica
began theological studies at the Bishop Tucker Theological

College College, Mukono. Towards the end of that year, Geraldine attended a meeting at Mengo, Kampala, where, to her delight, she met her Girl Guide friend, Euniya Katungi and Euniya's uncle, Erica Sabiti. He, with others, accompanied her back to Gayaza.

During the Christmas holidays, in 1933, Geraldine was invited by Euniya to the Katungi family home in Ankole. Her father had no hesitation in giving her permission to accept the invitation. It was not until Erica asked her to marry him that she realised that he had had a motive in arranging her visit there. Strangely, perhaps, Erica's proposal annoyed her. She had considered herself to be a family friend and had in no way anticipated this turn of events. She also wondered what would be the reactions of her father. Tragedy led to Geraldine changing her mind about Erica's proposal.

Euniya's mother had suffered with polio as a child. In addition to Euniya, she had several small children. On New Year's Day she contracted a fatal illness and died very quickly. This was a great blow for the family and Geraldine felt very keenly the plight of the smaller children, suddenly left without a mother. At the same time, Geraldine's feelings for Erica changed and she felt that it would be right to marry him.

Due to regulations governing those who undertook teacher training, Geraldine could not leave her teaching post until she had completed two years after her training. The Principal of Makerere College, which validated the Certificates awarded by Gayaza High School, was a friend of Erica. He understood Erica's situation, especially relating to the five boys and three girls he had inherited, and gave his permission for the marriage. The Headmistress at Gayaza was not happy with this exemption, with the result that Geraldine gained her Teaching Certificate but was never awarded the prized Gayaza badge which all students traditionally received.

During his training at Mukono Theological College, Erica was given a wider field and more opportunities to preach and teach about the Jesus who had done so much for him. He found that very satisfying. At the same time, something else was happening. "As I trained, the conviction produced in my heart at this time, thinking about the love of Jesus, and thinking about my life in relationship to Him, was that I was a great hypocrite. I was leading a life of sin, sin for which Jesus had come to die, and I knew that what He did on the cross was for my redemption from sin. I had a very deep conviction of sin. I was proud and rebellious when the Holy Spirit touched me and showed me the areas in my life the Lord wanted me to surrender and commit wholly to Him for cleansing with the precious Blood. I resisted with hardness of heart. I felt I was not able to be ordained for the Ministry, so I went to the Bishop, who was a friend of mine, and also to our class tutor for the Ministry, and told them that I had decided that I should give up training for ordination because I was too sinful."

The Bishop and the Tutor both assured Erica that, far from being wrong, it was good to have that sense of unworthiness in order for God to have His way in him. He accepted his friends' counsel and decided to go ahead and be ordained, but the decision brought him no peace of mind.

Erica was one of the first group to be trained in English at Mukono. He was ordained a Deacon in the Church of Uganda in 1933 and he worked for a year in the Cathedral Church at Namirembe. So well was his ministry received, and so good was his English, that he was asked to help with the next group of ordinands.

On completing his ordination, Erica was put in charge of the church at Bweranyangi, one of the largest parishes in his home area in Ankole. He and Geraldine, now his wife, worked hard and, numerically at least, the church grew.

An incident during this time brought home to him the shallowness of his spiritual life. "One Christmas Day", he wrote, "I had Communion with over 700 people. I was in the church from 9 am till after 3 pm. I was convinced that I was doing something to repay the love that Jesus had for me when He died on the Cross. The following day I went to the Rural Dean, who was a man of God, and told him what I had done over Christmas. I remember his words to me that day. He said, 'God wants quality, not quantity.' That was a challenge. My life was like a tree with leaves but no fruit. When Jesus came to a fig tree to see if it had leaves and fruit, He found nothing but leaves. My life was like that. He did not curse my life as He did the tree. He blessed me, but the conviction continued. He was touching areas of my life that I was not willing to surrender to Him."

In 1936, Ankole felt the effects of the Revival which had started not far away in the southwest of Uganda and in Rwanda. Teams of Christians visited the district around them with their testimony to a living Jesus Christ who had saved them and was enabling them to live in a joyous moment by moment fellowship with Him.

That year, two teachers from Mbarara, Anania Murumba and Elieza Mugimba, came to Bweranyangi where Erica and Geraldine were working. "I found that all over the parish people started getting saved," Erica said later, "and I praised the Lord for that."

Geraldine's first reaction was to reject the testimony of the visiting team. "I do not have this sort of sin or need," she argued with herself. Then she knelt to pray and was conscious of the Holy Spirit pointing out to her that she really was a 'child of Adam'. "I saw that, even if I was not conscious at that point of anything I had done wrong, nevertheless I was a child of Adam and, as such, I was under a curse as Adam was. So I repented and trusted in Jesus. I went outside the church and immediately gave my testimony to the fact that I had been born again. A light shone in my heart and life and I saw my own sin. It was then that I was convicted of friendships that were wrong, and of having photos and letters from other boy friends. Erica knew nothing about them even though they were in the house. He was amazed when I told him these things but, although he had read about Revival, he stood at a distance from it until the Lord touched him and opened his eyes."

Erica recognised immediately the change in Geraldine. "She met those who had caught the fire and she came back another person," he said. "There were many things she started to put right with me. She was rejoicing and happier than she used to be. Instead of being happy with her I was hard and tried to make it difficult for her."

Geraldine's comments on Erica's spiritual state at that time are very perceptive. She realised that "Erica loved Jesus from a very early age and had a deep calling to follow Him, but many thought he would never be saved. Some felt he was so good that he did not need to be saved, whilst others felt that he was so deeply interacting with others and so involved in various discussions that he could never come to faith. In those days, before he came to Christ, he worked so very hard in his own strength, and wherever he went, he was trusted and respected by those in leadership positions, by District Commissioners, Governors, the Kabaka of Buganda and the Omugabe of Ankole. He was highly respected as a person and for his academic and linguistic abilities. Until he came to Christ, he basked in the glory of this, but after he met with Jesus everything changed, and the once respected man became despised."

Miss Patty Drakely, the Headmistress of Gayaza High School, had opposed Geraldine being excused the normal two years teaching service in a school before being married. Geraldine related how, "Patty Drakely, who had not wanted me to leave the school to be married, was later brought to see her own need of a Saviour, and after she was saved she came and apologised for her hard attitude to me, and we became the greatest of friends!"

For two and a half years Erica continued in an unhappy state. He preached the Gospel, however, and people in the parish were being saved.

In 1939, Erica was asked to accompany the Bishop of Uganda on a visit to the churches in Rwanda and Burundi. There he met Christians who, though less educated than he was, were experiencing a reality of which he knew nothing. He bowed in repentance and his life was transformed.

Family life

From that time onwards, the lives of Erica and Geraldine were a testimony to the life of God in them, in their family and in their church. Individually and together they testified to the amazing grace of the Lord Jesus in saving them.

Enid Kanyangyeyo, Erica and Geraldine's eldest daughter, expressed the appreciation of the Sabiti children for their parents. "As a child I grew up looking up to my father as the most wonderful father in the whole entire world. I still do. My father was a most wonderful father, teacher, friend and also husband to my mother.

"I loved my father very much because I would confide in him. He was my mentor, my friend as well as being my father. I hated it when I had to share him and his time with a lot of 'balokole'. I felt they took up much of the time he would have spent with us, his immediate family. My brothers and sisters and I went to boarding schools at an early age and I felt that holidays should be family time. He travelled quite a lot for his church job and for balokole meetings. I did not like sharing *my* Dad with balokole who also called him 'daddy'. I resented it. But now I understand. He was, in a sense, a spiritual 'father' to them.

"When he was home, he spent time with us to make up for the time he was away. My father never preached to me as other *balokole* used to do. He advised me, counselled me and gave me guidance, as any other parent would do. In many ways he showed me that, as a girl I have to work hard in school, have a profession and grow up as an independent woman. I should never rely on my brothers or future husband for financial support. He showed me that he trusted my judgement about my choice of school and my future career. He encouraged me to fight for my rights. He taught me love and respect for him and my mother because he respected me. My father never worried about me when I turned into an adolescent that I was going to have boy friends. He trusted me. My father never hit me or showed great anger towards me. He gave me great confidence and self-respect.

"As I grew up I saw my mother totally differently from my father. Most of the time we were home with my mother. She tried hard to bring us up as the children of the Church as well as of 'balokole'. She was a strict disciplinarian. That turned me into a rebellious girl who was always getting into trouble with my mother.

"My parents were very loving and caring. They wanted me to have everything good. Most of all they wanted me to grow into a useful, beautiful, cultured, highly educated woman. I attribute all my success now to them and their upbringing. Being a good teacher, a good mother of four children brought up single handed, giving them education, teaching them how to be independent thinkers and making decisions for their future—all these good things are what I learned from my parents and that is what the children have learned from me.

"I have never ever seen or heard my parents have any form of fight, be it verbal or physical. I used to think that they had no differences. My parents were not rich at all, but they knew their priorities. They vested in our well being and education. Boys and girls were all given equal opportunity.

"My parents' lives have had positive effects on me, and not only me but also on my children's lives. In my own quiet moments, I pray to God as my father and mother taught me to pray. I trust God as I was brought up to. Although I do not go to Church on Sundays, personally I know that God is there and He cares. As I mentioned the things I rebelled about when growing up, I have allowed my children to do. I find I am more close to my children than I was to my mother. Father had a special place in my heart and I miss him a lot."

Godfrey Gariyo Sabiti shared the other children's appreciation of their parents as "very loving, very hard-working". However, he, with the others, felt that they suffered from the generosity of the Sabiti household. "Ours was a 'many people family'. My parents opened their home not only to children of their poor relations but also to those of the 'brethren'. They also welcomed many young men and women who were given accommodation in return for growing food, drawing water, gathering firewood and washing and dressing us children, as present-day nannies and babysitters do, while our parents were away. What was missing was individual discussions with my parents on issues of the ways of the world and growing up in general. Ours was a large home and our parents gave more time to the spiritual development of the large family. Generally, I missed the lack of 'space' to enjoy my parents when I was very young.

"What I learned most from my parents is humility, even when being looked up to; to let others elevate you so you do not need to pull rank. Material things are useful and good to have, but we can be very comfortable with little. I remember that, when we came home for holidays from school, we had to account for the clothes that we had taken to school at the beginning of term. If I had lost anything without a valid explanation, I would have to do some chore at home as replacement for what was lost. I learned darning socks and sewing buttons on my clothes when I was ten or eleven years old and I could patch a shirt before my mother ran it on the sewing machine. I also learned to deal with people in a transparent way or 'walking in the light'. This was very important as it involves saying 'sorry!'

Dora Sabiti also has happy memories of her very active parents, despite the extended family in which she was brought up. "As I was growing up, I always knew my parents were one and that they shared everything with each other. However, they never put me in an unpleasant position, so I always felt comfortable to talk to either Mama or Dad individually. Sometimes I believed it was a one to one conversation that would remain between just the two of us. As I look back I feel that this was a special gift of trust and sharing that they raised us with. Mama and Dad also raised us with their unconditional love and they taught us to have respect—respect for ourselves, for each other and for everyone else whom we would encounter in our lives.

"In a country full of tribalism and classification, I was raised in a loving, warm and unique world of *Abaishemwe* (the 'brethren'). For example, while attending school in primary 2 and 3, in my social studies class we would be asked to say our tribe, clan and one of the things our clan considered taboo. In the entire class of about twelve children, I was the only one with no idea of what all this meant. The teacher then gave me homework and my assignment was to find out what my tribe, my clan and my clan taboo were by the next day of class. On arriving home around 4 pm, tea time, I had the chance to ask both Dad and Mama, as well as other family members who were there for tea, to help me with my homework assignment. Dad and Mama seemed slow to give me an answer but one answer did come up unopposed: 'Tell them your tribe is *Oweishemwe* (Born Again), your clan is *Okujunwa* (Salvation) and your clan taboo is *Ekibi* (Sin).' I was very contented with this answer and I became busy memorizing the above in the order it was given to me.

"The next day in class I was the first one to raise my hand proudly, knowing that I had a very good answer for my homework problem. When I stood and gave my answer, to my amazement, the whole class laughed at me. My teacher, who was also saved (Omukuru Monica), calmed the class down and thanked me for my effort. I look back now on this memory and realise that I was extremely innocent, happy and trusting as I grew up. I also realize that my parents protected that innocence with love and I trusted them with unquestionable confidence. In this case they protected me from encountering the barriers associated with drawing generalisations about any group of people and they protected me from meeting the barriers associated with tribalism early in my life. They also prepared me for the battles I have to encounter today in the United States.

"As a child I remember being scared of the darkness, especially at bedtime. I was put to bed between 7:30 pm and 8:00 pm. It would take another half an hour to an hour of screaming before I would fall asleep. This screaming would annoy the entire household, of course, except my Dad. He would always come to my bedside, without condemnation or anger, and would find out why I was screaming. We would pray together and ask God to keep away whatever was bothering me. He would then sit outside my bedroom door until I fell asleep, reassuring me that nothing would happen. I look back and see his eternal patience and the security I had in his loving presence.

"As I grew into my teen years, I remember several times trying to straighten out problems by taking a short cut. Time after time I would try going through Dad hoping that he would help by talking to Mama and resolve the problem for me. This was interesting because any time I came to him, Dad would always listen to me objectively without judging—even if he was busy in the office, he had time for me. At the end of my story he would thank me for sharing my side of the story with him and simply ask me, 'Don't you think you should share your story with Mama as soon as possible?' This would take me by surprise. My parents taught me that there is no short cut to true repentance.

"In my eyes, Dad and Mama's faith in God was always there in their daily actions towards each other and towards everybody else. They were not pushy people, yet they were firm in their beliefs and they were comfortable and happy in their lives. Their faith was expressed in very many different ways that, if you knew them, you would be proud to be part of that faith and part of their family.

"Growing up, there was a song with the words: 'Read your Bible and pray every day.' Dad and Mama did just this. They started their day at about 4 am reading the Scriptures and praying. There were also weekly meetings at our house when everybody who lived in the household, in the neighbourhood, or who were in the family of *Abaishemwe* at that time, gathered. All people from near and far gathered outside under the moonlight in the compound sharing testimonies, scriptures, prayers and songs together. The compound was filled with people and children. Children, who were ideally supposed to be in bed—

but who could sleep with all that excitement? Though I was the last born of seven, I was always older than at least six of the many children who were at these weekly meetings! The only way to escape bedtime and join the meetings was to insist on having something to say. When I first began attending the meetings I would invent a story based on what I heard the elders saying, but with time I began to understand, and longed to be a part of the communion that was shared. I began to start looking within myself and became saved. The road has not been easy and I have faced many challenges in my spiritual journey.

"As I grew into a young woman, the world lured me and I grew cold spiritually," Dora adds, as she tells of a man she thought was going to marry her. But he forsook her when he learned that she was pregnant. "In His love and mercy," she continues, "God restored me to Himself. He blessed me with a daughter who was fortunate to enjoy both her grandparents and receive their unconditional love. In 1985, then 10 years old, while on her summer vacation, she was confirmed into the Christian family by her Grandfather, my Dad. We were fortunate and blessed at this time because Dad was just recovering from a minor stroke. Dad gave my daughter and two of her cousins an intense training in the Scriptures so that they could learn what it meant to be a Christian and *Oweishemwe*.

"On her return to the USA, I encouraged her to attend confirmation classes at the Episcopal Church we attend, in order to see the difference between Episcopal beliefs and Evangelical Anglican beliefs. Within the first week of classes, she found there were some practices in this particular Church she did not agree with. She immediately voiced her concerns to me and then talked with a family friend who put her in contact with the Rector of the Church. I was shocked to hear my daughter disagreeing with the Rector. She simply stated: 'My Grandfather is an Archbishop. He is saved, and he taught me differently...' 'Looking back I see that my father had a profound influence on my daughter's beliefs and values.

"Nkwanzi's personal commitment to the Lord, her testimony and dedication to reading the Scriptures and, most importantly, her peace of mind in everyday life, have been a challenge to me as we share and pray together and continue to praise God."

After many years of married life, Geraldine has testified to their—Erica's and her—life together in the home and in their ministry. "We have been through many trials and difficulties over the years, not only in the work, but also in a variety of ways. It has sometimes been very difficult when people have not wanted us or we have been misunderstood. But one thing that has helped us tremendously has been the oneness that the Lord has given us together.

"We have supported each other not only in the work but also when we have been physically weak. I was very weak after I had the children, but my husband really encouraged me, and he helped me in every way he could. But latterly it has been Erica who has not been well, and he has been extremely weak physically.

"Despite this self pity, the Lord helps us to get on and help each other, and this comes from the love He has given us for each other. Sometimes we find self love comes in, and I want my way, and I push so as to get it. Then my husband wants his way! But God helps us to share these things 'in the light' and to ask for each other's forgiveness, and the Lord refreshes and releases us. Our Lord does not change! As Scripture says, 'even to your old age I will carry you'. These things have helped us so much. Sometimes I find that my self pity, and self love, actually reduces the love I have for my husband, and then I get tired of helping him in the various ways that he now needs. But I go on trusting the Lord and casting my cares on Him, and then I find that He is even more precious."

When Erica and Geraldine retired to Kinoni, they named their house *Akibaho*, meaning 'He (God) is still there'. Then they added *Akibawe*—'He is still the same.' It was that sense of the living presence of God, who is ever the same, which marked their lives and their home right to the end.

Ministry in Revival

The effect of Erica's transforming visit to Rwanda and Burundi on his life and ministry is best recounted in his own words. Referring to the nominal Church of Uganda as it was in the years before Revival came, Erica said, at a convention in Mbarara in 1978, "I myself was in that Church, I was a Pastor serving at Bweranyangi Church. My wife had gone somewhere to get some treatment for her illness, and she had met with Jesus. When she came back and told me what had happened, my pride stopped me from listening to what she was saying. I thought I was educated and understood a lot, and I trusted in my own intelligence and understanding. I had just been ordained as a priest, and I was travelling a great deal because the parish was very large. But God saw dead bones, as Scripture says, and the question for me was, 'Can these bones live?' My answer was, 'Oh Lord God you know.'

"Although I struggled for a while, God went on speaking to me. ... Not many miles from Bweranyangi, at a place called Mitooma, a local chief came drunk one evening, holding his beer in his hand. God spoke to him in his drunken state and we heard him crying aloud saying, 'God has arrested me.' And he brought the beer and said, 'I will not drink again!' The wind of God was blowing.

"Near Mitooma, at Kashenyi, there was a senior church teacher who was having a drink problem. He had been drinking excessively and he found that he had a kind of paralysis in his arm and could not move it, and there he was stuck with the bottle in his hand and he could not put it down! His wife tried to pull it down for him, but it was stuck and would not move. She suggested that they should pray, and as they prayed the hand was released! He had things in his home to do with witchcraft and he got hold of these and early in the morning he came to Bweranyangi and knocked on my door. I cannot rehearse it all, but we saw wonderful things happening. That was the Spirit of God blowing but the wind of the Holy Spirit had not entered me.

"People thought I was a wonderful Christian, very devout and helpful. Bishop Cyril Stuart invited me to go on a visit with him to Rwanda and Burundi, and so we travelled together to those countries. He also invited William Nagenda to go with him. William had been touched by this wind of God's Holy Spirit. At that time he was working in Rwanda. William talked to Bishop Stuart, and explained that many of his clergy were not saved. Bishop Stuart smiled and said that he knew that there were clergy who were not saved, but he commented that some were good and others not so good! He loved me and counted me as one of his 'good' clergy, and gave me as an example of a 'good' ordained man, but I was a big hypocrite and a man-pleaser, and I went along with the Bishop, and approved of his remarks about my being a 'good Christian'.

"Then, at Gahini we found Banyarwanda who were not dressed as well as we were, and who were not so well educated, but they had peace. I was invited to preach and I preached about the Blood of Jesus. One Munyarwanda, dressed in his traditional dress, said to me afterwards, 'You have preached about the Blood of Jesus, but I do not think you have really experienced it in your own life.' What he said was true. Then another person came to me and took me aside in the prayer room and said to me, 'You seem to be happy, but not quite happy.' I replied and admitted that I had no peace.

"At Gahini, a lady missionary took me into a corner and said, 'I think that you are despising these people, but I tell you that God is using them. They have God's Spirit.'

"At the second church centre, meetings were held for those who could speak English. One of the missionaries took the Bible readings on Peter's first letter. He reached the verse where it says, 'Unto you who believe, He is precious.' He spoke about the preciousness of Jesus, the Man who did everything for us.

"There was a song that they sang there. The words melted my hard and proud heart. I gave up what I was holding onto. But again the devil got in and said, 'You are too sinful to be forgiven, you are not speaking the truth. You can never be forgiven.' As I was in that state, I seemed to hear a voice speaking to me directly, saying, 'You are accepted in the beloved.' Jesus had accepted me! I was through with fears and I started a new life. The words of that song are:

> Oh, teach me what it meaneth,
> That Cross uplifted high,
> With One, the Man of sorrows,
> Condemned to bleed and die.
> Oh, teach me what it cost Thee
> To make a sinner whole;
> And teach me Saviour, teach me
> The value of a soul.
>
> Oh, teach me what it meaneth—
> That sacred crimson tide,
> The blood and water flowing
> From Thine own wounded side.
> Teach me that if none other
> Had sinned, but I alone,
> Yet still, Thy Blood, Lord Jesus,
> Thine only, must atone.

"Before I went to Rwanda I had escorted my wife to the roadside as she was going to visit a relative. When we parted I did not know if she would come back. I returned from the safari with the Bishop. My wife did come back from her time away. We did not sleep the whole night. I was repenting and putting things right with her, I told her how proud I had been, proud of being a clergyman, and many other things."

Erica returned to Uganda to face change. Although he had been well-liked in the whole area, he now faced opposition. He and Geraldine were called in to church committees where strong criticism of the 'revived brethren' was voiced. Even bishops supported those criticisms. "It is wonderful," commented Erica, "that every time we were faced with such condemnations and oppositions, the Lord helped us to just keep coming to Him and to have peace with Him, and in the end we found that, despite this opposition, the church started appointing us to responsible places. I can remember the time when we sat at a committee to decide who should be the Rural Dean over a certain area. I hardly had any expectations, with such opposition, that I would be appointed. The Assistant Bishop was in the chair, meaning to oppose our appointment. We were asked to go out of the committee meeting. To my surprise, when we sent back into the room, I found that I had been appointed to the Bweranyangi deanery."

Looking back on the years at Bweranyangi, Erica said, "When we went there the responsibility was great, but we were given a lovely field to work in and we met many people who were testifying to the saving grace of God, and many caught fire and started spreading the Good News. It is well over thirty years since we were there, but we still meet with people with whom we enjoyed fellowship then and who are still walking with the Lord—some with grey hairs."

While at Bweranyangi, Erica, and Bishop Festo Olang, a 'brother in the Lord from Kenya', were invited to visit India as a team. That country was then one country, as it had been in colonial days. "There were brethren there that we shared our experiences with," wrote Erica, "and there were many who were brought to the Lord. And not only in India, but beyond Uganda, we went to Tanzania and many other places. It is wonderful when you meet people of different denominations, Baptists, Mennonites, or any other denomination, and you meet people of different tribes who have been to the Cross and who have accepted the Lord Jesus Christ, and we find that we are brothers and sisters in Christ, and we plead together for the broken world - a nationalistic world - a tribal world - a denominational world, and we are one in Christ—those who have been saved and redeemed by the precious Blood of Jesus."

To his surprise, Erica was appointed Suffragan Bishop in the Rwenzori diocese, in west Uganda. Erica recorded his impressions of that appointment. "After being Rural Dean for several years, I was appointed to be an Assistant Bishop. This was very naturally opposed again. We did not think that any of the Bishops at that time would appoint us to that position, because we were accounted to be people who were dividing the church by preaching the saving Gospel.

"To our surprise we were sent to England to work under the Bishops in different areas. In the north, we were sent to Bradford, an industrial area, with Bishop Donald Coggan, who afterwards became the Archbishop of Canterbury, and to the south, to a rural area with Bishop Maurice Wood. We worked there and the Lord kept us humble and helped us to testify to what the Lord had done. It was a joy meeting people in England who had the same experience as we had. After a year in England, getting experience with the Bishops and in parishes, we returned to Uganda. To our surprise, instead of being made an Assistant Bishop we were made a full Bishop of the Rwenzori Diocese. There we remained as Bishop from 1960 until 1966."

Erica introduced an energetic programme of self-help in this area, recorded the English *Daily Telegraph*: "During his years in Rwenzori, Sabiti had to carry out a major reorganisation of the diocese following an earthquake, and his churches also had to cope with many refugees from Rwanda and Sudan. He initiated the Christian Rural Service. This involved church workers going around in pairs on bicycles to teach simple methods of agriculture and hygiene in the villages, and to spread the Christian message. Sabiti's 'Young Farmers Scheme' was designed to encourage young men to work on unexploited agricultural land, rather than migrate to Kampala and other cities where there was neither work nor housing for them. His opposition to the political tyrannies of his time was courageous and he was fortunate to escape the fate of his martyred successor in the archbishopric, Janani Luwum."

In 1965, the expatriate Archbishop of the Uganda Province, Leslie Brown, retired from his office. The event was accompanied by much ill feeling. One source of discontent was his unwillingness to print the name of the Kabaka (King) of Buganda in the revised version of the Luganda Prayer Book. "The other grievance was that I had retired at a time when no Muganda bishop could be elected as Archbishop," he wrote in his autobiography. "Bishop Nsubuga had been a bishop only a few months, Bishop Tomusange was too old. So there was a good deal of anger against me on this score in Kampala."

"It was then up to the Ugandan Bishops to choose among themselves who would become the Archbishop," said Erica. "I had my choice among the Bishops, but I had no thought at all that a man so opposed by many would be thought of as the next Archbishop, the first African Archbishop of the whole Anglican Communion, and in this case, of the Province which, in those days, consisted of Uganda, Rwanda, Burundi and Boga Zaire. The Province was very big!"

As stated in the obituary to Erica in the English 'Daily Telegraph', "His election to the Archbishopric in 1966 was the consequence of the admiration and trust which he evoked wherever he went."

"Erica Sabiti was the first Ugandan to be the Archbishop of the Province," recorded John Bikangaga. "He was elected to follow on the last expatriate Archbishop of the Province - the Right Rev. Leslie Brown. He was the first African Archbishop of any Province in the Anglican Communion. He had the task of leading the way and providing a foundation for the Independent Province of the Anglican Church in Uganda. With the departure of Archbishop Leslie Brown many expatriates left. It was Erica's task to fuse the Mission Agency from overseas with the Church in Uganda.

"Under the Constitution previously drawn up, it was decided that the Archbishop should be not only the Archbishop of the Province but also a Bishop of his own Diocese. It was assumed that the Archbishop would be selected from a Diocese near Kampala, and therefore he would be able to lead the Province as well as his own Diocese. When Erica was elected to be Archbishop, he became

Archbishop of the Province of Uganda, but remained Bishop of Rwenzori Diocese, which was some 200 miles away!

"The Baganda went to great lengths, including barring the Archbishop from entering Namirembe Cathedral, to ensure that he had no right to be Bishop of a local Diocese. The disagreement reached such heights that the Baganda were demanding that they should split away from the Province and form their own Province.

"At this point the then President of Uganda, Idi Amin, asked to see all the Bishops in the Church of Uganda so that the dispute might be settled. At the end of a long day's meeting President Amin withdrew to one room with his cabinet, and left the church leaders to see if they could come up with an answer to their problems. When they resumed again after the break, the church admitted that there was still a deadlock. Amin then decreed that the Archbishop should be in charge of the Diocese based at Namirembe, and that the Bishop of Namirembe should become the Bishop of Mukono. It was from these discussions and decisions that the eventual solution was reached—to make All Saints' Church, Kampala, the Cathedral Church of the Diocese of Kampala."

At this time, Idi Amin had many supporters. He even gained credit for having tried to bring peace within the Church of Uganda, where the rift had deepened to the extent of the Baganda calling Archbishop Sabiti a traitor, and threatening secession from the province. It was assumed that General Amin would restore the kingdom of Buganda, which Obote had abolished, and put the Kabaka's son on the throne. He surprised the church leaders when he summoned all the bishops and diocesan councillors of the Church of Uganda to a meeting in Kampala, following an earlier gathering in Kigezi. He ordered them to straighten out their church differences.

Bishop Festo Kivengere, in *I Love Idi Amin*, recalls the meeting: "For two days we sat and looked at one another, and the differences remained. But on 28th November, the Lord gave us a message from Philippians. We saw that we were men *going up*, each one thinking about his reputation and demanding his rights. But that day, we caught a vision of the Man *coming down*—Jesus. 'Who, being in the form of God ... made himself of no reputation, and took upon him the form of a servant, and was made in the likeness of men: And ... he humbled himself even to death on the cross.'

"What a change He made! In the presence of Him who *came down*, our dear Archbishop, Erica Sabiti, and each of the nine diocesan bishops, went down in confession of the sins which had contributed to the divisions in the church. A great melting by the Holy Spirit came upon us all. President Amin has always, since then, laughingly reminded us that 'he saved the Church!' But we know that Jesus, the *One-coming-down*, did it." [149]

While Erica Sabiti's first priority and love was preaching the Gospel, he acted with great insight and vigour in seeking to meet the great needs of the Province. As a leader he considered himself to be the *'primus inter pares'*, the 'first among equals'. He valued teamwork and respected the worth and contribution of each member. The greatest obstacles in Uganda appeared to be to maintain unity within the territorial and social divisions within the Church. He initiated and promoted many activities of the developing Province.

These, as assessed by John Bikangaga, were:

1. *The education of the clergy.* Whilst Erica himself was highly educated there were few other clergy with adequate qualifications. At this time Makerere University was progressing rapidly with advanced degree courses being available, but there was no degree in Theology. Erica asked John Bikangaga to chair a committee to look at the 'Crisis in Christian Education' in order to work out guide lines for the training of clergy. Although Erica placed the spiritual before the academic, he had a high respect for scholarship where it served rather than fought the purposes of God.

2. *Finance.* The Province faced a dwindling income from overseas funds and it was, therefore, necessary to draw up a long- term plan in order to look at ways and means of

increasing church giving and creating income earning projects. This ten year plan was called 'Survey and Administration and Finance of the Church in Uganda'.

3 *Church land.* In an old document dating back to 1900, an agreement had been drawn up by which 52 square miles of land had been given to the Church of Uganda (then the Native Anglican Church). Erica, as Archbishop, wanted this and other issues to be investigated. This made him extremely unpopular with the Baganda in whose area this land was placed at the beginning.

"Erica led the Church through traumatic and tempestuous times. It was recognised that he was the only one who was fitted for that great task at that time. His inner spiritual strength remained unshakeable. He was always calm and his quiet faith and firmness held him through this very demanding and difficult period. Some of the experiences were extremely painful for Erica and for his family, but he never wavered in his calling to serve his Lord and the Church, which had brought him and so many others to the knowledge of their Lord and Saviour. Sometimes during those days people noticed that his face was shining as he walked with Jesus in the midst of the fires."

Erica was also very concerned about the separatist movement called *okuzukuka* (awakened). While in hospital in October 1969, he wrote to Simeoni Nsibambi and Joe Church: "I want to share with you that I have been very concerned with the state of things as they are among the brethren. ... Without my saying it, you both know that something has gone wrong with Revival today. Seeking a remedy for this is as much a challenge to you both as it is to me. I admit that, within ourselves, we have no remedy. The guidance I have received while on this bed in hospital is to go back to the Word of God, this time not to seek how the Holy Spirit came upon the early church. The Holy Spirit has come upon His church in this country and many of us have tasted of the water of life. What I think we need is to seek afresh the simplicity of how to be saved and, after being saved, how to walk with the Lord. ... Let us go back to our simple word of salvation and the simple way of walking with the Lord in daily repentance and cleansing."

Erica said little in public about his duties as Archbishop but he was always ready to speak about Jesus, his Master, and to give his testimony to the life of Jesus in all that he did—officially in the public eye and privately in his personal life and home.

He travelled a great deal and was well known as a preacher and lecturer in England, Canada and India. From 1966 to 1974 he was an Episcopal Canon of St George's Cathedral, Jerusalem. Erica had recognised the qualities of Janani Luwum and had consecrated him as a Bishop. It was to him that Erica handed over his office of Archbishop.

As others saw them

Erica and Geraldine were most closely observed by those who were in contact with them in their home and in the ministry of the Church.

Mrs Betty Kanyamunyu, a daughter of Ernest Katungi, Erica's elder brother and guardian, naturally saw a great deal of the Sabiti family. "Erica was known for his great love of people. His life was marked by his kindness to very many. In our extended family he had a special way of giving everyone a pet name, and he always used that when he met each one. He gave Christmas presents to each person, and he is remembered by his soft, loving voice, which never changed even when he was preaching.

"For me personally he was a great help and support. I had left the Lord's ways, and was back-slidden, but when I had my son I came back to the Lord. I do not think I realised what a blessing his life was to me until he parted from us, and I cannot say how much I missed him and his wisdom and his prayers for us all."

Miss Nancy Chase was on the staff of Bweranyangi Girls' School when Erica and Geraldine were responsible for the church in that area. "Erica was Rural Dean when I arrived. He had no car and I often acted as his chauffeur. Frequently, he would see someone at the side of the road and ask to stop. "I must speak to ...." he would say.

"He and Geraldine were always available with wisdom and support for me. Their loving influence in Ankole meant that I felt surrounded by love and support and the challenge of the brethren. Without it I would not have survived spiritually. Theirs was a very open home and people came to them constantly for help and fellowship. Geraldine was a very competent home-maker and agriculturist. Erica looked after the church money and Geraldine handled their personal money in order to keep the two completely separate. An action, the wisdom of which I did not realise until years later, was that, if Erica needed to call on me after dark, he always came with someone else. There was never even a breath of scandal.

"When he became Archbishop, I used to write to him and Geraldine because I loved them and wanted them to know of my prayerful support. To my amazement, I had a number of personal letters from Erica. He and Geraldine stayed with my parents in England on two separate occasions and Erica found time to visit my youngest brother when he was at Cambridge."

As a Bishop and later Archbishop, Erica came into contact with fellow bishops from all the dioceses of the Province, as well as church leaders from other Christian denominations. One of those who worked with Erica was Dick Lyth, Bishop of Kigezi. "Erica was known by everyone to be kind, gentle and humble," he said, "but those who worked with him closely knew he could be tough and sometimes even difficult and contrary, even with us, his fellow bishops. He was, however, always ready to repent and forgive.

"He was always faced with great problems in his ministry. As Bishop of Rwenzori, he faced dislike, even malice from the people there, as he was from a different tribe. The Baganda dioceses were all against their own Archbishop Brown. When he left, Erica, as his successor, faced many problems and grievous opposition for at least two years, but the Lord gave him wonderful courage and confidence.

"On one occasion, President Idi Amin told Erica to call the clergy and church councils from all the dioceses—about 500—and God used that meeting in His wonderful way, to bring firstly the Bishops and then their people into forgiveness and fellowship. There was great rejoicing and praise.

"Increasingly, Idi Amin faced problems in the country and Erica showed great courage in those difficult circumstances. One day, on the bench of Bishops, Janani arrived in tears, having heard news of some of his people being drowned in a river by Amin's men. After the meeting, Janani told his fellow-bishops that he was going to put on his robes, take his staff and walk to Amin's office—if he was going to be shot, he would be shot! We all prayed. Then Erica said that they all—the Bishops—would walk with Janani to Amin's office. Erica phoned Amin to say we were coming, but this was too much for Amin because of the publicity. Amin said he would come to the Archbishop's house, which he did. Erica spoke to him humbly and politely but with confidence, speaking for all of us, and handed him a letter from us all. Amin promised to do what he could."

Josephine Stancliffe (later Haslam-Jones) was a missionary at Kigeme in Rwanda, when, on a visit to Kampala, "I met Erica Sabiti for the first time. I had only been in Africa for a year. One afternoon, while walking on Namirembe Hill, I saw Erica. He greeted me and asked me who I was and where I was working. In a short time, we were able to praise the Lord together. He was going to England a few days later, and I mentioned that my parents would be going to the Ruanda Mission Annual Meeting in London for the first time, and that they had not been in favour of my coming to Africa as a missionary. He said, 'I will see them.' And he did! They were thrilled. It meant a great deal to them. I met Erica again over eleven years later, at his home near Mbarara. He said, 'Hullo, Josephine.' How did he remember me after all those years? People mattered to him."

Kathleen Mawer was the missionary Headmistress of a girls' boarding school in Uganda. "I loved the Lord," she wrote, "and had given my life to Him, I just did not know the wonder of His salvation. ... I was praying very much to know whom I could ask to take School Prayers during Holy Week. One day an African clergyman came to the school, and asked to see some of the young children he knew, so I sat him in my sitting room and sent the children to him. Some little while later I wanted something from my desk, so I peeped through the window to see if he had finished. And there were those children, sitting on the floor, looking up into his face, just absorbed. And the Lord said in my heart: 'He's the one to ask to take prayers in Holy Week.'

"I'm ashamed to say I replied, 'I can't ask him, Lord. He's in 'Revival' and I'm not.' There was quite a big Revival movement there in Uganda, but alas, I think all the missionaries and most of the Christians kept right away from them. Looking back, I just cannot understand why. They were sometimes noisy, singing praises, and they were very free in their testimonies, and would often challenge folk, asking: 'Are you saved? Do you know Jesus as your Saviour?' But they had such joy in the Lord.

"For two days I struggled in my heart, and then God helped me and I wrote to Erica and said, 'I know you are in Revival and I'm not, but God has told me to ask you to take prayers in Holy Week. If you will come, I am willing to listen to anything you have to say."

"Well, Erica came. The first day I invited him to tea with me, and there he asked me:

'Do you really, love the Lord?'

'Yes,' I replied.

'Do you really believe your Bible?'

'Yes,' I answered.

'Are you glad that Jesus died?'

"I was horrified. How could anyone be glad that Jesus had to die that terrible death. That night I searched and searched my Bible, trying to show that I was right and Erica was wrong. God showed me that if we were to be redeemed, Jesus had to be willing to die for us, to bear all the guilt and nastiness of our sin. Next day, Erica came to tea again and I tried to say, 'You were right and I was wrong,' but

I couldn't get a word out. Soon he got up to go, and asked if he could see any children or teachers that wanted to see him that evening. I said, 'Yes,' and that I'd be there. Poor Erica's face fell—that wretched headmistress would stop them being free! Then, with the children and teachers together, the Lord helped me. I went over to Erica and said, 'God has shown me, you were right and I was wrong.' He took my hand and said, 'Praise the Lord. I feel that you are a sister in the Lord now.'

"To be honest, the joy didn't come right away, but about ten days later Erica and his wife had to come the 15 miles from their village to a meeting, and I invited them to stay with me. My guest room was on one corner of my bungalow and my sitting room at the other end. Early that evening, a lot of the African Brethren came to see Erica and Geraldine ... and no one came to see me! I became horribly jealous. When the others had gone, I went to tell Erica and Geraldine that supper was ready but after we had said grace, I said, 'I am sorry. I'm too bad to eat with you. I have been horribly jealous. You have your supper and I'll go to my room.' Erica looked at me with such love and said, 'Does it take Jesus any time to forgive?' 'No,' I replied, ' but I've been horrid. I'd better go to my room.' Then Erica said, 'When Jesus forgives, does He leave any stain?' And it was then the truth of this salvation really began to be real to me.

"That was in April 1947. I have been a different person ever since. It's so wonderful to know that we can come back and back to Jesus... just as we are, whenever He shows us that we have let Him down, and there at His feet, ask His forgiveness and the cleansing of His precious Blood.

Zeb Kabaza knew Erica and Geraldine well. "One of the outstanding characteristics of Erica's life", he wrote, "was that he knew how to cope with disappointments, opposition and being misunderstood. On one occasion he had got everything prepared so that he could accompany William Nagenda and Yosiya Kinuka on their first visit to the UK in 1947, but to his great disappointment the Diocesan Council did not give him leave to go.

As with other disappointments he was never bitter, and he knew how to bring his reactions and feelings to the Lord for His cleansing and forgiveness.

"He was a very able man intellectually, and both he and William gained the highest education that was available at that time, both going to Makerere to study, in the days before University recognition had been given to it. He therefore became one of the best educated clergy in the country. He had a real grasp of theological issues, which was rare amongst Ugandans. After he came to Christ, his preaching remained centred on the redemptive work of Jesus Christ on the Cross.

"He was acutely aware of the dangers of living a superficial Christian life, and he made every effort, both by teaching and preaching and by example, to move people on to maturity in their daily walk as Christians. He lived in days when some unusual things were happening in the church, but he was never impressed by exuberance that was not based on the Cross and Christ's work for us there. He was always a softly spoken man, but he was, nevertheless, a great talker!

"He loved talking to young and old alike, to those who were highly educated as well as to the completely uneducated, and his willingness to associate with the uneducated meant that he was sometimes despised and unwanted. But his happiness in sharing with everyone irrespective of their educational background, clan, tribe, colour or religious persuasion meant that people were confident in him and really listened to what he had to say. He became a model for many—educated and uneducated alike. It was because of him and people like William Nagenda, that no one could say: 'Salvation is only for the ignorant.' He appeared to be a gentle character, but he was very strong and resolute for what he believed to be right.

"In the days when he and Geraldine came to know the Lord, there were very few saved people in the rural areas, and folk who became the Lord's in these areas had very little help in their spiritual growth, (it should be noted that many of them were illiterate). Many of them came to stay in their home. Their home at Kinoni was conveniently situated on the main road from Kampala, and many people would call by for refreshment and encouragement. By this time, he and Geraldine had a growing family, and so sometimes some of the saved girls from the village areas would come and help them. This gave these young girls a great opportunity to grow in the faith, and many of these people have grown to be mature leaders in subsequent years.

"Erica was a great student of God's Word, and could often be found poring over the pages of Scripture and other Christian writings, ever eager to learn more of Jesus, his Saviour. This love of Scripture kept him from legalism on the one hand and on the other hand gave him an open heart to Jesus and His people."

For some people, Erica's ability to make things simple was remembered by the illustrations he used:

"There was a man who lost his way in a forest. It got dark and he didn't know which way to turn. As he was in this state a man came along who was dressed in very bright clothes. He held a *red thread* which he handed to the man who was lost. He advised the lost man to hold on to this thread and never to let it go, as it would lead him out of the forest. The man clutched on to it, delighted to know that there was a way out of his lost state. For a time he held tightly to the *red thread* as he was led through the dark forest paths.

"Then, as he was walking along holding the *red thread*, he saw, on the path beside him, what looked like a glistening *golden egg*, and he bent down to try and pick it up. However, he could not grasp the *golden egg* and at the same time hold on to the *red thread*. In the end he decided that he would leave the *red thread* momentarily, pick up the glistening *golden egg* very quickly and then get back the *red thread*.

"So he let go of the *red thread*, and reached down quickly for the glittering *golden egg*. As he bent to pick it up he found it was only a bubble! Disgusted he stood up and began to look for the *red thread* he had been holding, only to find that it had disappeared high up in the trees, well out of his reach! Erica would then go on to explain that the world, like the *golden egg*, sometimes glistens like gold, but it is really like a bubble which would burst. If, to grasp the *golden egg*, we let go the *red thread*—the Blood of Jesus—we will lose our way."

Another illustration was of a caterpillar which lived inside a maize plant. The caterpillar was warned by other caterpillars that the plant would be cut down and he would be killed. The caterpillar replied: "It is all right, I will get out later." Then the maize was cut down and the other caterpillars came and said, 'the maize cob will be taken off the stem and what will you do then?" He replied: "It is all right, I will get out later." Then the maize cob was taken off the stem and lay on a table. His friends said to him, "Don't you realise that the maize cob will soon be cooked?" He replied, "It is all right, I will get out later!" Then the maize was cooked and he perished.

"How many people say: "It is all right, I will get out later, or I will come to Christ later," Erica would point out, instead of realising that "now is the time of salvation".

As people listened to words such as these, spoken on many different occasions, they heard not only the voice of a man but the words of God. One of the addresses which Erica loved to preach was based on the words of King David to the elders of Judah, "Why should you be the last to bring the king back to his palace." (2 Samuel 19:11)

Erica and Geraldine complemented each other perfectly although they were, in many ways, different. Erica was a great family man who loved to have many children and young people around him. Geraldine's organising abilities made this possible. Their very strengths necessitated close cooperation and frequent repentances. When Erica referred to his work as Bishop and Archbishop, he often used the word 'we' naturally. He and Geraldine were truly 'one' in Christ, in marriage, in parenthood and in their different but complementing ministries.

The later years

Janani Luwum was installed as Archbishop on the 9th June 1974, and Erica Sabiti immediately entered into full retirement. He and Geraldine moved to Kinoni, in his native Ankole. From there, they exercised a wide ministry, ever faithful, in public meetings and in private, in personal contacts and relationships, to their Lord and Master, Jesus Christ.

A tribute to Erica in his last days as Archbishop of the Province of Uganda, Rwanda and Burundi appeared in the biography of his successor to that office, the martyred Janani Luwum. "Archbishop Erica Sabiti, a man who walked closely with his Lord and Master, Jesus Christ, guided the Church of Uganda through the turbulent years 1966-74. His own life had been transformed as a young pastor when the flame of revival had swept through Ankole in southern Uganda. Now frail in body, though not in spirit, dogged by recurrent illness, he pondered deeply over the question of his retirement. He knew he was not indispensable. But his position was not an easy one. He was afraid for his successor and the possible division over his selection. Prayerfully Erica Sabiti sought the Lord's guidance and it was just before the Provincial Assembly in August 1973 that he felt that the Lord had given him the green light. Accordingly he announced his intention to retire in May the following year."[J56]

In 1982, Erica was interviewed for his recollections of his years of service. He said: "It is now eight years and two months since I retired from the active services and the administration of the Church, yet I have felt the need of keeping at it, sharing Jesus with those who know Him and with those who do not. The souls of men are what Jesus came into the world for, and they should take the priority in the lives of all those who have come to know Him.

"Oh, how very much I feel for my brothers and sisters who are still active in the Lord's work and are entrusted with the ministry of sharing Jesus with other people. I feel for them and I pray very much that they may be aware of the dangers of what a friend of mine some years back called 'the barrenness of a busy life and the busy-ness of a barren life'. There are too many activities in the church today which take a kind of priority in the mind of the ministers and bishops to promote the ways of the church by trying to raise money for things—for many good projects in the church. These are all right in their own way, but it is not the main thing and in the long run it creates this barrenness in the church. May God help our ministers.

"My wife and I praise the Lord for the way He has helped us since we went to the Cross. We keep remembering that dreadful place where the Lord found us. Isaiah writes (51:1): 'Look to the rock from which you were cut and to the quarry from which you were hewn.' We remember that God found us in the miry clay, and picked us up, took us to the Cross, made us His children, and then He reminds us that we need to grow as children of God. God does not mean that we should stop there, but we must grow, ... and the way to grow, as Peter has said, is to desire the 'spiritual milk' on which the 'babies of God' feed. This is the Word of God.

"God has helped us to keep a Quiet Time each morning, when we come to the Word of God, the Bible, and ask Him for His grace to help us to understand what He is saying to us. For the last forty years we have kept this time. To begin our day we go to the throne of grace before starting our work, listen to His Word and then turn to prayer, using what He has taught us in the Word and praying that what we have learnt may not be just head knowledge, but that we may be changed, as Paul said, 'from glory to glory'. We are still saved, and we are growing by feeding on the milk of the Word of God. I feel for people who are Christians without understanding the Bible. Now, we are in Jesus's hands. As the chorus says: 'We are marching to Zion, that beautiful city of God.'"

Erica's health deteriorated in later years, but ever at his side was his beloved, Geraldine. Many people continued to come to their home, which was near a main road, for counsel and encouragement.

Erica Sabiti died peacefully at home on 17 May 1988 at the age of 85, leaving Geraldine, three sons and three daughters. After the funeral, Geraldine wrote: "The feeling of loss of Erica is not something that is small, not small at all, and is really something almost impossible to bear. Many times I have found myself feeling cold spiritually. We always shared everything—all our thoughts. Now I find myself having to make decisions on my own, but the Lord is helping me to repent and to go on trusting Him more and more, knowing that 'He who has started the good work will complete it'. The work of the home is still a very big responsibility and then there are God's people here, and also our children and our grandchildren."

"God did, indeed, complete His work in the life of Geraldine," wrote Zeb Kabaza. "She looked after the grown-up family and their children—praying, counselling, admonishing and encouraging all around her.

"Ten years after Erica's death Geraldine arranged a thanksgiving service for what the Lord had been to, and done for, her and her family during those ten years. Many people came from Buganda, Tooro, Kigezi and Ankole for the mini-convention. Many tributes were given to the lives and testimonies of both Erica and Geraldine and, which would have given joy to the heart of Erica, Jesus Christ was given the central place and the Gospel again proclaimed.

"Geraldine had for many years been aware of a weak heart. In 1999 she suffered a series of heart attacks and passed into the presence of her Lord on 30th November of that year. Her funeral was a remarkable time of affirmation of the way her life had witnessed to the saving power of Jesus Christ. The Archbishop of Uganda asked that her funeral be delayed so that he could attend and he preached at the service in Namirembe as well as one in Mbarara.

Although Erica and Geraldine have gone to be with their Master, their testimony continues, from the highest levels of the Church of Uganda to the many individuals to whom they were, in truth, 'a dear brother and sister in Christ'.

Conclusion

In the Preface, some characteristics of the East African Revival were noted as 'seen from the outside'—the merging of two streams of Revival - the European/North American and the African, and the merging of two cultures—the industrialised white west and that of the agricultural black Africa. Even more powerful in their impacts were the characteristics of this Revival as seen 'from the inside', by those who entered fully into what God was doing.

a. *No great names and no 'loners'*
In the East African Revival, there were no widely acclaimed great preachers of the order of John Wesley, George Whitefield, Jonathan Edwards and Charles Finney. *None stood out* from everyone else as powerful leaders, but rather, *all submitted* to each other in the fellowship of which they formed a part. Their differences lay in their personalities, their backgrounds, their family situations and their cultures. Their similarities lay in the genuineness of their experience of God, their understanding of, and commitment to, the fundamental truths of the Gospel and to each other.

Zeb Kabaza has pointed out that "one of the reasons there has not been a book focusing on these people until now, was the fear of making an idol of anyone, or of hero-worshipping them. People have not modelled their lives on them. Through them, people wanted to follow *Jesus*, not *them*. For example, Nsibambi did many unusual things, but no one took this up and did what he did." There were no distinctions encouraged such that people could say, "I follow Nsibambi," or "I am one of Nagenda's group".

There were no 'loners' in the leadership. Zeb Kabaza had many opportunities of seeing these men and women at work and noted the close way in which "they worked together as a team. If you went to one of them to discuss something they would ask if you had discussed it with any of the others. They shared a lot by correspondence when they did not see each other, and we never, ever heard them talk of each other behind each other's backs. Oneness is one of the very, very precious things that the Lord has taught us, and taught particularly through these brethren. Once Jesus is the centre, you do not want to lift yourself up above others so that Revival becomes 'Barham' or 'Kinuka'. It was never called 'Joe Church's Revival'. None of them was a speaker whose eloquence drew the crowds, yet there was something which came across when they spoke to crowds or chatted to individuals which testified to the fact that 'they had been with Jesus'."

This oneness of heart and mind between those of different cultures has not been a general characteristic of all revivals, but it happened in striking ways in East Africa. It was not surprising, perhaps, that God should give a deep sense of fellowship between previously antagonistic Rwandans and Burundians and between Baganda and Banyoro of Uganda, but it was quite unexpected that English and African men and women should be as deeply understanding of, and committed to each other as they became then.

This brought about a radical change in the attitudes of many missionaries as they observed the oneness between , for instance, Joe Church and Yosiya Kinuka, and between Lawrence Barham and Ezekieri Balaba, as they not only shared a speaker's platform, but welcomed each other into their homes.

b. *'Satisfied with Jesus'*.

A phrase frequently used by these men and women was: being 'satisfied with Jesus'.

Joe Church illustrated this truth by comparing it with a train which consists of an engine pulling a number of carriages, like the trains that plied between Mombasa and Kampala. The carriages, on their own, are powerless. Jesus is that 'engine' and the carriages are: victory, healing, fruit of the Spirit, gifts of the Spirit, etc. If you have Jesus, the rest follow. If you do not have Jesus, the 'carriages' become distractions or hindrances.

William Nagenda illustrated the same truth by speaking of the Devil's work as *dragging* people away from Jesus before they are 'saved'. Then, when they are 'saved', his work is *pushing* them to want more than Jesus.

Being 'satisfied with Jesus' was a driving theme in the living and preaching of these pioneers. "They put Jesus Christ in the centre. Other things that were not of Him, no matter how good they might be, they would not encourage, saying that they would lead into error," commented Zeb Kabaza. "So if you emphasise brokenness or prayer or fasting, anything, however good it may be, if it goes beyond the compass of the Cross, it becomes an error. For instance, the laying on of hands for the sick, however good it may be, is not the message, and it can become a gimmick. They were always careful not to emphasise spiritual gifts. They recognised them and they praised the Lord for them, but they did not make them special messages. For example, when William was sick, some people suggested that he had hands laid on him. His reaction was that he did not know what the Lord wanted, whether for him to be healed or not. He allowed prayer, but not in a special way. And that was general for every spiritual gift. As people fixed their eyes on Jesus, He would give gifts as He saw fit."

Joe Church often quoted the words of Paul: "I determined to know nothing among you but Jesus Christ and Him crucified". It was a simple message, too simple for some people, but it was a 'saving' message.

A criticism was levelled against them that they never went beyond 'repentance' and 'the Cross' and so neglected the 'fullness of the Spirit' and the 'gifts of the Spirit'? The reply was simple. 'You cannot go beyond repentance and the Cross!'   'Repentance' is the most radical, continuing need of both the 'saved' and the 'unsaved'. It is a *daily,* even *moment by moment* experience to recognise the thoughts, attitudes and aims which are of 'the world', 'the flesh' or of 'the Devil', confess them to God and seek His forgiveness. Only when a person is in a right relationship with God is it *safe* for him or her to use the gifts He offers or to serve Him in any way.

The basis of God's forgiveness of the repentant sinner is always the same—the Cross of Christ, and particularly that aspect of the death of Jesus Christ which is referred to as the 'shedding of the Blood of Christ'.

So important was the moment by moment fellowship with God that, while interest was shown in how a person repented of his or her sin and trusted in Christ for salvation in the past, this was usually quickly followed with: 'Are you repenting *today*? Are you trusting Christ *now*? Do you know God's forgiveness *at this moment*?'

The 'receiving' of, the 'fullness of', and the 'baptism with' the Holy Spirit were made gloriously simple: 'When the Blood of Jesus cleanses, the Holy Spirit fills.' It is a person's relationship to Jesus Christ which determines his or her experience of the Holy Spirit. When people 'see Jesus', they can truly be 'satisfied with Jesus'. Where this is absent, there is error or distraction from the truth.

When any of the team appeared to be adding or subtracting from the simple Gospel, they would lovingly pursue that person with prayer and gentle admonition. They were, themselves, quick to submit to the 'light' received in the fellowship. 'No one person is an infallible interpreter of the Holy Spirit' became an underlying principle. They recognised that, however much God was using them, they could make mistakes. Their safeguard was living close to Jesus, keeping close to their colleagues in the fellowship and repenting of any sin that came in to mar that fellowship, even when they were physically separated from each other by distance.

"They did not lecture people, but they shared from their experience," commented Zeb Kabaza. "If anyone fell spiritually they would weep with that person and try to help him and show him Jesus, and they were quick to show their own failings." When a person went to one of the African couples to seek counsel about some wrong-doing that he or she had committed, he or she was never met with an accusing figure. Usually they would begin by sharing with them where they themselves had failed and where they had had to repent and ask for forgiveness from God and from those they might have offended. They could then, as sinners together at the 'foot of the Cross', seek to find God's mind about the present situation. They never forgot that the accusing 'pointing finger' was accompanied by the 'three fingers' pointing back to them.

c. *Letting God work.*

These pioneers insisted that it was God who acted and not them. It was not that God worked apart from them, but it was for them to rest in 'the finished work of Christ'. "Each one of them emphasised it in his own way," wrote Zeb Kabaza. "I remember Nsibambi reading to me a portion of one of the old, old talks. It was on *'Resting faith'* and *'Wrestling faith'*. 'What we need is a *'Resting* faith' in Christ's finished work,' he said, rather than *'Wrestling,* struggling faith'. For example, you do not *repent* unless you appreciate what Christ has done for you, otherwise what you do becomes *penance.*"

The Luganda word *kufuba,* meaning 'to strive', took on a special meaning in the revived fellowships. It came to mean 'striving in the flesh' or working to achieve what only God can do. God was sovereign in all that He did. These pioneers were able to preach God's truth and then relax. When God confirmed their preaching by extraordinary conviction of sin or by joyous forgiveness, accompanied sometimes by extraordinary physical manifestations, this was recognised as something which God does, and to try to produce those effects by human striving was *kufuba*.

Remarkable evidence of 'letting God work' was provided by the 'teams of witness' which were a feature of the Revival. People who experienced the reviving power of Jesus Christ in their lives felt impelled to visit their friends, nearby villages, churches or schools, and tell them of what Jesus had done for them and warn them of the eternal danger of rejecting Him. God worked in amazing ways in the ministry of the pioneers and other leaders, but He also worked among the ordinary Christians who had an extraordinary up-to-date testimony of the living Christ.

d. *A high acceptance of women as of equal status as men.*

Wherever there have been genuine Christian conversions, there has been a raising of the status of women, in the home in particular, but also in church activities. What was distinctive in the Revival was the way that women were accepted, not only as equal in being admitted to the team meetings where arrangements for activities were planned, but their views were accepted as of equal worth as those of the men. While leadership in the speaking ministry was largely retained by men, the leadership role in discerning what was needed and in planning events was seen to include the views of women as well as of men.

There was a special power in the testimony and ministry when a man and his wife were truly a team in everything that they did together. This represented a remarkable and notable change in the usual husband/wife relationship in African culture. Even the greater equality of status in European society, enjoyed by the missionaries, did not guarantee oneness in a marriage. The oneness of Joe and Decie, and Lawrence and Julia, was a powerful testimony to a living experience of Jesus Christ in the home, as was that of Simeoni and Eva, William and Sala, Yosiya and Dorokasi and Erica and Geraldine. 'Light' and 'love' in the home are marks of Revival.

e. *Grooming for leadership.*

A striking feature about these pioneers, commented Zeb Kabaza, "was their concern to 'groom' people to take leadership. They would emphasise the need to be responsible. That meant having that desire to go deeper into the Scriptures and to know Christ much more."

Far from trying to keep their leadership to themselves, they appeared to go out of their way to encourage younger Christians not *to imitate them* but *to follow in their footsteps,* by deepening their knowledge of the Scriptures and becoming fully established in the faith and so fulfilling God's purposes for each one of them.

All these pioneers, African and European, were great readers. Lawrence Barham was probably the most highly trained in an academic discipline, but they all respected scholarship and read books which were available to them. Simeoni Nsibambi and Joe Church, in particular, were well acquainted with the works of Charles G Finney and other writers on Revival. Evangelical theological works were recommended to young questioning Christians. They were encouraged to think deeply about their faith.

h. *God-filled horizons.*

It was perhaps, natural that the missionaries horizons should be filled by their calling to serve God. Many of the African leaders also showed this same characteristic. The Kingdom of God was as real, if not more so, than the physical world in which they lived. This occasionally gave rise to the criticism that they were too 'other-worldly'; that they had no 'small talk'; that they were only interested in people's spiritual relationship with Jesus and not in their social circumstances. This was a misunderstanding. Human events were real and important for them, but only as seen in the light of spiritual truth. Simeoni Nsibambi, William and Sala Nagenda and Eric Sabiti were noted for their concern for the physical health and welfare of people. Erica was concerned for the right use of the land. These concerns were seen as part of the outworking of spiritual life.

Among those who felt that they suffered from the seeming spiritual preoccupation of their parents were some of the children of these pioneers. The testimonies of the children of both missionary and African families range from a deep gratitude for their parents' great love and concern for them, to a feeling of being neglected because their parents appeared to put other people first. This kind of criticism is not unique to those whom God uses in pioneer circumstances, and they are certainly not immune from it.

These men and women were primarily 'citizens of heaven' and they were often misunderstood by those who did not live in the 'real world' which filled their horizons.

Here then, are the stories of six couples, very ordinary in many ways, but men and women whom God used in extraordinary ways. They have now gone to be with the Master they served. Their memory lives on in some who are still alive today. Even more important, the message of Revival is still alive in East Africa today. Despite the ravages of the Mau Mau in Kenya, the Idi Amin regime in Uganda and the Hutu/Tutsi conflicts in Rwanda and Burundi, there are still those in these countries who put Christ at the centre of their lives, are 'walking in the light' with each other, repenting when sin is recognised, are living in fellowship with each other, and are demonstrating that, in Christ there are no ethnic, racial or colour barriers. Many are those who have suffered, and there are those who suffer today because they will not align themselves with those who discriminate in racial or ethnic ways.

There may not be the widespread manifestations of Revival in East Africa today as there were in the late 1930's and 1940's, but there is still revival in the hearts of many men and women who testify in their lives daily to the reality of the Good News of 'Jesus Christ and Him crucified'.

Only eternity will tell the number of those who will sing in heaven, "Worthy is the Lamb", because of the testimony to Jesus, the Lamb of God, of the men and women whose stories have been told here.

References

A   *America Letter*   Dr J E Church
C   *The Coming of the Rain*   Kathleen Makower   Paternoster
E   *A Call to Ethiopia*   Dr J E Church and Mr William Nagenda
F   *Fire in the Hills*   H H Osborn   Highland Books
FK   *Festo Kivengere*   Anne Coomes   Monarch
G   *A Grain of Mustard Seed*   Lindesay Guillebaud
                                            Ruanda Mission (CMS)
I   *Tour in India and Pakistan*   Dr J E Church
J   *Janani - The making of a martyr*   Margaret Ford   Lakeland
K   *The East African Revival Movement*   MTh Thesis
                                            James Katarikawe
N   *Diary of the Nyasaland Tour*   Dr J E Church
P   *Pilkington of Uganda*   C F Harford-Battersby   Marshall
PL   *The Promised Land*   Dr J E Church and Mr William Nagenda
Q   *Quest for the highest*   J E Church   Paternoster
RN   *Ruanda Notes*
RR   *Road to Revival*   A C Stanley Smith   CMS
WN   *William Nagenda - A Lover of Jesus*   Dr J E Church

Index

The names of the *Pioneers* appear in this index only where they occur in
sections other than those which bear their names.